M000310636

Breakout: How Atari 8-Bit Computers Defined a Generation

Breakout: How Atari 8-Bit Computers Defined a Generation

Jamie Lendino

Ziff Davis LLC
New York, NY

Ziff Davis LLC
28 East 28th Street
11th Floor
New York, NY 10016

© 2017 Jamie Lendino. All rights reserved. No part of this book may be reproduced in any form by any electronic or mechanical means (including photocopying, recording, or information storage and retrieval) without permission in writing from Jamie Lendino or the publisher.

Edited by Matthew Murray.
Cover design by James Jacobsen and Jose Ruiz.
Cover photo by Paul Maljak.

Printed and bound in the United States of America.
Second printing, December 2017

ISBN-13: 978-0692851272
ISBN-10: 0692851275

To the two most important and amazing people in my life: My wife Allison and daughter Siena.

Contents

Introduction

My childhood circled around video games in general, but specifically, around one computer: the Atari 800. It's impossible to overstate Atari's impact on personal computers and especially gaming. While Apple and a few other companies delivered personal computing for the first time, Atari was the first to bring arcade-like graphics and sound into the home.

This book serves as a celebration of Atari 8-bit computers and what made them special, with a heavy emphasis on gaming. It's a look back at how the computers, peripherals, and software worked, and why the games were so good. In a world of always-on social media and ad-filled websites, where the idea of "just develop your own game" seems hopelessly complex, the simplicity and sophistication of a tightly coded "to the metal" Atari program is intoxicating—and you didn't need to have dedicated artists with such a low pixel count.

Hopefully, reading this book will trigger some pleasant memories of your own. Perhaps you had an Atari computer yourself and miss it. Maybe you even still have or use an Atari computer today. In the 1980s, Atari computers never really got their due. Let's see if we can finally fix that.

Who Cares About Old Computers, Anyway?

Today's obsession with retro computing is unmistakable—and it's safe to say our memories are a little rose-tinted. With fast multicore processors, phones, apps, cloud storage, social networks, and streaming media, it may seem surreal to wax lyrical about a particular oversized hunk of plastic, metal, and chips. By today's standards, any computer from the late 1970s had a tiny amount of unreliable storage and low-resolution graphics, and most of them took forever to load programs. If you were "there," though, you know full well why these computers were special. If you weren't, imagine the ability to control every last feature of the hardware, without layers of software abstraction on top, and in a way that rewards detailed study the more you work with it. The graphics were simple and distinct, and in its beautiful minimalism the machine was both easy to program and difficult to master. Early software sparked your imagination in a way even the most realistic high-definition graphics today can't quite pull off. Many enthusiasts I've talked to over the years feel the same way.

I was born in 1973 and was fully immersed in the home computer revolution as a kid. I got my first Atari computer, a 400, when I was eight years old. Until then, all of my entertainment options were too defined for me. I'd play a board game, and the rules were the same each time, and if I changed them, the basic structure still remained intact. My imagination may have run wild when I was playing with Lego, but the bricks were always the same each time, and thanks to the laws of physics, they always worked the same way. Beginning with the computer, suddenly I could make new games out of thin air, either by typing in programs from books or creating my own. Every cartridge and disk made the computer do something different than it had done a few minutes earlier. It was as if you could make your own bricks, and make your own physics.

None of this sounds crazy now. But consider how unprecedented video games, and the ability to play lots of them or program your own, were back then. Remember that computers had already been around for several decades, but they used to take up entire rooms, or at least portions of rooms by the 1970s. They used to cost tens or even hundreds of thousands of dollars. The members of the informal Homebrew Computer Club of the mid 1970s in Menlo Park, California had the right idea. They were the first to see the creative potential in writing your own code, and running it on hardware *on your desk*, rather than having to line up at a university or work in a big company to use a mainframe system. They worked to make computing more accessible to everyone. Because of this, within a few years' time, a kid like me could own and experience a real computer every single day, without having to share it with strangers.

Computer memory was still extremely expensive, though—you could only store a few games or text-based documents on a fragile floppy disk, which meant no digital music, photos, or movies. This was even before CDs and VHS tapes. Music came on records and cassettes, you had to bring film from your camera to a store (and wait) to get printed photos developed, and you could only see movies in the theater. Back then, just about anything digital and affordable was a revelation. Sure, we had our computer-tech-infused science fiction and space adventures—*Star Wars*, and soon after, *Tron, Blade Runner,* and William Gibson's novel *Neuromancer.* The concept of cyberspace would soon become a thing. But what we didn't have yet, at least until the late 1970s, was the ability for walk into a store, buy a complete personal computer system, and bring it home to learn to program or play video games.

One of my favorite books, *The Hitchhiker's Guide to the Galaxy,* starts off with a line about humans on Earth being so primitive they "still think digital watches are a pretty neat idea." Imagine the jump from a digital watch to your own personal computer. If you're younger than 30 and reading this, trust me: It was amazing.

Why I Wrote This Book

Obviously I wrote this book because I am a huge Atari computer fan, but there's more to it than that. Putting this book together evoked many good memories. Throughout the writing process, I discovered that what was driving me was nostalgia for a wonderful time and place. They say you can't go home again, and it's true in some sense; life is different when you're in your 40s with a family, a job, and responsibilities. A part of me misses having untold hours to disappear into Ultima IV: Quest of the Avatar (and only half of which was waiting for the maps to load). But when I was 12, I also didn't have much else going on aside from homework. Finding this kind of free time today would be impossible.

In addition, I stumbled on some things that reminded me that it wasn't cool to be a computer nerd in the 1980s. My general impression is that it's more acceptable to be a geek today. I remember feeling lonely a lot of the time I spent on the Atari. That said, I met some lifelong friends through the bulletin board system (BBS) I ran on the Atari 800, and also talked to countless other people online with whom I've since fallen out of touch. It's never usually just about the thing (computer, kind of car, book club); it's always about the people, and often that becomes the most important part. And for me—I'd argue for some two million of us, if somewhat difficult-to-prove sales figures are to believe—the Atari 8-bit was central to our lives.

Figure I.1: Me in 1986, in front of my Atari 800, with an Ultima IV: Quest of the Avatar map on the wall. I still have the map.

How This Book Is Organized

This book is roughly divided into three sections. The first five chapters cover the mid 1970s to the late 1980s, spanning the birth of the Atari 8-bit platform, the challenges Atari faced, and how the platform evolved over time. Chapter 6 is entirely about the games, which for many people are the most important part of the Atari experience. If you want to skip straight ahead and read about those, go for it! Finally, the last four chapters cover the Atari 8-bit platform as it is today: what it's like to collect the machines, which ones you should choose, what modifications are available, and the best emulators on today's platforms.

Finally, a few notes on conventions throughout this book. Generally speaking, I refer to 8-bit Atari computers as the Atari 8-bit; I wanted to continue in the tradition of the 20-plus-year-old Frequently Asked Questions list (FAQ), which has circulated around seemingly forever thanks to the tireless efforts of Michael Current, its publisher. Saying just "Atari computers" would also bundle in the 16-bit ST, the 32-bit Falcon, and a rather sorry bunch of PC compatibles from the late 1980s and early 1990s that no one needs to remember. While I had and also loved a 520ST for many years, this book focuses entirely on the earlier 8-bit experience.

Tense—as in the written-word sense—is an issue when you're talking about computers that came out 30 years ago, but that people also use today in different ways, not to mention your thoughts about them then (in the 1980s) and now. People can play Atari 8-bit games quite easily on emulators or otherwise modified Atari hardware even now. There are multiple ways to approach tense, and none are perfect. As a general rule, I use the past tense for the first five chapters of the book covering the tenure of the Atari 8-bit, and then switch to present tense for the real meat of the book—the games—and the community, collecting, and hardware mods available today.

A few other quick notes: I also refer to modem and transfer speeds as "bits per second" or "bps," even though in the 1980s everyone (including me, and incorrectly) said "baud." Finally, I edited some quotes very lightly for clarity and consistent style within the book, but otherwise left them intact.

With that, let's look back at the start of an incredible home computer revolution, one that became intertwined with a golden age of arcade gaming.

1 | Atari 400/800

The history of Atari the company has been told and retold. Most of the time, it's with a focus on either of two things: its coin-operated arcade machines like Breakout, Asteroids, and Missile Command; or its game console lineup, starting with home versions of Pong in 1975, but most notably with the Atari Video Computer System (VCS, later known as the 2600) in 1977. I won't rehash every last thing about Atari and its various levels of corporate dysfunction and pot smoking in this book, as others have already done the same. But we could do with a brief refresher of how we got the computer in the first place.

In a nutshell, it was originally about succeeding the VCS with something better. But then it got complicated.

Nolan Bushnell and Ted Dabney incorporated the Sunnyvale, California–based Atari on June 27, 1972. This was after the two launched Computer Space, the world's first coin-op arcade game, under the name Syzygy Engineering, and several months before the release of the coin-op Pong. The following year, Bushnell bought out Dabney, and provided financial backing for a group of engineers working under the name Cyan Engineering, located a few hours away in Grass Valley. Atari purchased Cyan Engineering in 1975 and renamed it the Grass Valley Research Center.[1] This is important for our purposes, because four key players for the design of the Atari computer emerged from this group. Ron Milner and Steve Mayer developed the VCS prototype. Joe Decuir debugged it and created a new, gate-level prototype. Decuir apprenticed for Jay Miner, who served as

---

1. Atari 8-bit FAQ

the lead chip designer for the VCS, and later went on to design the Commodore Amiga.

Separately, in 1976, one of Atari's early employees worked on the Breakout arcade game with his friend, which turned out to be a huge success. Later, the two developed a home computer design using borrowed Atari parts. Bushnell turned down the design and wanted to stay focused on video games. The two friends, Steve Jobs (Atari employee number 40) and Steve Wozniak (who had been working for Hewlett Packard), went on to form Apple.[2]

Eventually, it became clear that Bushnell needed more capital to launch the VCS, so he sold Atari to Warner Communications for $28 million in a deal with Warner exec Manny Gerard. The transaction ensured there was enough money to finish developing, release, market, and distribute the VCS.[3] Bushnell remained chairman and chief executive officer of Atari, but tensions between him and Warner remained high, and Bushnell was eventually forced out before the end of 1978.

After Atari launched the VCS in 1977, the Cyan Engineering team at Grass Valley Research immediately got to work on its successor. The team believed the VCS had roughly three years of life before it would become obsolete[4], and wanted to fix its most obvious flaws: Make it faster, give it more memory, and vastly improve its graphics and especially sound capabilities.[5] "[We knew we had to] support 1978 vintage arcade games," Decuir said in a presentation at the first Classic Gaming Expo in 1999.[6] "We knew we would need to leapfrog the 2600 before somebody else did. [We had to] support home computer character and bitmap graphics. We saw the Apple II, Commodore, and Radio Shack appliance machines coming."

The project was known internally as Oz, and Milner, Mayer, and Decuir headed it up. George McLoed designed what would become the Atari computer's Color Television Interface Adapter (CTIA) chip, which like the VCS's Television Interface Adapter (TIA) chip, could generate two-dimensional, on-screen sprite animation in hardware for faster performance. And a new Pot Keyboard Integrated

---

2. Atarimuseum.com/computers/computers.html
3. Atari 8-bit FAQ
4. 8-BitCentral.com
5. Ibid
6. www.atariarchives.org/dev/CGEXPO99.ppt

Circuit (POKEY) chip, designed primarily by another Atari engineer named Doug Neubauer, would deliver rich four-voice audio for complex music compositions and sound effects, as well as allow for four-port joystick control.

The First "Trinity"

By the mid 1970s, it became clear that microprocessors were the way to go over the discrete logic design found in early arcade machines like Pong and Breakout. The MITS Altair 8800 jump-started the home computer revolution in 1975, thanks in part to its reasonable $399 price in kit form. Just about everything was extra; the Altair didn't even come with a keyboard, much less a display. Still, for the first time ever, the Altair made it possible for anyone to own a real computer for not much money. Other companies soon joined in with their own kits. By the end of 1976, some 40,000 personal computers had been sold already, with MITS, IMSAI, and Processor Technology making up about half, and dozens of other smaller companies selling the rest.[7]

At this point, there were still no prepackaged computers available. Sure, you could buy the Altair 8800 or a competing kit, and check the box to pay extra for the company to assemble it at the factory for you. But there was nothing standalone and self-contained—nothing you could just bring home from a store, plug in, and start using.

This all changed in 1977, thanks to the arrival of the first so-called trinity of personal computers, the Radio Shack TRS-80, the Commodore PET 2001, and the Apple II. Tandy launched the TRS-80 in New York City on August 3. It cost $399 on its own and $599 with a 12-inch monitor, with a $49 cassette recorder for storage.[8] The TRS-80's architecture was based around a Zilog Z80 microprocessor running at 1.77MHz. The first machines came equipped with 4KB of RAM. The TRS-80 benefited from the thousands-strong Radio Shack retailers already open, meaning it had a comprehensive dealer network from the get-go. The TRS-80 went on to see serious popularity over the first several years of its life.

---

7. arstechnica.com/features/2005/12/total-share/
8. Wikipedia, TRS-80.

Commodore's monster PET 2001 started at $795. The PET 2001 looked like something straight out of the movie *2001: A Space Odyssey*. The machine contained a 1MHz MOS 6502 CPU, 4KB of RAM (though Commodore bumped it to 8KB by early 1978), a built-in cassette recorder for loading and saving programs, and an integrated monochrome display so you could see what you were doing and what the results were. Many people complained about the feel of the chiclet-style keyboard. I became quite acquainted with it in my fifth-grade computer class in 1983, as our elementary school's lab was stocked with PET computers. I don't remember caring at all how the keyboard felt, other than that it was different than the Atari I had at home and therefore neat.

Then there's the Apple II, the one most people remember. It was the slowest seller in the beginning, thanks to its high price ($1,298, sans floppy drive or monitor). But it eventually became a juggernaut in home, business, and education environments. Steve Jobs and Steve Wozniak released the Apple II in June 1977. The brilliance of the Apple II's design, which was based on that of the Apple I, can't be overstated. Wozniak knew how to get as few chips as possible to do as much as possible, while Steve Jobs ensured the machine was wrapped in friendly, stylish packaging. The Apple II contained a 1MHz MOS 6502 and 4KB of RAM. Like the TRS-80 and Commodore PET, the Apple II output to a 40-by-24-character display, but unlike those machines, the Apple II also displayed color. This innovation—huge at the time, if you can believe it—turned out to be key to the machine's popularity, and became vital for both gaming and educational software.

Early personal computers delivered on the promise of a packaged, fully contained system. But all of the popular machines, like the Altair 8800, Apple II, TRS-80, and Commodore PET, had limited graphics, sound, and memory. They also lacked software libraries. Dan Bricklin's VisiCalc, the first electronic spreadsheet program, became the killer app for the Apple II in businesses large and small. VisiCalc let executives and accountants ditch their calculators and pencils and play out fictional business scenarios to see what would happen before any money was spent. But most people buying these machines ended up writing their own software using BASIC (short for Beginner's All-Purpose Symbolic Instruction Code, a popular programming language) for the first couple of years, itself an incredibly rewarding activity. Games with good graphics were few and far between.

On the gaming front, the Atari VCS was the first console to bring cartridge-based arcade gaming home—pull out a cartridge, plug in a different one, and you have a different video game to play. But the VCS was even more limited in power, and since it wasn't a full-blown computer, it was impossible to program unless you worked for Atari.

Candy and Colleen

Back at Atari in March 1978, amid conflict with Bushnell, Manny Gerard (the Warner Communications exec) installed Ray Kassar, a fabric industry executive with an eye on the home computer market, as president of Atari's consumer division.[9] Kassar ordered the engineering team to turn the planned VCS game console successor into a real home computer. This meant adding programmable BASIC, a keyboard, a character set, and support for external peripherals such as a disk drive and printer.[10]

Figure 1.1: The Atari 800's internal expansion riser with the MOS 6502B processor.
Credit: Evan Amos/Wikipedia

With its new marching orders, the engineering team developed the Alpha-Numeric Television Interface Circuit (ANTIC), a chip to control bitmapped graphics and character support in a variety of modes, with different levels of resolution and color. The chip would work in conjunction with CTIA's video output. The engineers were well aware of the limitations of the Apple II, the PET, and the TRS-80.

9. Atari 8-bit FAQ
10. 8-BitCentral.com

They wanted their computer to be just as good at gaming as consumers would expect from the Atari brand, while simultaneously delivering a real computing experience.

The final design had five large-scale integration (LSI) parts: the MOS 6502, ANTIC, CTIA, POKEY, and the 6520-based Peripheral Interface Adapter (PIA, the auxiliary 16-bit chip that delivers interrupt control for peripheral I/O and manages the joysticks). Atari employees also coded the operating system. "There [was] a period at Atari when there were no [VCS] games coming from Larry Kaplan, Alan Miller, Bob Whitehead, and myself," said David Crane, an early Atari employee who eventually went on to cofound Activision with the other three men he named. "As the most senior designers at Atari we were tasked with creating the 800 operating system. This group, plus two others, wrote the entire operating system in about eight months."[11]

"I'm very proud of the OS we created for the Atari 400/800," said Alan Miller. It was similar in complexity to QDOS, the OS that Microsoft licensed a couple of years later, renamed MS-DOS, and sold for the IBM PC. "However, the Atari OS was much better designed in terms of its user-friendliness and it had a much, much richer graphics subsystem and many fewer bugs."[12]

Next, Atari needed a BASIC for the computer. The company signed a contract with Shepardson Microsystems to write a version of BASIC that could fit into 8KB, as well as a file management system.[13] The way Atari got there is fantastic in retrospect. "A funny story from this time that Al Miller likes to tell has to do with the Atari BASIC cartridge that was to ship with the system," Crane said. "Atari had contracted with a young programmer named Bill Gates to modify a BASIC compiler that he had for another system to be used on the 800. After that project stalled for over a year, Al was called upon to replace him with another developer. So, while Al is the only person I know ever to have fired Bill Gates, I suspect that rather than work on Atari BASIC, Gates was spending all his time on DOS for IBM. Probably not a bad career choice for him, do you think?"[14]

---

11. www.gooddealgames.com/interviews/int_David_Crane.html
12. www.digitpress.com/library/interviews/interview_alan_miller.html
13. Atari 8-bit FAQ
14. www.gooddealgames.com/interviews/int_David_Crane.html

Atari ended up deciding on making two computers, famously code-named Candy and Colleen after two attractive secretaries at the company. In December 1978, and despite warnings from Bushnell, Atari announced that it was forming a Computer Division, separate from consumer electronics and coin-op.[15] The next month, at the 1979 Winter Consumer Electronics Show (CES), Atari officially unveiled two 8-bit home computer models: the 400 (formerly Candy) and 800 (Colleen). Both machines had cartridge slots, which immediately marked them as stand-ins for game consoles—instantaneous program loading!—along with four joystick ports and heightened graphics and sound capabilities.

Figure 1.2: The April 1979 issue of *Creative Computing* on Atari's new computer line.

On the low end, Atari pitched the 400 as a kind of hybrid game console and entry-level computer, albeit with non-upgradable memory. The 800 was considered the real computer, with modular RAM and ROM, a second cartridge slot, a monitor output (including separate luma and chroma pins), and a mechanical keyboard.[16] The names 400 and 800 came from their initial base memory—4KB and 8KB—although Atari also bumped the 400 to 8KB by the time the first shipment of machines hit Sears stores in November. "The Atari 400 was a game machine with a flat keyboard," Decuir said. "The Atari 800 was a full computer."[17]

Part of what made Atari computers so accessible was that it was possible to hook them up to a regular television, and not only to a dedicated computer monitor the way you had to with the Apple II. The company bundled a television switch box adapter with each machine—which meant that the machines needed to comply with FCC

15. Atari.com, 1972-1984 page
16. 8-BitCentral.com
17. www.atariarchives.org/dev/CGEXPO99.ppt

regulations for frequencies in the television range, unlike competing models. As a result, Atari built both computers with extremely heavy cast aluminum shields to minimize radio emissions from the hardware. The machines received FCC approval in June 1979.[18]

Unfortunately, the shielding made it difficult to work with the insides of the computers. In lieu of expansion slots (aside from memory) like those the Apple II had, Decuir developed an ingenious, shielded serial input/output (SIO) interface for attaching peripherals in a daisy-chain configuration.[19] Atari's SIO was an early plug-and-play system for external peripherals. While the cables were huge and thick by today's standards, and the connectors large, they worked securely and reliably, and were impossible to plug in the wrong way thanks to the connector's defined trapezoidal shape. The SIO port made it extremely easy to connect powerful peripherals to the computer anyone could set up. The downside was that each peripheral had to have its own brains and internal interfaces, which drove the cost higher, and since the connection was proprietary, only Atari computers could use Atari peripherals (though this began to change when various interfaces and third-party adapters hit the market a couple of years later). The worst irony is that later in 1979, the FCC changed the rules to allow Class B electronics, or those intended for residential or home use, without the shielding.[20]

Thanks to the combination of joystick ports and full QWERTY keyboards, game designers could develop complex simulations and role-playing games the likes of which had never been seen before.[21] The first was Star Raiders, introduced concurrently with the Atari 400 and 800 and arguably the killer app for the platform; other famous original Atari 8-bit titles like Rescue on Fractalus! and M.U.L.E. came later.[22]

The Atari 400 was supposed to cost $499.95, but the price was bumped up to $549.95 by the time it launched. Atari positioned the 800 on the higher end, at $999.95. Both machines came with a manual, a power supply, the aforementioned TV switch box, a CXL4002 BASIC cartridge, and the book *Atari BASIC: A Self-Teaching Guide*.

---

18. Atari 8-bit FAQ
19. 8-BitCentral.com
20. www.atariarchives.org/dev/CGEXPO99.ppt
21.www.ign.com/articles/2014/12/24/happy-35th-birthday-gaming-pc
22. Ibid

The 800 also included a 410 Program Recorder cassette drive. Sears received the first shipments in November 1979, and *Electronic News* (December 10, 1979, p. 83) reported retail stores were having trouble getting in stock initially.[23]

In fact, Atari pulled a fast one to make the deadline for the famed Sears catalog. From Jerry Jessop, an Atari employee from the late 1970s to the mid 1980s:

> *The first official small shipment of the 400/800 was on August 29th 1979...These were hand built pilot run units to Sears that needed to be in stock by Sept. 1 so they could be placed in the big fall catalog. The units were placed in the Sears warehouse and then immediately returned to Atari after the "in stock" requirement had been met.*[24]

It's been widely reported the 400 was the bigger seller of the two original computers, though hard numbers are tough to come by. "With the introduction of the Atari line of computers we are seeing a third generation of microcomputer, not just from the hardware end, but also from a marketing approach," John Victor wrote in the first issue of *Compute!* magazine. "These computers are slightly cheaper than those of the previous generation. The major difference is in the configuration and the application for which the systems were designed. A [recent article] described the Atari computers as hybrids—a cross between a video game and a small computer."[25]

In an interesting side bit of history, IBM itself may have cemented the popularity of Atari computers. IBM, increasingly concerned about the burgeoning personal computer market eating into its minicomputer business, considered rebranding the 800 as an IBM PC. But when the company visited Atari headquarters to explore the possibility, IBM businessmen were "literally put in a box and run through the assembly line by unorthodox and sometimes stoned Atari employees,"[26] leading IBM to decide it should build a computer all its own instead of trusting those clowns. If the day had gone down

---

23. Atari 8-bit FAQ
24. www.atarihq.com/atcomp/8bitfaq.html
25. *Compute!*, Fall 1979, p. 62
26. arstechnica.com/features/2005/12/total-share/

differently, one could only imagine how the computer industry would have unfolded.

Figure 1.3: The Atari 400. Credit: Evan Amos/Wikipedia

Atari 400

The Atari 400's svelte dimensions were just 4.5 by 13.5 by 11.5 inches (HWD). Of the personal computers available on store shelves in 1980, the Atari 400 was the one you wanted to bring home after seeing *Star Wars: The Empire Strikes Back* in the theater—or at least after popping a hazy bootleg VHS copy of it into your fake-wood-paneled VCR, and watching the movie for the fourth time on your living room's 25-inch color TV. (Obviously I'm not drawing the latter example from real-world experience.) The 400 was clearly a product of its X-Wing–influenced time period. It had some of the same angular lines as the Commodore PET. It looked both different from and more attractive than the Apple II. The 400 was made lower, longer, and wider—similar to what automakers do to improve the look of their automobiles from one generation to the next. The Apple II featured rounded edges and a larger footprint. The 400's low profile and angular creases looked sharp and arresting in comparison.

"I designed the case for Candy," designer Doug Hardy said in an interview in Marty Goldberg and Curt Vendel's thorough and compelling book, *Atari Inc. Business Is Fun* (p. 462). "I think I have the patent for it too." He said the design was started right after the VCS went into full production, and that Candy was meant as the eventual replacement for the VCS. "Candy was meant to be a laptop computer. This is before [LCDs] and such. What I mean is, it was designed to be able to sit in your lap, but connected to a TV. It was a game console, but could use the same cartridges as the other system [the 800] and it had a keyboard."

Part of what made the 400 such a nice-looking machine was also its biggest downfall: the dreaded membrane keyboard. Atari had originally planned the keyboard design so the entire family could use it without fear of easily damaging it. This entailed a keyboard without vulnerable openings around each key—meaning the machine wouldn't succumb to the first glass of juice spilled on it, and little kids couldn't pull off the plastic key caps and accidentally swallow them.

The 400's keyboard did have some devotees. Just kidding! Everyone hated it. While you couldn't argue with the spill resistance, it was just too difficult to touch-type on with alacrity. Even typing short BASIC programs on it was a giant pain. I didn't know what carpal tunnel was when I was eight years old, but I knew that typing on this thing required significant effort. (My awesome dad exchanged our 400 for an 800 within a week.) Within a couple of years, an entire cottage industry of third-party manufacturers opened up making add-on mechanical keyboards for the 400, and they sold a lot of them. It didn't matter too much; the main thrust of the 400 was as a glorified game machine. It could play more complex titles than the VCS.

"We wanted the systems to be able to play complex games, for example—Star Raiders, so having some kind of a keyboard was always a feature in the Colleen and Candy designs," Decuir said.[27]

The horrid membrane design aside, the layout of the QWERTY keyboard was well thought out, with a dedicated numeric row along the top, and a long space bar at the bottom with Shift keys to either side. The overall look was a little bit odd and cluttered, though, thanks to the shaded orange and brown color scheme, as well as icon labels on the keys for the computer's graphical character set. Four recessed function keys sat to the right: System Reset, Option, Select, and Start. In the middle of these was a red power LED. Pressing

---

27. *Atari Inc. Business Is Fun*, p. 462

KB 400™ $89.95

Exact Atari™ keyboard layout — Full Year Warranty

New! Speed Blaster™ rapid fire joystick add on $12.95

16k ATR8000 .... $299.95		8" Drives .... CALL
64k ATR8000 w/CP/M ... $449.95		4-Connector Drive Cable $35.00
OS/A+ 4.1 .... $ 49.95		2-Connector Drive Cable ... $25.00
1—5¼" Tandon Drive $249.95		8" Drive Adapter $19.95
2—5¼" Tandon Drives ... $449.95		Parallel or Serial Cable $29.00

SEND CHECK OR MONEY ORDER TO:

PLEASE ADD:
$2.50 Postage & Handling
COD —$2.00 additional
Illinois Customers
5% Sales Tax
Amerbank
Express Accepted

TELEPHONE
309/343-4114
Weekdays 9am-5pm
Saturday 9am-12pm
Central Time

ATTO-SOFT

832 E. Third Street
Galesburg, Illinois 61401

KB 400 & Speed Blaster
are Trademarks of Atto Soft.

Atari is a Trademark of Atari, Inc.

Figure 1.4: A September 1983 ad in *Antic* magazine for one of many Atari 400 keyboard add-ons.

System Reset triggered a warm start, where the machine stayed on and rebooted; sometimes it still kept the currently loaded program in memory, if instructed to do so once loaded the first time. A cold boot, in contrast, was when you powered off and on the machine entirely.

The right side of the machine featured the SIO port for connecting peripherals, a sliding hardware power switch, and a power input. There was no composite monitor port on this model, so you had to use the included switch box and a Phillips screwdriver to connect it to a television for monitoring purposes. On the top of the 400, the center panel popped open via a plastic pull switch to reveal a single cartridge slot, labeled "left" (to correspond with the 800, which had both main "left" and secondary "right" cartridge slots). The panel also contained a second power switch underneath it and along the edge. Whenever you opened the cartridge door, it was the same as powering off the machine using the main switch.

The 400 shipped with 8KB initially; a 16KB version debuted at the 1981 Winter CES, and became the only version available by the middle of the year.[28] Shortly after production of the 400 (and 800) ended in May 1983, Atari unveiled an expansion kit, which would upgrade both 8KB and 16KB versions of the 400 to 48KB.[29]

---

28. Atari 8-bit FAQ
29. Ibid

In retrospect, this initial machine could well have been the successor to the VCS—a proper game console as originally conceived. The VCS flourished for several years anyway, and Atari would finally get around to making the 400/800-style console in the 5200 SuperSystem and XE Game System in 1982 and 1987, respectively—letting crucial years in the home console market slip by in the interim.

Figure 1.5: The Atari 800. Credit: Evan Amos/Wikipedia

Atari 800

Most of what I said above about the 400 also applies to the 800; I'll stick to the differences in this section. Like its lower-cost brethren, the Atari 800 was made of a thick, textured plastic, but it looked noticeably different. The 800 was larger at 4.5 by 16 by 12.5 inches, with a curvier and more organic enclosure designed by Kevin McKinsey. It looked more business-like, but was still nice enough to sit on a desk at home. And even more than the 400, at 10 pounds, the 800 was pretty heavy—although later revisions weighed less, thanks to less internal shielding and a simpler circuit board design.

Unlike the 400, the 800 featured a raised, full-stroke mechanical keyboard, which was much easier to type long programs on. At first glance, it's obvious the keyboard was a huge improvement over the

400's, thanks to its design and cleaner layout. Much has been said about the way Atari played a little fast and loose with manufacturing techniques throughout the run of a particular piece of hardware. One of the consequences of this approach was keyboard feel, which you can easily test today by trying several 800s—it's almost guaranteed each one will type a little bit differently. Despite the variances in quality between individual keyboards, every 800 I've typed on over the years has been comfortable. Some were a little stiffer than others, but as a group, they were suitably clicky, springy, and accurate. And my first (dearly departed) model had one of the best keyboards I've ever used.

In addition to the main (or "left") cartridge slot, the 800 also included a second right cartridge slot, as I alluded to above. This was an interesting idea at the time, allowing you to plug in and run two different programs concurrently (provided they together fit within the machine's total RAM). The concept didn't gain much traction. Only a few programs made use of it, such as the ACE-80 80-column display device, and developer and disk utilities like Magic Dump and Monkey Wrench.

The Atari 800 was expandable to 48KB using up to four proprietary memory cartridges. Internally—and unlike the 400, or any future 8-bit Atari—there were four modular slots you could use to swap out the 10KB ROM (if necessary) as well as add memory. You could just pop up the 800's lid to access all four slots, which made the computer simpler to upgrade. Competing machines required opening the entire case with a screwdriver and installing exposed memory chips.

Eventually the market spoke, and it didn't care so much for expansion. Initial Atari 800 units shipped with one 8KB memory cartridge and two empty expansion slots, but during the summer of 1980, Atari bumped the stock 800 memory to 16KB.[30] Later versions of the 800, particularly from 1981 onward, shipped maxed out with 48KB, to better distinguish it from the 400 and hedge against increasing competition. The last run of machines included the cards installed without their enclosures for better heat dissipation, and without the thumb tabs used for removing them; instead, the modules were screwed down with a plastic strip across the top.

---

30. Atari 8-bit FAQ

For video, the Atari 800 came with a 5-pin monitor port, unlike the 400. This meant you could hook it up to a dedicated computer display for a sharper picture, in monochrome or in color, although Atari didn't sell an OEM monitor at the time.

In the beginning, the 400 and 800, plus some of the peripherals, were shipped in plain cardboard boxes. By 1981, Atari was shipping machines in the more familiar silver boxes with silk-screened logos and color images of the products. Atari also cut the price of the 400 from $549 to $399 and doubled the stock memory to 16KB, in response to the then-new 16KB, $299 Commodore VIC-20 home computer. The last 800s, produced in early 1983, sold at $679 and then $499. Production of both computers ended in May 1983.

Architecture Overview

Most of the material in this section is derived from what is widely considered the original text for Atari 8-bit computer programmers: *De Re Atari*. Atari employee and early evangelist Chris Crawford wrote the first six chapters of the book, and they explain in detail how the system works. The book also covers the operating system, manipulating disks, storing data on cassettes, and so on; a variety of other Atari employees wrote these sections. I've seen this book described as arcane, but I've always found it pretty clear, and there's no need to go into huge amounts of detail for our purposes. I'll footnote as I go, but I want to try and distill just the purest, most relevant pieces of the book to better explain the architecture of the computer. I want to highlight what made this computer special, how different it was from its predecessors, and how ahead of its time it was when compared with later machines.

The Atari computer consisted of a wide array of components, including its motherboard, memory, enclosure, keyboard, cartridge slots, and ports. But just four chips made up the computer's breakthrough design. Three of them were unique.

Most early home computers, like the Commodore PET, the Apple II, and the Radio Shack TRS-80, had a main CPU, along with a peripheral interface adapter and some memory, as discussed above. The Atari's CPU was a version of the same chip powering the Apple II, Commodore PET, and many coin-op arcade machines. The MOS 6502 was an 8-bit microprocessor with a 16-bit address bus, and normally ran at 1MHz. The Atari 400 and 800 contained a slightly modified MOS 6502B, which ran at 1.79MHz instead of 1MHz as in the Apple II and Commodore PET. The Atari 400 and 800 also included three additional chips—ANTIC, CTIA (later GTIA, for Graphic Television Interface Adapter), and POKEY. These chips offloaded various processes from the CPU and handled them separately. That freed up the 6502B to focus on pure computation.

Figure 1.6: *De Re Atari*, the first real guide from Atari employees on how to program the machine – more than a year after the computer hit the market.

The three additional LSI chips gave programmers many more tools to work with. As Crawford wrote in *De Re Atari*, "mastering the Atari 400/800 Computers is primarily a matter of mastering these three chips." You could write a much more sophisticated game for an Atari computer than you could for an Apple II or TRS-80. You could also port an existing TRS-80 or Apple II program to the Atari, and the result would be similar (and we saw this with some truly good games like Choplifter and Spare Change, which I'll get to later on). But for a program to be truly Atari-native and exploit the hardware to the fullest, the programmer had to rewrite the code with the Atari's more advanced chipset and features in mind.

Inside each 400 and 800, underneath all the shielding, there were three main component boards. The largest was the motherboard, which ran front to back. It contained the joystick ports, 22-pin and wire connectors for the power supply board, a 2-pin speaker connector, POKEY, and PIA. Above the motherboard, you'd find the four main ROM and RAM module slots. The power supply board held the on/off switch and power jack. The Personality board, which was positioned vertically on the motherboard, contained the CPU, ANTIC, and either CTIA or GTIA.

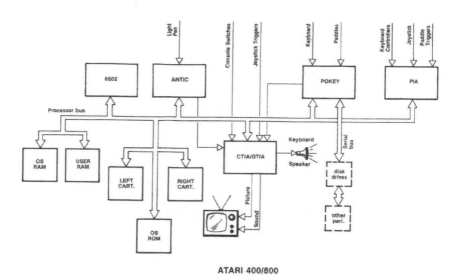

ATARI 400/800

Figure 1.7: A block diagram of Atari 8-bit hardware. Credit: *De Re Atari*, p. 1-3

ANTIC was a full microprocessor, with its own instruction set, as well as a program (which Atari called the display list) and relevant data.[31] The display list contained where the screen data was located, what graphics modes to use, and what options to use, if any. The 6502 wrote the display list and data into RAM; ANTIC then retrieved it using direct memory access (DMA) and translated the instructions to feed into CTIA.[32] ANTIC controlled vertical and horizontal fine

---

31. *De Re Atari*, p. 3
32. Ibid

scrolling and light-pen registers, and was a vertical line counter and DMA controller.[33] CTIA was the television interface chip. CTIA converted commands into a signal, which then went to the television or monitor. CTIA also handled color and player-missile graphics (more on these later), and had hardware collision detection. Both ANTIC and the 6502B itself could control CTIA, but ANTIC did most of the heavy lifting.[34]

The TRS-80 and Commodore PET had just one graphics mode, as Crawford explained in *De Re Atari*, with 1KB RAM allocated to the image in the form of 8-bit (or 256) characters. The Apple II had three modes instead of one: 8-bit text (like the TRS-80 and PET), low-resolution graphics with 4-bit nibbles, and high-resolution graphics with a 7-bit bitmap. The Atari used 14 graphics modes, each with varying resolutions and color support; plus, you could mix them so part of the screen had text and part had graphics. The ANTIC chip let a programmer move the display graphics anywhere in RAM, even while a program ran. If you wanted, you could make every raster line of the TV image use a different graphics mode. There were some modes you couldn't access via BASIC; you could only access them directly using machine language.

The Atari computer, as a result of all of this, gave the programmer many different tools to create advanced graphics. Crawford gave the example of using one graphics character set for one planet, another for space, and a third for a different planet; the program changed the character set in real time to display new scenery. In the Atari 8-bit version of Space Invaders, the programmer animated the invaders by switching character sets.

Before the Atari computer, graphics animation consisted of moving image data through the screen RAM area, which led to choppy graphics or overly complex calculations, as Crawford explained. The Atari 400 and 800 had something called player-missile graphics, which let programmers easily code high-speed sprite animation independent of the background and of each other. Player-missile graphics solved the problem of having a two-dimensional image in one-dimensional memory, and then having to perform complex calculations to produce animation. Player objects were also one-

---

33. *Antic*, April 1983, p. 19

[34] *De Re Atari*, p. 3

dimensional, and mapped directly to the screen, while the computer handled putting it into an 8-pixel-wide space and them moving it through one-dimensional memory for vertical motion. Horizontal motion was as simple as changing a single number in the horizontal position register. The computer was also the first to support hardware collision detection, which let you check if possible collisions have occurred between players and missiles on screen.

The CTIA chip as originally designed didn't last long in production. Beginning in November 1981, the 400 and 800 came equipped with a GTIA chip instead of CTIA. The GTIA chip, also designed by George McLoed (for "George's TIA"), meant the machines were capable of 256 colors instead of 128, and had three additional graphics modes; this remained true for all future 8-bit Atari computers as well. For a time, Atari authorized a GTIA upgrade for earlier CTIA-equipped 800 machines; you could have the upgrade performed at various service centers across the country. Today it's pretty rare to stumble on an 800 with CTIA, although it could happen, especially since many people don't realize exactly what they're selling in estate sales, pawn shops, and the like. There's no technical reason to want a machine with CTIA graphics now; in fact, Atari designers had intended the GTIA chip to be in the original design, but couldn't complete it fast enough for the first run.

Let's take a closer look at POKEY, the Atari 8-bit's dedicated four-voice sound processor. "The Atari 800's architecture evolved as an upgrade of the 2600," Neubauer said in an October 1986 interview in *A.N.A.L.O.G. Computing.* "Conceived primarily by Steve Mayer, Joe Decuir, and Jay Miner before I arrived at Atari, the original plan for the POKEY chip called for keyboard interface, audio, and paddle controllers."[35] Mark Shieu, Steve Stone, and Delwin Pearson also worked on the chip.[36]

POKEY was a capable synthesizer—and vastly more sophisticated than what came with any other computer at the time. For each musical note, you could control the waveform, pitch (frequency), volume, and duration. The chip worked in three modes: four voices with up to 256 pitches each, two voices with up to 65,536 pitches each, or one voice with 65,536 pitches and two voices playing back

---

35. www.atarihq.com/othersec/library/neubauer.html
36. Atari 8-bit FAQ

one of 256 pitches.[37] There were also eight noise and distortion settings, and each voice could be played back at one of 16 volumes.[38] POKEY also handled keyboard input, the serial I/O bus, paddle controller input, and interrupt (IRQ) requests from peripherals. It included a random number generator and a timer.

Before the Atari computer, no home computer could produce more than one voice of audio for basic sound effects. The Atari was the first machine that could play polyphonic music as well as detailed, more realistic audio effects. I always found it strange how the newer Commodore 64's SID chip is more widely recognized today, given that SID could only support three voices instead of four (albeit with a wider range of notes). Atari, once again, was years ahead of the competition. As we step through some of the best games to grace the 8-bit platform later on in this book, the quality of the sound effects and music comes up repeatedly. Crawford understood the special place good sound had, and made an excellent pitch for it at the end of the chapter in *De Re Atari* on POKEY. He wrote the following in 1981; I'm including it here because it's a good first draft of what video games were to become:

The programmer must also understand the broader role of sound in the complete software package. Moviemakers have long understood the importance of mood-setting background music. The recent space adventure movies by George Lucas are excellent examples. When the villain enters the room you know immediately to fear and hate him from the menacing background rhythms accompanying his entry. You gleefully clap your hands when the hero saves the princess while gallant music plays in the background. Likewise, horror films can frighten you by merely playing eerie music, even though the action may be completely ordinary.

Space Invaders issues a personal threat to its player and victim with its echoing stomp. As the tempo increases, knuckles whiten and teeth grind. When a Zylon from Star Raiders fires a photon torpedo you push frantically on the control to avoid impact. As it bores straight for your forehead, time slows and you hear it hissing louder and louder as it approaches. Just before impact, you duck and dislodge yourself from your armchair.

---

37. Atari 8-bit FAQ
38. Ibid

Impressionistic sounds affect our subconscious and our state of mind. This is due possibly to the fact that sounds, if present, are continuously entering our mind whether or not we are actively listening. Visual inputs, on the other hand, require the user's attention. If we are distracted from the TV set, we cease to concentrate on the picture and the image leaves our mind. Sound therefore offers the programmer a direct path to the user's mind—bypassing his thought processes and zeroing in on his emotions.

It wasn't until the Commodore Amiga and Atari ST arrived that we began to see computers exceed what the Atari 8-bit was capable of. A computer with a 16-bit processor and bus may have been the envy of the technological world in the early 1980s. But when you have four separate processors, each dedicated to specific tasks, there's a tremendous amount you can accomplish even with "just" 8 bits. Sadly, in the case of the ST, it wasn't a clear break; there were certain things the Atari 8-bit could still do better, which is part of why the company continued to struggle. These machines did well for what they were, but once the PC began to "game" as well as the Amiga, the PC's much wider software compatibility meant the platform would eventually run away with the gaming market as well.

Today, PCs with dedicated graphics and sound chips are common. Veteran PC builders may recognize this as similar to having a PC with a GPU and a sound board. In fact, a standard 286-12 clone in 1989 with a VGA card and a Sound Blaster card would be a good analogue, as it represents the first time a PC-compatible became more powerful for all-around gaming than an Atari computer 10 years its senior! (Even then, the PC lacked hardware sprites.)

First Peripherals

By themselves, the Atari 400 and 800 couldn't do much, so it was up to you to buy a couple of extra products to get a complete system. Atari sold peripherals for data storage, for playing games, for printing output such as letters and program listings, and more. If you were buying the computer for the first time, you probably wanted at least one peripheral for data storage and one printer. Otherwise, all you could do with the machine was play games on cartridges. Thanks to the aforementioned SIO interface, it was easy to connect peripherals to the computer and expand your system.

The first thing you'd need was some type of storage system for saving your programs and documents, and the least expensive way to get it was with the 410 Program Recorder. At first glance, aside from its matching clay color, the 410 looked like a tape recorder you'd find at the local Radio Shack (may the retail chain rest in peace). The 410 loaded prerecorded programs from cassettes, and it also let you store and retrieve BASIC programs you created or typed in from a magazine. The 410 was a dual-track design, meaning it could play back audio instructions or music while simultaneously loading new data into the computer. Think of the cassette recorder as a miniaturized version of the massive reel-to-reel tape recorders used with mainframe computers of the 1960s and 1970s.

Figure 1.8: The Atari 410 Program Recorder. Credit: Bilby/Wikipedia

Cassettes were never the ideal medium for important data storage. Tape was prone to damage and decay. You had to rewind and fast-forward to just the right spot to get to where the program was stored, hence the three-digit, analog tape counter display. The 410, and all program cassette recorders to follow in Atari's lineup, stored 100,000 bytes on a 60-minute cassette and transmitted at just 600 bits per second.[39] While short programs could load and save in a few mo-

---

39. Atari 8-bit FAQ

ments, the majority of longer and more sophisticated software could take many minutes to transfer.

There appear to have been several iterations of the 410 Program Recorder. Earlier models looked like light-gray-painted generic tape recorders—shown in early Atari color brochures, and I've since seen one for sale on eBay—whereas the later model you see in most of the catalogs looked more like a proper peripheral for the 400 and 800. Every 410 contained a hardwired SIO cable, meaning it had to be at the end of an SIO peripheral chain.

The $599 Atari 810 was where the real storage action began. It was equipped with an MOS 6507 CPU—the same microprocessor in the VCS—and supported 5.25-inch floppy disks, the same size the Apple II and Radio Shack TRS-80 used. The 810 ran at 288rpm and was considerably faster than the 410; it transmitted data at 19,200 bits per second (bps). The drive shipped with Disk Operating System (DOS) 1.0 at first. Then, in 1981, it began to ship with the much more commonly used DOS 2.0S.

Figure 1.9: An Atari 800 parked next to an Atari 810 disk drive in my office. Superfluous Fios modem on the left.

The average 5.25-inch floppy disk, when formatted with an Atari computer, could store 88KB per side (88,375 bytes, or up to 60 pages of text or program code). Usually, though, you didn't see a kilobyte readout. Instead, most Atari 8-bit users remember sectors as the unit of measurement for file size. There were 128 bytes in a sector; you could fit 18 sectors on a track, and each single-sided, single-density disk had 40 tracks. Most people only paid attention to the sector count—707 per side, once formatted—because the drive handled the rest internally. You had to buy special double-sided disks if you wanted to use the other side. Enterprising owners figured out that if you punched a square-shaped hole in just the right spot, a single-sided disk became double-sided, at the slight risk of possible data loss on the second side (since the second side wasn't subject to the same quality control during manufacturing).

Beginning in October 1981, Atari began shipping 810 drives with ROM C, with a new, 20-percent-faster sector layout, and a Data Separator Board for improved reliability.[40] There were also two physical versions of the drive, with different door open-and-close mechanisms; the MPI version (produced from 1980 to 1982) had push-button eject, which slid a door up, while the Tandon version (1983) had a door where the center flipped open.[41]

A rare, massive version of the 810, the 815, contained two separate floppy drives in one enclosure. It debuted at the 1980 Summer CES, and aside from the doubled-up drive mechanisms, operated in the same way as the 810 (6507 microprocessor, 19,200bps transmit speed, and so on). Only approximately 60 were ever made[42] and were hand-built;[43] Atari apparently had trouble building them, so they fulfilled preorders and then abandoned the model entirely. Some of these survive in the wild, as is evident on Atari forums.

Atari also made several printers for its new computer line. The 40-column 820 printer, when stacked up on top of an 810 disk drive as it was shown in early Atari home computer ads, looked like it belonged with the system. Inside was a 6507 microprocessor (like in the 810 disk drive), a 6532 RAM I/O chip, and 2KB ROM.[44] The 820 plugged directly into the computer via an SIO cable. It could print 40 characters per second in upper- and lowercase on what was then standard-size adding-machine-style paper with its dot matrix impact print head. The utility of such small paper output was certainly questionable. While it matched the width of the computer's 40-column text display, it was still more for listing out programs you were working on or handling basic finances, than for typing up serious correspondence. The companion 40-column 822 Thermal Printer did a nice job with charts and graph plotting, and like the 820, the 822

---

40. Atari 8-bit FAQ
41. Ibid
42. *Atari Inc. Business Is Fun*, p. 478
43. Atari 8-bit FAQ
44. Ibid

connected directly to the 400 or 800's SIO port. It printed on thermal paper at 37 characters per second, and 40 characters per line, with upper- and lowercase and point graphics.[45]

The Atari 825 was the real workhorse of the first product lineup. This early 80-column dot matrix printer (introduced in at the 1980 Winter CES) was pretty slow, and generated decidedly middling-quality output at a rated 50 characters per second. But the 825 supported standard-width letter paper and stationery. This meant you could do actual work with it, and see your BASIC programs in more detail. Atari sourced the 825 printer from Centronics and rebranded it. As a result, the 825 didn't plug directly into an SIO port the way the 820 did; instead, you needed the Atari 850 Interface as a go-between, thanks to the printer's Centronics parallel interface. On the plus side, the 825 had both pin and friction feed, so you could use regular or perforated dot matrix paper. It also had a double-width mode for heads and captions.

Atari's first modem, the acoustic-coupled 830, debuted at the 1980 Winter CES. It may not have been much from a technical standpoint—honestly, it was a pain to use, compared with later modems—but it did open your Atari to an entire new world of what was then called telecommunications. The 830 consisted of a base and two foam cups, which cradled your regular telephone receiver. The 830 transmitted data (as sound) to and from the phone line at speeds up to 300bps. You just had to make sure to keep quiet once you finally connected online, or otherwise it would "hear" the noise, garble the signal, and disconnect you. The modem also required the 850 interface to connect to the computer.

The 835 Direct Connect Modem debuted at the 1982 Summer CES, and was the product Atari should have introduced in the first place. It resolved the biggest problems of the 830. It plugged directly into your phone line, which eliminated external interference. On the other end, it also plugged directly into the 400 or 800 via an SIO cable, and therefore didn't require the 850 interface. The 835 featured auto-dial, so whenever it encountered a busy signal because someone else was already logged into a particular online service, it would keep trying on its own. The modem still lacked auto-answer, so you

---

45. Atari 8-bit FAQ

couldn't use it to run your own BBS, and the bundled Telelink II software didn't enable file uploads and downloads.

Atari's peripheral lineup wasn't bad overall, but there was still the need for a real interface to existing third-party peripherals. Enter the 850 Interface: Debuting alongside the 825 and 830 at the 1980 Winter CES, the 850 gave you four 9-pin RS-232C serial ports and a 15-pin Centronics parallel port. This interface was necessary if you wanted to use many popular third-party modems and printers. For example, in my case, this interface let me run my BBS using a modem with auto-answer capabilities, which I wouldn't have had with any of Atari's own modems (more on this in chapter 3).

The Atari 400 and 800 were big game machines, so the need for controllers was paramount. The 9-pin joystick ports worked natively with the CX40 joystick, which debuted in 1977 with the VCS and became something of an industry standard. It even worked with the Commodore VIC-20 and Commodore 64. The CX40 is still my favorite joystick, but the model was not known for its reliability. I always found its directional control precise, and the fire button delivered positive feedback and was satisfying to press repeatedly.

Potentiometer-based controllers were also important for some games. The original CX30 paddles, which came with the VCS, also worked well with compatible 400 and 800 games. The paddles were a two-in-one design, terminating in a single 9-pin connector, but still allowing for two players. Notably, you needed the paddles for some early 8-bit games like Super Breakout, Kaboom!, (optionally) Clowns & Balloons, and a few others. Finally, you needed a trackball if you were going to play Centipede or Missile Command the right way. The CX22 wasn't as full-featured as the one made available in 1982 with the 5200 SuperSystem game console, as it lacked extra buttons and a numeric keypad, but for the Atari 400/800 versions of these popular games, it did the trick.

At this point, the groundwork was laid. Atari had the machines, the peripherals, and as we'll soon see, the software. Let's take a look next at some of the things you could do with an Atari computer the day you brought it home.

2 | Using Your Atari Computer

When you use a computer, phone, or tablet today, chances are you're familiar with what it's capable of. You may want to read news, watch a TV show on Hulu or Netflix, listen to music, check your email, see what your friends are doing on Facebook or Twitter, or Instagram some new photos. But it wasn't always this way.

Consider how much has changed just in the past generation alone. A popular graphic currently going around social media contrasts a 1993 electronics store flyer advertising all the individual pieces of equipment you needed for various tasks, versus a smartphone of today that's capable of doing all that and more. Gadgets like a CD player, a VCR, a camcorder, a point-and-shoot camera, and an answering machine are all obsolete (with the obvious exceptions for professional-level gear in some cases). In the early 1990s, computers ran word processor, spreadsheet, and desktop publishing programs, and you could play games and get online with them. All of the other stuff came later.

Now imagine how primitive computers in the 1970s were. Enthusiasts were just discovering what the machines could do; back then, there still wasn't any prepackaged software for word processing, desktop publishing, or managing your money. Atari wanted to address that with its new computer line. Many early programs were designed to help you around the home, or assist you in running a small business. User-friendliness was a brand new concept. One of the most distinctive things about Atari's home computer lineup was the packaging and advertising, which tried to appeal to the average person not already into computers: "Introducing the Atari Personal Computers. You Don't Have To Be a Genius To Use One." Under Kassar's direction, the advertisements mentioned, but played down, the 400 and 800's impressive gaming prowess, and instead focused on more mundane tasks like organizing your finances, learning new languages, and educating your kids. The real magic, though, was in programming the computer and gaming.

Figure 2.1: My first Atari desk in December 1983, after originally sitting on the floor in front of our console TV. I used a 13-inch Magnavox TV before I got a real monitor. (Pardon the backwards date stamp—the photo was stuck to another one when I found it.)

Getting Started

Let's say you bought an Atari computer, a peripheral or two, and some software, and you took it all home to set up. The 400 and 800 both came with hardwired video output cables, along with TV switch boxes you connected to the back of your television. This would let you intercept the signal from a dead channel in your area—usually channel 3 or 4. Whenever you wanted to use the computer, you would switch the box from TV to Computer, and then power up the machine. This worked the same way as early video game consoles like the VCS.

The 800 also came with a composite monitor jack, as mentioned earlier, which meant you could also use a computer monitor directly with a cable. Some people went this route, and purchased a monitor from another company. This is because Atari didn't sell a dedicated monitor for the computer. Mostly, it didn't matter. As long as you had a small TV set around—13 inches was a popular size at the time—then you were fine.

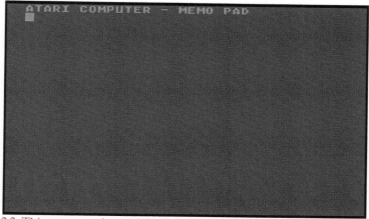

Figure 2.2: This was as useless as it looked. Still comforting to see it today, though.

When I first got started with my Atari computer, I hooked it up to the console TV in our family room (or "den," as we called it then). The TV delivered a giant 25-inch color picture for playing games and typing in programs. To use the computer, I sat at a marble-and-imitation-gold-leaf coffee table, the kind you'd find in a lot of houses with Italian grandmothers living in them. I typed and looked to the right to see the results on the screen, which was absolutely fantastic for a developing 8-year-old's neck muscles. Eventually, my ever-supportive parents set me up with a real desk and chair. First, I used a small 13-inch Magnavox TV set (also with fake wood paneling), and then a beloved Commodore 1702 computer monitor.

The original 400 and 800 didn't come with BASIC built in. The machine did do something when you turned it on, though: It made its trademark raspberry sound through the TV speaker and launched into ATARI COMPUTER MEMO PAD, a simple scratch pad you could type into. (Remember, this was back when using all caps for commands was still normal. It wasn't until the Internet, first on Usenet and later the Web, that all caps became synonymous with shouting.)

Memo Pad, for all intents and purposes, was completely useless. You couldn't save anything you typed. You couldn't program in it. All it did was let you type characters on the screen and see the results. I suppose if you were coming from a typewriter, as many people were in the 1970s, or emerging from the sea for your first steps on an earthly landmass, it was pretty novel. In the end, about the only thing Memo Pad was good for was indicating that your Atari could boot up on its own and was working normally. Since we all prefer to actually use our computers for something, let's move on.

Cartridges, Cassettes, and Floppy Disks

The easiest way to load and run programs was with cartridges. Atari computers didn't accept VCS cartridges—a sticking point during the design stage at the company. Instead, the 8-bit line brought its own slightly shorter, but thicker, plastic cartridges, which were notable for their internal mechanism to prevent dust from getting on the contacts. You could buy all manner of Atari 8-bit software in cartridge format, including programming languages like BASIC, educational programs, and (eventually) hundreds of games.

As with VCS cartridges, you couldn't erase an Atari computer cartridge—the software was permanently burned into the cartridge's circuit board. They were extremely durable and loaded within milliseconds of turning on the computer. Many Atari computer users built up a collection of cartridges, although some preferred the rewritability of cassettes and floppy disks.

I won't quote much from the manuals of Atari products in this book, because then why not just read the manuals? But I do want to highlight a particular section of the 800's original instruction booklet, which described cartridges as follows:

Many programming languages, games, and applications come in the form of a cartridge. These cartridges contain the actual program or programming information required to perform the desired functions. The programming language cartridges contain the instructions and other types of code making up that par-

ticular language. When you write a program, you are organizing these instructions into a meaningful procedure that the computer can understand and then execute. The game cartridges contain the entire program for that game. To begin playing the game, all you had to do is insert the cartridge, turn on the television, make sure the TV Switch Box is on COMPUTER (GAME), and turn on the computer. Then follow the game instructions and have fun!

This passage encapsulated the mentality of using an early personal computer. You didn't think of it the way you think of a phone with apps, a desktop browser with bookmarked websites, or even a PC with games installed. You thought of the computer as something that executed instructions, and those instructions were collected into programs for specific things you wanted to do. It may sound like semantics, but at that time, the home computer was a new, unexplored frontier. A computer wasn't just an appliance you used to balance your checkbook, print your homework, or play Missile Command. A computer was something you could learn to control, to harness to your exact specification. A computer contained multitudes.

Figure 2.3: An early Atari computer brochure showing cartridges, cassettes, and disks.

Cassettes were the primary user storage medium on the budget end of the spectrum. They consisted of differing lengths of magnetic tape, and let you keep a permanent record of your programs, at least until you erased them yourself—or unless you made it permanent by snapping the protective tabs out of the top. Cassettes were inexpensive, and let you store multiple programs on each one provided you kept track of the tape counter. The downside was speed; you had to forward or rewind each cassette to begin loading or saving a program, and the data transfer process itself could take a long time—which, if you were an impatient kid, could feel like years.

The norm for storage with the first wave of personal computers in the late 1970s and early 1980s was the 5.25-inch floppy disk, and it was no exception with the 400 and 800. If you were lucky enough to have a disk drive, it enhanced the experience of using the computer. Floppy disks were much faster than cassettes for both loading and saving data, and more sophisticated programs tended to come on them. Using disks also made it easier to store data you created, such as your own BASIC programs or AtariWriter documents.

Disk errors were a common source of frustration. You learned early on that you either had to made backup copies of your disks or risk of losing data—much more frequently than what happens today. Worries about data loss abound throughout Atari literature. The manual for the Sirius Software game Bandits read, "If 'BOOT ERROR' appears on the screen after booting, try the disk on another Atari 800 to verify the disk is good. All of our disks are tested prior to shipping," after which you were informed that the company would replace any defective disk with a new one for $5 as long as you sent back the original. And while it may seem odd that Sirius Software wouldn't replace a defective disk out of the box, the manual acknowledged how disks sometimes just go bad over time and need replacement. Or maybe you spilled your juice on one. It was a fact of life, and we learned to live with it.

Atari's disk operating system was developed by SMI and OSS.[46] Starting with version 2.0S in the fall of 1981, it consisted of two files: DOS.SYS (39 sectors), which booted the system on startup, and DUP.SYS (42 sectors), which you would use to bring up the main menu to look at files, run them, duplicate disks, and so on. In total, the two files used up a little more than 11 percent of a typical single-

---

46. Atari 8-bit FAQ

sided, single-density 5.25-inch disk. DOS had the ability to write itself to any new disk you wanted; this way you always had a copy on hand.

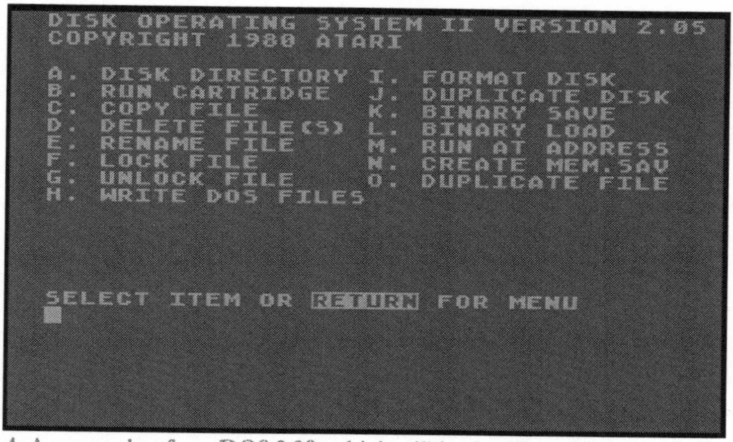

```
DISK OPERATING SYSTEM II VERSION 2.05
COPYRIGHT 1980 ATARI

A. DISK DIRECTORY     I. FORMAT DISK
B. RUN CARTRIDGE      J. DUPLICATE DISK
C. COPY FILE          K. BINARY SAVE
D. DELETE FILE(S)     L. BINARY LOAD
E. RENAME FILE        M. RUN AT ADDRESS
F. LOCK FILE          N. CREATE MEM.SAV
G. UNLOCK FILE        O. DUPLICATE FILE
H. WRITE DOS FILES



SELECT ITEM OR RETURN FOR MENU
```

Figure 2.4: A screenshot from DOS 2.0S, which will be familiar to anyone who owned an Atari computer and disk drive.

The main screen (copyright 1980!) would be familiar to anyone who has used an Atari system before. It still gives me comfort to see it to this day. It offered options to display a directory of what was on a disk, run an inserted cartridge, manipulate files (copy, delete, rename, lock, unlock), and format or duplicate disks. You could also save the current contents of memory into a file called MEM.SAV before loading a new program. When you were programming in BASIC and not looking at the DOS screen, you could save or load programs to disk. All you had to do to get back was type DOS, and the main menu would reload into memory. Most people who bought an 810 or other disk drive after owning a cassette recorder for a while would immediately load each of their programs from cassette and then save them onto disk for faster retrieval.

Atari BASIC

The vast majority of Atari 8-bit owners who also programmed—which was most of them, as I've been alluding to—used BASIC to do so. BASIC may have gotten its start in 1964 at Dartmouth College as a math project. But it ended up defining home computer ownership for an entire generation. Back in the early 1980s, programming your computer was a big part of the ownership experience. Often, it was the main reason you purchased a machine in the first place. There were many ways to write programs on the 400 and 800, such as Logo, Forth, and if you were daring enough, assembly language. But the most common was with the included BASIC cartridge, thanks in large part to its clear, natural-language-style syntax.

True story: I distinctly remember my dad and I spending one Sunday afternoon typing in a flag program in BASIC. It was one of the first ones we did, right after we bought the computer. It seemed long at the time, though later I would spend several days typing in programs 100 times its size. When we finished, the program naturally didn't run at first; we had made at least one mistake somewhere, so we spent even more time figuring this out. When we finally got it right, we typed RUN, and—ta da!—it displayed a blocky, pixelated American flag on the screen, complete with white dots for stars. And that was it. "This is what we get for all that? You've got to be joking," my father said. After this episode, I was the one who typed in all the programs. I didn't mind.

From then on, I was off. I typed in code for more graphics demos, puzzle games, text adventures, disk utilities, printing projects—you name it, and there were probably a bunch of near-useless-but-still-fun programs I could type in or write myself. At the time, schools began adding computer labs; in my elementary school, we were issued big yellow binders full of exercises and programming examples to type in throughout the semester. We learned about avoiding spaghetti code (too many GOTO statements), how to design simple and clear user interfaces, and how to program rudimentary graphics and sound on what were even then considered obsolete computers.

The computer was a completely novel thing back in the early 1980s, and it was fascinating to learn to program it and watch it do things. *De Re Atari* encapsulated the pros and cons of Atari BASIC quite well. It let you make simple graphics, sound, joystick, and paddle calls in clean language. The USR command delivered embedded access to assembly language routines. Since the BASIC interpreter was in ROM (either on a cartridge, or for later XL and XE machines, embedded in the hardware), you couldn't accidentally modify the interpreter. Atari BASIC also let you read and write to disk or control peripherals. But as the book pointed out, Atari BASIC didn't support integers; it required 6-byte binary-coded decimal floating point, which slowed down math calculations, and you could only create one-dimensional string arrays.

Writing Your First Programs

Most Atari owners started programming in BASIC before moving on to other languages. BASIC programs were written line by line, with line numbers to identify where you were in the listing. Often, your first programs were short, and demonstrated some simple capability of the computer, such as asking you to guess a number the computer was "thinking of," drawing lines on the screen, or solving a math problem and displaying the result. Some of the early BASIC programming books were ideal for learning this, including *Atari BASIC: A Self-Teaching Guide*, and even the blue three-ring-punch manual bundled with the Atari BASIC cartridge.

As you became more experienced, you could write longer and more detailed programs, with subroutines, arrays, and more advanced functions. For example, the Atari computer excelled at playing games, so it was natural for many enthusiasts to try their hand at programming one of their own. Some books offered tutorials on making games specific for Atari computers—you needed these if you wanted to take full advantage of the hardware. Other books showed how to make text-based adventures you could adapt for Atari computers with a little modification for standard BASIC syntax.

The Atari computer supported character graphics, which displayed white shapes on a blue background and could be triggered with various keys on the keyboard. Each computer came with a diagram of the keyboard showing where the symbols were located. When you pressed the Atari logo key, it triggered Inverse Video mode, which swapped the blue and white. Together, along with the regular upper- and lowercase letters and numbers, the characters made up ATASCII, which stood for the Atari Standard Code for Information Interchange. You could use them in your own programs. Later on, some developers made animation software to let you use these characters to build little movies, frame by frame, which played back at a defined speed. And BBSes run on Atari computers supported these animations, or "break movies" as they were sometimes called, and you could see them if you also owned an Atari computer. All told, character graphics were pretty nifty, and because they were built into all Atari computers, they were accessible and easy to use.

Figure 2.5: *Atari BASIC: A Self-Teaching Guide* was a popular book on programming for the Atari 400/800. It's how I got started.

One reason the Atari 8-bit played arcade-style games so well was the aforementioned player-missile graphics. Any *Star Wars* fan worth their salt knows what a TIE fighter looks like, and if you were programming with player-missile graphics, you'd see a lot of them in the example code. Both machines also had what you could call early screen savers built in, although they weren't called such at the time. After a period of inactivity, the computer would begin shifting through various color schemes, so as not to freeze any one exact image on the screen for too long. (This was known as "attract mode," named after the standby modes arcade coin-op games used to attract passersby, but in the Atari computer's case, it was really just a screen saver.)

If you did a lot of BASIC programming on the Atari, you invariably came across PEEK and POKE commands. PEEK let you check the value of a particular memory location, and POKE let you change it. These made program listings a bit more difficult to read, and consisted of large groups of numbers separated by commas. But they served a real purpose: While you could often accomplish the same tasks without PEEK or POKE, they used less or no memory and executed more quickly. Remember, BASIC was an interpreted language; PEEK and POKE were faster ways to get at the machine's actual capabilities, without requiring slow translation between easily readable BASIC code and incomprehensible machine language code.

Microsoft's Basic for the Atari came on floppy disk or cartridge (with the latter gaining the "II" moniker). Atari was purportedly going to use Microsoft Basic for the 400 and 800 at launch, but the software needed too much memory. It also wasn't quite compatible with Atari BASIC programs—*Antic* magazine noted it required PEEK commands for the joysticks—and didn't let you abbreviate commands. It also lacked compiler support, and was little used. It was, however, sold in an Atari box, and called Atari Microsoft Basic, somewhat confusingly.

BASIC and other entry-level languages were fine for hobbyist programming, easy to learn, and quite powerful once you learned to get under the hood. But BASIC had something of a less-than-stellar reputation among true power users at the time. You had to run BASIC first, and then run your code on top of it. As a result, games programmed in BASIC tended to be sluggish and unresponsive compared with those written in assembly, which was tougher to learn, but gave you direct access to the hardware. Anyone looking to maximize the potential of their Atari Computer headed straight for assembly language, using either Atari's Macro Assembler and Program Text Editor or Assembler Editor, or a third-party environment.

Compiled BASIC was a solid intermediary step. Datasoft and a few other vendors sold BASIC compilers for the Atari 8-bit; each read BASIC code, converted it into machine language instructions, changed floating point calculations to integer, and then spit out a compiled version of the program you could execute directly (and more quickly) without needing to load BASIC into memory. The downside was that, while it did in fact speed up code tremendously, it still wasn't quite as fast as what you could do natively in assembly language.

Part of the problem with learning assembly was that it was tough to look at someone else's code, since it was already compiled (or assembled) into machine language. This is where having the ability to disassemble code helped, and fortunately, Atari's Assembler Editor cartridge was up to the task. I myself spent the most time programming in BASIC, although I tried all of the other methods. I always wanted to get better at assembly language. Today, assembly programming is almost unheard of; there are far easier ways to access the machine directly using APIs, and anything you write in a higher-level language like C or C++ can be ported across many platforms more easily.

Forth was particularly attractive to anyone who wanted to program advanced graphics and sound capabilities without learning assembly language; portions of the code were compiled as well. Logo was an educational programming language based on LISP, and particularly lent itself to building artificial intelligence systems. Logo let you build lists of words and used so-called turtle graphics, and was easier to grasp than some of the more difficult concepts in BASIC. PILOT (for Programmed Inquiry, Learning, Or Teaching) also employed turtle graphics, but it wasn't based on LISP. Instead, it featured eight basic commands that let you manipulate text. You could also code in C on Atari computers, using a compiler from Deep Blue.

Today, you can't just power up a PC or Mac, boot into the OS, and start programming. You need a programming environment, a new project to set up, and you need to learn how to do all of this. While you're learning it, there are a million apps you can run, websites you can visit, or other things to do to distract you, because using a computer no longer almost requires you know how to program in some fashion, the way it did when the Atari 8-bit was in its heyday. Obviously people today are learning to program even as kids the way I did (except with newer languages like Python). But it's not the same as just happening on some BASIC code, liberally sprinkled throughout the instruction manuals and magazines dedicated to your favorite computer, and being able to try it out in a matter of moments. Also, get off my lawn.

Early Atari Software

In a series of product catalogs beginning with the release of the 400 and 800, Atari offered an assortment of off-the-shelf software it called "ready-to-use programs"—because often, at the time, you had to type in or modify software yourself for it to work properly. It's amusing to think about now, but off-the-shelf software was only a couple of years old at the time the 400 and 800 were released. Unfortunately, even though Atari kept the design of its computers a secret and wanted all software developed internally, the early selection for the computers was limited.[47] Right from the start, it was clear that Atari didn't know exactly what it wanted its new computer line to be.

From a retail standpoint, though, Atari products were inviting. One of the few bright spots was the distinctive art design. As was typically the case with Atari products, the people creating the beautiful artwork found on software manuals and boxes went uncredited. Some of it, such as the art on the Disk Operating System II Reference Manual, contained a signature buried in the corner. But most of it was done anonymously. The artwork served a real purpose: In a time when rudimentary screen graphics could only go so far, even with the then-advanced capabilities of Atari computers over the VCS and Mattel Intellivision, beautiful box art let the imagination run wild—a concept software developers like Infocom, with its text-based adventure games, later exploited.

Veteran Atari 8-bit enthusiasts know the company went through several different art design periods during the life of the platform:

- Black cartridge boxes and original cardboard-colored computer boxes, with a dark blue for BASIC and DOS manuals, and beautiful, color sketched artwork (1979-1981);
- Silver computer boxes, with rainbow logos and regular photographs (1982-1983);
- Silver-with-lines XL period boxes across the whole line (1983-84); and
- Dark gray and red XE period boxes (1985+).

---

47. www.gamasutra.com/view/feature/132160/atari_the_golden_years__a_.php

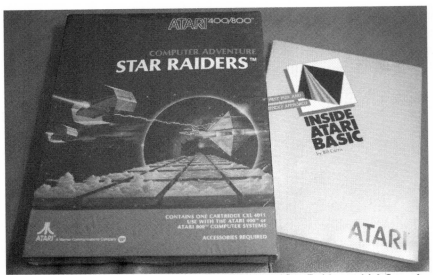

Figure 2.6: Contrast an early shrink-wrapped copy of Star Raiders, which I am the proud owner of, with a later Atari BASIC manual that mimics Atari's late-800/early-XL-era style.

Tim Lapentino's October 2016 book, *The Art of Atari*, sheds much more light on the subject, albeit with a focus on Atari consoles. It's beautifully made and well worth buying a copy.

Let's quickly look at some early software products before we get to the truly good stuff (the games) in Chapter 6. Atari's first word processor, imaginatively named Atari Word Processor, debuted in 1981 and utilized a graphics mode for previewing text in 80 columns. Well, "preview" is too strong of a word, as the computer didn't have the resolution for this without an aftermarket 80-column card. Instead, you would just see lines representing the overall layout of the printed text. The program supported basic editing commands, including moving chunks of text, but it had a stiff interface with separate Create and Edit modes. If you bought into the Atari early, you likely had either this, Letter Perfect, or Text Wizard.

Atari's own AtariWriter, released in 1983, was more popular. It's the word processor I used the entire time the 800 was my main computer. AtariWriter cost just $79.95 at its introduction, and since it was a 16KB cartridge, you could use it with either the 400 or 800. The interface looks clumsy to someone coming from today, but it worked well for the time, especially given the limitations of a 40-column screen width. AtariWriter let you write and edit in the same mode.

You could adjust the margins, line spacing, and justification, or print in two columns; use superscripts, subscripts, headers, and footers; and cut and paste text. There was also an Undo function—a serious novelty for anyone coming over from a typewriter. It didn't let you type over existing text; you could only backspace it or insert new text. But for the price, it was an excellent word processor.

Before the 400 and 800 hit the market, Atari showed off a series of educational cassette tapes at the Summer CES in 1979, covering a range of subjects including physics, auto mechanics, and economics.[48] The company expanded this catalog over the first couple of years, taking advantage of the 410 cassette recorder's ability to simultaneously stream data and audio. It's not clear how many people purchased any of these programs, but I'm betting on a relatively small number. On the other hand, speed-reading was a big deal in the 1970s and 1980s, and Atari capitalized on it with a dedicated five-cassette course called (simply enough) Speed Reading, packaged neatly in a large binder with a workbook and marketed as a standalone Atari product. The lessons had both voice tracks and program components, and you controlled the speed of the lessons with a joystick. Atari claimed Speed Reading "was based on a method proven successful since 1975," without ever sourcing the claim or explaining what it was. Hint: It was baloney.

One of Atari's more popular early initiatives to drum up interest in the new home computer line was a series of instructional cassettes for learning other languages. If you bought a 400 computer, a 410 cassette recorder, and one of these packages, you could learn "conversational" Italian, Spanish, French, or German via an interactive lesson system, which played actual voice examples and then turned it over to you to repeat them. The program spelled out phrases on-screen while a voice track pronounced the words. Each course came with five cassettes and a workbook, just like Speed Reading. The system couldn't listen to you, but most don't even today, and the programs still offered the ability to learn a language in a brand new way.

Famously, all new Atari hires had to program a VCS game first. This extended to Crawford, even though he was hired for his computer programming experience. So after he finished one—his game Wizard was never packaged and released—he coded two interesting

---

48. m.current.name/atari1979

nuclear power simulators for Atari computers. The first one was called Energy Czar, which put you in the role of guiding the U.S. through an energy crisis (a timely task in 1981). It was a primitive form of SimCity-like games, which had you raise or lower taxes, keep people happy, and monitor the nation's energy levels, economy growth rates, and overall public approval ratings. Scram was Crawford's second title, and simulated the inner workings of a nuclear power plant. The game let you first construct a plant, and then operate it in the face of a series of crises, including earthquakes and potential meltdowns. The game also purported to be an educational title, with tutorials on thermodynamics and nuclear safety.

Two other popular cartridges covered drawing and music. Atari's Video Easel cartridge let you "paint" on the computer screen. I spent many an afternoon drawing with it and experimenting with different colors and shapes using an Atari joystick, even before I got a Touch Tablet. Interestingly, this program had a mode to expand on your creation and add to it. You could watch this happen in real time. It also included preprogrammed pictures and the game of Life, which started with a small picture and then evolved on its own as time progressed. Many Atari ads showed the computer running Music Composer, which helped teach music to kids and adults alike. The program let you type in notes, and then play them back on screen. You controlled the pitch, octave, duration, and loudness of each note. The POKEY chip's four-voice polyphony made it possible to put together some surprisingly intricate compositions, especially with some creative, intentional "note stealing," where you would drop out a note or two from a chord to introduce an additional melody or other instrument at the same time. You could also save your compositions to either cassette or disk.

Magazines

Many big-name publications covered the launch of the Atari 400 and 800 in 1979 and 1980, including *InfoWorld, Creative Computing, Byte,* and the then-new *Compute!* magazine. Atari didn't see its first dedicated third-party publication until 1981, though. Originally called *A.N.A.L.O.G. 400/800,* and then *A.N.A.L.O.G. Computing,* it quickly became a go-to read with each issue, and well known for its tendency to publish machine language code instead of BASIC programs like other publications at the time. And it spared no expense in trashing the computer competition:

> *The color TRS-80 is a joke in comparison to even the 400. The APPLE II is archaic in technology next to the 800, and any other micro on the market just can't match the Atari's built-in computing power. Many computer stores won't carry the 400 or 800... 'there just isn't any software available,' well we receive software and new products at an almost daily basis at the A.N.A.L.O.G. office, so much that we have a difficult time reviewing it all. I am very impressed with the amount of really good software available in just a year's time.*[49]

Next, there was *Antic: The Atari Resource,* my own personal favorite. Each monthly issue had plenty of BASIC programs to type in. I killed a lot of evenings and Sundays in elementary school doing just that. Launched in April 1982, *Antic* magazine was a primary resource for anyone who wasn't already part of a local user group or online, and remained so even if you were.

I was an *Antic* Magazine subscriber for nearly its entire eight-year run. In addition to all the code in each issue, the magazine's staff developed an easy error-checking system called Typo. You could type in code by hand, line by line, and then run Typo to see if you got it right, based on a sophisticated analysis. Typo II, which debuted later on, made it even easier. It would check line-by-line as you typed, so you'd know you made a mistake immediately, and you'd know almost exactly where it was. I spent many an afternoon typing in games like Galactic Gloop (February '84) and Escape from Epsilon (June '84).

Like *A.N.A.L.O.G., Antic* contained tons of tips and tricks to help you get the most of your Atari computer. Example topics included ways to speed up and optimize cassette storage, reviews of popular games, tutorials on getting online with a modem, and endless articles on learning to exploit the graphics and sound capabilities of the 400 and 800. And any magazine reviewing video games, like *Computer Gaming World* or *Dragon* magazine (for role-playing games), would certainly mention any big or even exclusive Atari 8-bit titles.

---

49. *A.N.A.L.O.G.* issue #1: marvin3m.com/video/atari.htm, via Gamasutra.com History of Atari

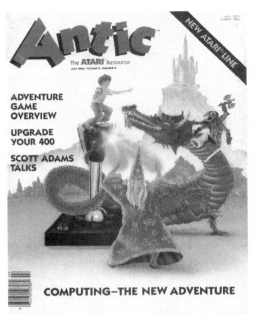

ADVENTURE
GAME
OVERVIEW

UPGRADE
YOUR 400

SCOTT ADAMS
TALKS

COMPUTING–THE NEW ADVENTURE

Figure 2.7: I read this magazine every single month, and usually typed in most (if not all) of the programs included in each issue.

Atari issued its own house-organ quarterly magazine beginning in early 1981 called *The Atari Connection*. It featured product news, technical tips, and quotes from happy Atari computer users. It was more of a brochure to get you to buy Atari products than an actual magazine. There were 16 issues in all, from spring 1981 through winter 1984. This publication was separate from *Atari Age*, the awesome VCS bimonthly that the dearly departed Steve Morgenstern launched in 1982 and published through 1984 for Atari Club members.

User Groups and Events

Atari also launched numerous outreach-style programs to educational markets and the community at large. In 1981, the company created the Atari Institute for Educational Action research, which awarded stipends and Atari products to individuals and nonprofits developing uses for computers in schools, community programs, or the home.[50] The following year, Atari opened the Video Adventure Center, which

---

50. Atari 8-bit FAQ

included an arcade and Atari store, at Marriott's Great America Theme Park in Santa Clara, California.[51] The same year, Atari began holding its Computer Camps in several locations across the country.

In 1983, Atari launched "Computers: Expressway to Tomorrow," an assembly program for junior and senior high schools. It delivered entertainment and computer education, along with a live host that would take students through the possibilities of computers in society.[52] The company also expanded the Marriott Theme Park with a video kaleidoscope and computer painting "Tone Tunnel," and even sponsored a Club Med Atari computer vacation getaway in the Dominican Republic.[53] Later the same year, Atari launched "Catch On to Computers," a program with General Foods for delivering equipment and educational software to schools collecting Post cereal proof-of-purchase points.[54] And Atari opened the first Atari Adventure Center in St. Louis, Missouri; it was a video arcade and a public computer classroom and lab with XL machines.[55]

The Atari Program Exchange (APX) (1981)

Atari wasn't known for its open-mindedness with regard to evangelizing its computer platform, and often actively kept schematics and programming details secret. It did foster the growth of the Atari Program Exchange, a library of several hundred programs in a variety of categories, from business and finance to games and developer tools. As with *The Atari Connection*, the company published an APX catalog four times per year. All you had to do to get on the list was send in a warranty card (back when people did this). Atari also courted hobbyist programmers to submit their creations, in return for possible royalties from sales in the catalog and a portion of $100,000 in annual prizes (including $25,000 in cash and $75,000 in products).

Unfortunately, APX didn't get off to a good start internally. "The guy who cooked up the idea, Dale Yocam, was trying to explain to the management there are a lot people out there who like to write programs and if we can publish these programs for them, it's a win-

51. Atari 8-Bit FAQ
52. Ibid
53. Ibid
54. Ibid
55. Ibid

win," Crawford said. "The management was not very interested in it. He put together a business plan for it and said, 'Look, we only need a little bit of money and this thing can be self-sufficient and it might make some money.' They very grudgingly agreed to let him do it. And so he did it and very quickly made it into a monster success. It was a major profit center for Atari. They rewarded Dale for his initiative by bringing in another guy to be Dale's boss... so Dale, in disgust, quit about a year later."[56] The APX program ran until Atari shut it down in 1984; the company returned all software rights to their respective owners. Afterward, *Antic* magazine tried to pick up the pieces with its own software-publishing arm.

There's more I've left out here. But by visiting user groups, reading *Antic* or *A.N.A.L.O.G*, or otherwise engaging with the community at large, using an Atari computer in the early-to-mid 1980s made you feel creative and inspired. Each magazine issue came with multiple programming projects you could try and/or build on, computerized art contests (which look downright primitive now, but were impressive at the time), utilities to aid your programming, and more.

Atari Starter Kits

Atari eventually realized that it wasn't at all clear to the average person what they needed to buy to get started with a computer. In 1981, the company began to offer accessory kits to help beginners get up and running with their basic Atari system and television set. Here's what each of the six kits included, and in all cases you could also buy each of the bundled products separately as well:

The Programmer: A BASIC Computing Language cartridge, the BASIC Reference Manual, and *Atari BASIC: A Self-Teaching Guide*, all geared toward teaching you to program the Atari computer for the first time. This was a potent combination, although 400 and 800 packages available at retail outlets often came with one or more of these products already.

The Entertainer: Two joystick controllers, a Star Raiders cartridge, and either a Pac-Man or a Missile Command cartridge (depending on when the kit was put together). This was a fairly obvious and not particularly useful package. It didn't take much to figure out you bought

---

56. Steve Fulton interview with Chris Crawford, September 2007

each game cartridge separately, and to play games, you needed one or two joysticks.

The Communicator: The 830 Acoustic Modem, the 850 Interface Module, and the Telelink I cartridge, a simple program to connect online to other systems and send and receive information. Later on, this kit was upgraded to the Communicator II, which swapped the 830 for the 835 Direct Connect modem, along with Telelink II and 3 hours of free service on various information networks.

Figure 2.8: An early Atari brochure explaining the starter kits.

The Educator: The 410 Program Recorder, a BASIC Computing Language cartridge, and States & Capitals, a cassette-based educational game to teach U.S. geography, which I still remember playing with my dad in our den, on the floor, in front of the aforementioned wood-paneled console TV. The first time I played, I got just 12 states and one capital right. Successive plays eventually got me to the point where I could remember all 50 states, if not all 50 capitals. (Quick: What's the capital of South Dakota?)

The Home Manager: Included Family Finances and The Home Filing Manager, and required an 810 disk drive and 32KB of RAM. I never met anyone who used either of these programs, but they turned up in all of the early Atari product catalogs, separately and as part of this Home Manager kit. I list it here for completeness, but I don't suggest you go out and buy one unless you're trying to complete a collection of early Atari software.

The Bookkeeper: Atari's bookkeeping kit package highlighted everything wrong with Atari computers in a business environment. The kit came with 48KB disk software and an external CX85 hardware numeric keypad to plug into the 800. A June 1983 review in *Antic* said the software was slow to respond and didn't support double-density drives. The system also couldn't issue invoices or monthly statements, and it didn't let you compare budgeted values with actual expenditures.

3 | Atari Learns to Let Go

Once you bought your Atari computer and made it past the company's own product line, there was gold to be found in third-party peripherals and upgrades. Unfortunately, it took a few years before the third-party market began to flourish—and the blame lies entirely with Atari Inc. After the 400 and 800 launched, the company remained secretive about its computer in a misguided attempt to give its own in-house developers an advantage.[57] This was an unnecessarily deep wound to the platform at a critical time, when the company needed lots of third-party developers on board.

It frustrated Crawford, who was arguably the biggest early evangelist for the platform: "The attitude of the executives was, 'We want to make all the money on the software. We don't want any competitors.' They were having competitors with the VCS and the programmers were trying to explain that, 'No, that's not how it works, you need a big library of software, you need to encourage them.'"[58]

Nolan Bushnell famously conflicted with Warner Communications and got out of Atari soon after selling it. So it's no surprise to find he has similar feelings. "The big difference was Warner Communications against Steve Jobs," Bushnell said. "Warner could never win that one. I don't know if I could have, but I wouldn't have made the same mistakes Warner did. The main problem that allowed Apple to dominate was, in fact, not technology but business strategy. Steve was

---

57. arstechnica.com/features/2005/12/total-share/
58. Steve Fulton interview with Chris Crawford, September 2007

out evangelizing to software developers to build software for their machines. Our strategy with the video games was that we basically wanted to give away the hardware and make money on the software. That called for a quasi-closed system.[59]

"Warner thought that was the right way to do the computers business, too," Bushnell continued. "So they said, 'Not only are we not going to help third-party developers, we're going to sue you if you use our operating environment.' So everybody that wanted to get into the software business supported Apple over Atari. So basically Warner drove the coffin nail in the Atari 800, despite it having a clearly superior chipset, a better operating environment... We had a lot of innovations in the Atari 800 that became standard later on."[60]

This sentiment was pervasive throughout the company at the time. "All of us on the project strongly urged senior management to make the Atari 400/800 an open design and publish the operating system and hardware manuals," Miller said. "We felt this was essential to making the computer successful because it would encourage outside development and allow much more software to be developed than Atari could ever produce. Unfortunately, management decided to make it a closed system. A few years later that decision was reversed and the entire listing to the OS was published, but Atari didn't make any effort to sanitize the comments. So, you'll see comments in the [program] listing like, 'I hope this works!'"[61]

Eventually, developers began to band together and figure out what they needed to know. People like Crawford began to leak documents to anyone requesting them. "Initially they had never quite defined what it was that had to be kept secret," Crawford said later. "I was the programmer at Atari who had come in from the outside world and had more contacts with outsiders. I'd be working on Atari software and the phone would ring and it was somebody in Indiana saying, 'Can I get any of the technical documents?' and I would go over to the main area and get a few of the technical documents, photocopy them and mail them off... there were enough loopholes that I was able to send out some documents and not get fired."[62]

59. CNET News.com, "The return of King Pong," David Becker
60. Ibid
61. www.digitpress.com/library/interviews/interview_alan_miller.html
62. Steve Fulton interview with Chris Crawford, September 2007

Atari eventually got the message and got over its secrecy. It formed the Software Support Group in 1981 to foster third-party software development. "Our job [in the Software Support Group] was to provide technical support to outside programmers," Crawford said. "We had a whole package of goodies we provided for free. By the way, the main thing we did was this tour where I would travel around to cities all over the country. We would rent a hotel meeting room, and people could come in to these seminars where we taught them all about how to program the Atari and I did almost all the work here.[63]

"I had a real barnstorming style. My job was to wean people away from the Apple to the Atari. I was pushing that line really hard. Somebody in one of the magazines that had come to it said 'Crawford does a show like an old-time evangelist. You half-way expect him to start quoting the bible', and that is where the term 'software evangelist' arose."[64]

Atari employees were finally able to publish *De Re Atari*, and it's true that Atari 8-bit sales peaked in 1982 at 600,000 units.[65] But by this point, plenty of software developers were already flocking to the competing and more open Apple II, and later, the Commodore 64. This began to happen right as the first dedicated magazines like *A.N.A.L.O.G.* and *Antic: The Atari Resource* began to pop up around the platform, after more general computing publications like *Compute!* and *Creative Computing* grew in size. As Atari's veil of secrecy began to fall, some of the most notable third-party products began to hit the market. Let's take a tour through some of the best.

Third-Party Disk Drives

Some of the most popular third-party peripherals were disk drives, made by manufacturers like Percom Data, Rana Systems, Indus, and Astra. They offered features you couldn't get straight from Atari, such as double-density support, digital track and error code readouts, and in some cases, a built-in printer interface. For example, an early entrant in third-party peripherals for the 400 and 800 was Percom

---

63. Steve Fulton interview with Chris Crawford, September 2007
64. Ibid
65. jeremyreimer.com/uploads/notes-on-sources.txt

Data. It offered the AT88, one of the first double-density drives, which let you store 176KB per disk side instead of 88KB. The drive contained an I/O pass-through, so you could hook one into a system along with a standard 810 drive. The AT88 was particularly desirable at the time because it contained a parallel printer port, so you didn't need a separate interface for your printer. The AT88 was advertised for $599 in 1983.

Many Atari users preferred to stack two (or more) floppy drives together as part of their computer system. This way, you could play a game or run a two-disk program by leaving them both inserted at the same time. It also made file and disk copying a snap. The Astra Systems 1620 gave you this flexibility in one enclosure. It was single- and double-density compatible, meaning it offered the storage of up to four 810s chained together—all for $595 retail. A later revision changed the door mechanism to make the 1620 easier to close, and an entirely new model introduced in 1984 (the 2001) promised improved reliability and quieter operation, but was otherwise similar.

Distinguished by its slightly quieter beeps while loading sectors, the Rana Systems 1000 was another popular third-party drive from a company already known for its Apple products. The low-profile 1000 was faster than the Atari drives as well. It sported a two-digit red LED readout, status indicators, and buttons to display density, error status, and drive number. The LED readout also displayed what track the drive was currently reading to or writing from. In my own (and obviously anecdotal) experience, the Rana drives were a bit less sensitive to bad sectors than the Indus GT, and could often read a disk the Indus GT choked on with its dreaded error codes.

Then there was the sleek black $449 Indus GT. "Looks like a Ferrari. Drives like a Rolls. Parks like a Beetle." Pictured with a pair of leather driving gloves, the ballsy advertising slogan launched a seriously slick piece of hardware, complete with a two-digit red LED readout for status and error codes, and a soft-close, tinted plastic front panel cover to protect the drive and buttons from dust. Naturally, I had to have one, because the ad used car analogies, and even as a kid, I loved cars. I ended up owning three of these drives, which made it easier to run a BBS. The only problem was that you couldn't quite stack them without something to sit between them, because otherwise the dust cover door for the drive on the bottom couldn't fully open.

Trak drives were also quite popular, beginning with the AT-D2. Another third-party drive to contain a separate parallel port for plugging in a printer, the Trak AT-D2 cost less than $500 and offered double-density storage and a front-mounted control panel similar to what Rana and Indus drives offered. The control panel had a touch-sensitive disk protect switch and the *de rigueur* two-digit red LED track indicator. The AT-D1 was a lower-cost version; it only supported single-density read/write, but was otherwise similar to the AT-D2.

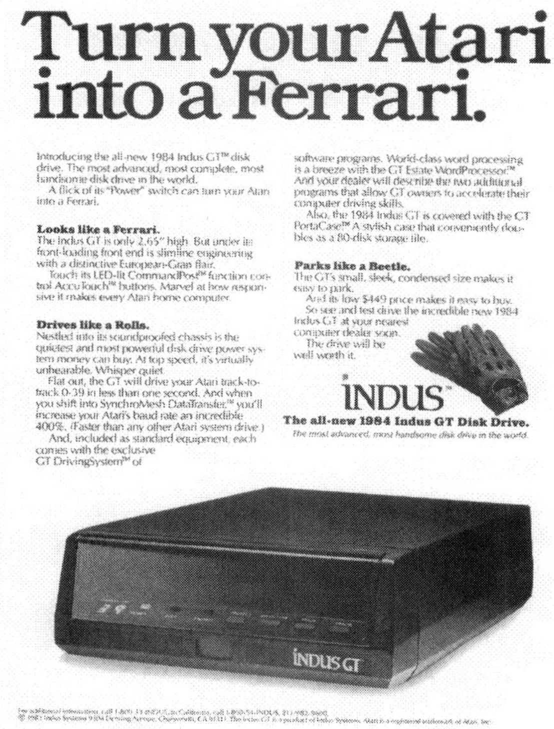

Turn your Atari into a Ferrari.

Introducing the all-new 1984 Indus GT™ disk drive. The most advanced, most complete, most handsome disk drive in the world.
A flick of its "Power" switch can turn your Atari into a Ferrari.

Looks like a Ferrari.
The Indus GT is only 2.65" high. But under its front-loading front end is slimline engineering with a distinctive European-Gran flair.
Touch its LED-lit CommandPost™ function control AccuTouch™ buttons. Marvel at how responsive it makes every Atari home computer.

Drives like a Rolls.
Nestled into its soundproofed chassis is the quietest and most powerful disk drive power system money can buy. At top speed, it's virtually unhearable. Whisper quiet.
Flat out, the GT will drive your Atari track-to-track 0-39 in less than one second. And when you shift into SynchroMesh DataTransfer™ you'll increase your Atari's baud rate an incredible 400%. (Faster than any other Atari system drive.)
And, included as standard equipment, each comes with the exclusive GT DrivingSystem™ of

software programs. World-class word processing is a breeze with the GT Estate WordProcessor™. And your dealer will describe the two additional programs that allow GT owners to accelerate their computer driving skills.
Also, the 1984 Indus GT is covered with the GT PortaCase™ A stylish case that conveniently doubles as a 80-disk storage file.

Parks like a Beetle.
The GT's small, sleek, condensed size makes it easy to park.
And its low $449 price makes it easy to buy.
So see and test drive the incredible new 1984 Indus GT at your nearest computer dealer soon.
The drive will be well worth it.

INDUS™
The all-new 1984 Indus GT Disk Drive.
The most advanced, most handsome disk drive in the world.

For additional information, call 1-800-33-INDUS, in California, call 1-800-54-INDUS, (I) (800) 9800.
© 1983 Indus Systems 9304 Deering Avenue, Chatsworth, CA 91311. The Indus GT is a product of Indus Systems. Atari is a registered trademark of Atari, Inc.

Figure 3.1: A 1984 ad for the Indus GT disk drive.

In 1984, Trak unveiled the AT-D4, a $649 model with support for double-sided, double-density disks. Finally, Trak's later Champ drive ($399) also worked with double-density disks, but came in at a lower price with fewer buttons and no digital LED track indicator on the front panel. On the plus side, you could add up to two auxiliary drives, and there was a factory turbo option available to enhance read and write speeds. Trak also packaged its own proprietary disk operating system; Trakmanager, a disk filing system program; and some games and utilities.

Third-Party Disk Upgrades and Utilities

Many smaller companies popped up offering chip upgrades to existing drives to make them faster and able to duplicate copy-protected disks. The US Doubler, developed by ICD, was a hardware kit to add double-density support to the Atari 1050 disk drive. It also added an UltraSpeed I/O mode, which was several times faster than a stock 1050 at reading and writing data. It consisted of two replacement chips and a software disk. The Impersonator, by Alpha Systems, let you create backup copies of your cartridges on disk. It came with a "dummy" cartridge—basically a circuit board you inserted into the cartridge slot to trick the computer into thinking it had a cartridge loaded, thus bypassing the copy protection most had built in. Unfortunately, rampant piracy was the norm on this platform, and more often than not, tools like The Impersonator were used to create tradable versions of otherwise expensive cartridge-based games.

Computer Software Services placed many ads in Atari magazines in the early 1980s, and one of the most prominent was an ad for The Pill, a cartridge backup device to let you save the contents of a cartridge to either disk or cassette. This meant you could store roughly 10 16KB programs on a regular disk, and give each one individual filenames. Each file was an executable you could just run straight from disk. The Impossible let you make copies of copy-protected disks. But in addition, it also removed the protection; it didn't just clone the original disk, but "unprotected" it in the process.

The well-loved Happy Computers company produced add-on upgrade boards for 810 and 1050 disk drives. The boards usually delivered a five-fold improvement in seek and write times. In addition, Happy upgrades remain prized for their ability to back up even copy-protected floppy disks. I'm sure that it, like sector editors and the tools I mentioned above, also contributed to the Atari 8-bit's piracy problem, but upgrades like these also gave honest owners peace of mind; floppy disks weren't reliable at the time. Happy-enhanced drives are still popular on the used market today.

Figure 3.2: An ad for Computer Software Services products.

The $79.95 SpartaDOS was a phenomenal product you may not have run into during the 400/800 years, unless you stuck around throughout the late 1980s. If you did, SpartaDOS may have transformed your experience using Atari 8-bit computers. It's the closest Atari ever got to feeling like MS-DOS. Unlike Atari's DOS, SpartaDOS had a command line UI in addition to a menu system. The commands were similar to those of MS-DOS, such as DIR, CHDIR, and DEL, and it supported wildcards and drive selection (D1, D2, and so on). You could also control the OS from other programs, such as AtariWriter, since SpartaDOS was in a separate cartridge. SpartaDOS also contained ARC for file compression, support for a RAM disk, and even an unerase function. A revised version called SpartaDOS X carries on; many Atari 8-bit enthusiasts use it today. News on the latest updates can be found at sdx.atari8.info.

The Indus GT disk drive came with its own DOS called Synchromesh. Any disk formatted in Synchromesh ran faster on the Indus GT than a regular disk. The only problem was you had to load

Synchromesh in first, before you could take advantage of the speed boost, which negated the benefit.

As your disk library grew, you may have come across some programs to help you organize your collection. Two personal favorites: If you had a lot of executable binaries across many floppy disks, Automenu was your friend (and there were others like this). It quickly and easily created a root menu, which would boot up almost instantly when you first inserted a floppy and turned on the computer. Then it would let you select from a list of what was on the disk. I also swore by Diskeeper to keep things organized. I had four Indus GT disk drive cases, each of which held either 60 or 100 disks (depending on the version and when it was produced). I used sticky labels and a black marker to number all of my disks. Then I used Diskeeper to remember where everything was stored. It was like book or music library cataloging software, except it was for Atari disks.

Other Products

There was no shortage of utilities for programmers looking to move beyond what Atari offered. Most were in software, but a few hardware options sneaked through. OSS Precision Software Tools bought Shepardson Microsystems, the company that coded the original BASIC and DOS for Atari, and then sold an upgraded version called Basic XL. It claimed to be twice as fast, and supported structured programming and enhanced graphics capabilities with improved player-missile support. I used Basic XL to run FoReM XL, bulletin board software. A free (public domain) version of Basic called Turbo Basic XL reportedly ran three to four times faster than Atari BASIC. It also came with a compiler that sped up listings by 15 or 20 times. I regret not getting the chance to try this out at the time. I had moved on to the Atari ST, but I certainly would have appreciated the huge speed boosts.

The Walling Co. Aprom was advertised as a general-purpose 16KB EPROM burner cartridge, which plugged into the 800's right cartridge slot. The idea was you could "burn" a program to it, and then run it at ROM speed. The cartridge booted with its own OS first, and could then work with BASIC or Assembler. The main kit cost $99.95, and you could also buy additional cartridges to store multiple programs.

The ATR8000 was a versatile box advertised in many issues of *Antic* magazine. It was known primarily for bringing CP/M compatibility to the Atari 8-bit, letting you use the computer as a terminal for it; it even had a Z-80 processor built in. The ATR also let you hook up standard disk drives, a parallel printer, and a modem, eliminating the need for an 850 interface and letting you use third-party disk drives. It also had an optional board to give you an 80-column display for use with CP/M, while another optional board added an Intel 8088 for IBM PC and MS-DOS compatibility.

Another area ripe for "disruption" (though no one called it this in the early 1980s) was Atari's home printer market. Atari printers were the most popular in the beginning, because they worked and retailers often packaged them for sale with the computers. But they generally offered only text output, and were slow and needlessly expensive. Newer third-party printers often delivered superior print quality, faster speeds, support for graphics and additional fonts, and other desirable features. The most popular brands were Epson, Okidata, Star Micronics, and Axiom.

Epson 80-column dot matrix printers, including the MX-80, FX-80, and FX-85, were widely regarded as reliable workhorses for the time, and were often seen perched next to Atari computers. I personally owned an FX-85, and ran my BBS with it faithfully spitting out updates on whatever each caller did when they dialed in. Each of the Epson printers had near-letter-quality modes, which were good enough for mainstream home and business work, if not quite as smooth as a typewriter's output. And unlike some of Atari's own early printers, the Epson models were capable of printing graphics in programs like Brøderbund's The Print Shop. You did need an 850 interface to connect one of these printers, though.

A few other brands developing dot matrix printers at the time didn't survive the way Epson did. Star made several quality printers for the Atari 8-bit line, most notably the Gemini 10X, which was known for its reasonable speed and output quality for the price. The 10X supported both friction and tractor-feed paper. Star also sold a companion STX-80 thermal printer and the Gemini 15, a 136-column legal-size model. The Axiom AT-100, an 80-column dot matrix printer manufactured by Seiko, plugged directly into Atari computers via the SIO port. It had a sleek, shallow-depth design and a smoked plastic cover, and delivered solid value for $299, if not the best print quality or speed.

Atari joysticks were arguably the most famous ever made for home computers and game consoles, at least until NES-style gamepads took over. But if you were around in the early to mid 1980s, you probably also owned or saw someone with the Wico Command Control bat-handle joystick, with its trademark red-and-black design and white button on top. These were excellent joysticks, if different in feel from the simplistic Atari models. I always favored genuine Atari CX40 sticks, but many people swore by Wico's. The company produced other variations, such as ones with an arcade-style red ball on top instead of the bat handle, and a flight-stick version with finger grips built into the handle. If you're looking for alternatives today, *Antic* ran roundups of models from Kraft, Suncom, Amiga (!), and Questar among others in the December 1983 and December 1988 issues, both of which are available for free online.

Touch tablets were also a popular item, and the KoalaPad was arguably more popular than Atari's own graphics tablet (which I'll cover in the next chapter). The KoalaPad let you input commands with your finger, as well as giving you a 4-by-4-inch drawing surface with an included pen. You connected the KoalaPad via a joystick port, and the pen had buttons on the top instead of on the side the way the Atari model did. In addition to the Atari 8-bit line, the KoalaPad worked with the Apple II, Commodore 64, and TRS-80.

One of the biggest problems with the Atari 8-bit computers, and the main reason business users didn't take them as seriously as IBM PCs, was the 40-character-per-line limit. It made word processing and working with spreadsheets difficult. Programs like Letter Perfect, AtariWriter, and VisiCalc had plenty of power, but you couldn't always see enough of what you were working on, or even see roughly what a printed document would look like on a page. One early, if expensive, solution was to replace the Atari 800's two 16KB RAM modules with one 32KB module and fill the last slot with the Full-View 80, a $350 board you hooked into a dedicated monochrome monitor instead of a regular TV set. The board was designed to work with Letter Perfect, and made editing and formatting documents easier. The ACE-80 also generated an 80-column display, and notably, came in a right cartridge version for the Atari 800 so you could use it while programming in BASIC (which would be plugged into the left cartridge slot).

Manufacturers like Mosaic offered memory upgrades for Atari computers: first, to bring 800s from 16KB to 48KB less expensively than what Atari charged (before the latter began shipping all 800s maxed out at 48KB), and then later to 64KB and even 192KB and 384KB. For the 400, Sar-An offered a $149.95 upgrade to 48KB. These numbers sound silly today, but at the time, the idea of being able to save hundreds of pages of text, or the information to play 10 or 15 different songs (using MIDI or other sound data), on storage media was considered a breakthrough. And you only needed some of it in memory at any one time.

Figure 3.3: RAM expansion kits for the Atari 400 and 800 were quite popular. Three of these 64KB Mosaic cartridges would bring an Atari 800 up to 192KB RAM.

As the 1980s wore on, more memory upgrades began to appear on the market. Perhaps the definitive article on this arrived in the

November 1988 issue of *Antic*. In it, the writer Dr. Lee Brilliant said to no longer bother with 400 and 600XL upgrades—some AtariAge forum members today may beg to differ. Nonetheless, Brilliant listed upgrades from ICD (the RAMbo XL) and Newell (the 256KXL), both of which are for the 800XL. The newer XE models worked with Magna Systems upgrades, and came in 320KB, 576KB, and 1088KB versions, though you couldn't do much with them aside from run a RAM disk. The 800 had the most options available, including models from Magna Systems (up to 1MB, though 256KB was more common) and Axlon.

Manufacturers such as The Alien Group, RealTime Electronics, and Street Electronics made third-party voice synthesizer boxes to enable the Atari computer to speak text aloud. They came with software to control the speed, pitch, and volume of speech, and whether punctuation should also be spoken. They were expensive—an early Street Echo box sold for $369.95 in *Antic* magazine—and while they were pitched as peripherals for game development, educational programs like spelling software, and aiding the handicapped, few were sold.

There was one exception, though: Software Automatic Mouth. Based entirely in software, S.A.M. was less expensive at just $59.95 and considerably more accessible, and also found its way into a number of games at the time. You could control S.A.M. with simple BASIC commands. Since it was software-based, it ate up most of the CPU, so the screen would go blank whenever it spoke. This was a small price to pay given the program's flexibility and audio quality, however, and I had tons of fun making S.A.M. say silly things and curse words and whatever else my 10-year-old brain dreamed up at the time.

There were several good word processors available for the Atari platform aside from the company's own products. Datasoft's Text Wizard included most of the same editing and text manipulation tools; what made Datasoft's package different was its separate Spell Wizard spell-checker, which boasted a dictionary of 33,000 words, spelling suggestions, and the ability to add custom words (all of which became table stakes later in the 1980s). Both sold in a package for $79.95 list. More popular still was PaperClip. *Antic* celebrated moving from Letter Perfect to PaperClip in its May 1985 issue, saying it was "by far the best word processor ever available for the Atari," despite its relatively low $59.95 list price. It offered one-key macros, a superior 40-column preview mode, support for 80-column cards, and a dual-window view for looking at two files simultaneously and moving text between them. One notable downside: It required a hardware copy protection key, which plugged into the second joystick port.

Dan Bricklin's famous "instantly calculating" (as per the box copy) spreadsheet program, VisiCalc, made its way over to the Atari 400/800. It supported 63 columns, 351 lines, numerous formulas, and even a rudimentary dual-window view, and you could output data to the company's VisiTrend/Plot program for charts and graphs. VisiCalc required 32KB to run, and also worked with Atari's numeric keypad (included in The Bookkeeper Kit or sold separately for $124.95).

The 800's right cartridge slot didn't see a lot of love, but a natural use for it was disk and programming utilities. Monkey Wrench II added 18 utilities for your BASIC programming sessions and 16 for machine language. Some of the best included automatic line numbering, the ability to scroll up and down through BASIC listings, and move and copy functions for lines of code. It also supported hexadecimal and decimal conversion.

If you had a computer and a printer in the 1980s, you probably remember The Print Shop. I went through more than my share of tractor-feed printer paper running this program. It was the easiest way to print signs, banners, greeting cards, invitations, and even letterhead on your own. The output never rivaled a professional service—you'd have to move to a Mac and an expensive laser printer, and decent, affordable inkjets for the PC didn't appear until the 1990s. But The Print Shop brought custom graphic design to the home and small business, and let you change the borders, add graphics, type in custom messages, and more. Given how much you can do with even free software today for the PC and Mac, not to mention the kind of print quality you get from even a $49 inkjet printer, there's not much reason to revisit the 8-bit version of The Print Shop except for nostalgia purposes.

Going Online

At some point after owning an Atari computer for a while, you may have gotten the itch to go online and "see the world," either to meet other enthusiasts, trade software, or get some information in what was then a high-tech and cutting-edge manner without newspapers or television broadcasts. BBSes were a way for people to meet each other, trade tips and hacks, swap software, and bond around their favorite activity—programming and otherwise using home computers. Some of them had specific themes, such as for movie or music fans, for Dungeons & Dragons players, and so on. Many BBSes offered cute animations when you called up and logged in, and as a system operator (or sysop) got to know you, he or she could add extra minutes or downloads to your allotted calling time, or add access to otherwise restricted message bases.

Early online services enabled primitive forms of banking and stock trading, such as CompuServe and the Dow Jones News/Retrieval Service. These required hourly charges; calling them on a regular basis could add up fast, and was certainly beyond the budget of a kid like me at the time. But most Atari users stayed on the free route and called local, personalized BBSes. To do this, you needed to buy and connect a modem to your computer, and then connect the modem to your phone line.

You also needed some kind of software for calling the bulletin boards. I often used Xmodem or Ymodem, but there were plenty of others, each with varying features and performance. The earliest popular modems ran at 300bps. That was slow enough you could see the text "paint" itself across the screen, 40-character line by 40-character line. It worked out to about 300 words per minute, which is roughly the average person's reading speed. (Some software offered a 110bps mode, which would mean you could download a new program once every eight months, or something.) Later, faster 1,200bps modems appeared, which sped up downloads considerably. You could still see text paint across the screen, but it was faster.

Third-Party Modems

Atari's own modems were all you needed for getting online. But third-party modems usually offered more features, sometimes at a lower price. The Hayes Smartmodem line was iconic—though I'm biased, since I had one. The RS-232C-based Smartmodem 300 was expensive, but it contained several key features Atari modems didn't have, including auto-answer, dial, and repeat. The auto-answer part meant you could use it to run a BBS of your own, and auto-dial meant you can keep trying a BBS if there's a busy signal without having to dial manually each time. A built-in speaker let you monitor the status of the connection—early shades of the "ping" and "sshhh" sounds people remember from dial-up AOL disks in the 1990s. An array of seven status lights gave you information about your current connection; eight lights for the 1,200bps modem, thanks to its High Speed light. Hayes kept the popular, finely honed metal enclosure with plastic end caps for many years, upgrading the internals all the way through 9,600bps with the Optima moniker.

Anchor Automation's Volksmodem was a frequently advertised budget modem. You have to love the name; it immediately conjures up the image of an inexpensive, reliable product, just like the Volkswagen Beetle. The small, basic Volksmodem ran at 300bps, came with an RS-232 cable, and has an audible cue for connections. It lacked the Hayes Smartmodem's auto-answer and auto-dial modes, though.

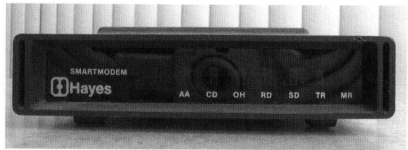

Figure 3.4: The Hayes Smartmodem 300 and the later 1200 were two popular third-party modems that worked with the Atari 800, provided you also had an Atari 850 interface for the RS-232C connection. Credit: Michael Pereckas/Wikipedia

Another budget option was the Microbits Peripheral Products MPP-1000C, a basic, tiny 300bps box without the need for the 850 interface, or even an SIO cable. It just plugged into your Atari computer's second joystick port. This model supported auto-dial and auto-answer, so you could use it to run a BBS if you were so inclined. A later version of this modem, the MPP-1000E, eventually became the Supra 300-AT once Supra Corporation purchased Microbits Peripheral Products in 1985. Supra Corporation went on to sell modems for personal computers of all stripes over the next several decades, and became known as Supra, Inc. in 1994.

Bulletin Board Systems (BBSes)

Once you had an Atari computer and a new modem, all you needed was the number of a BBS—preferably local, as back in those days, you'd get nailed with per-minute long distance charges—and you could call. Local hobbyist BBSes were free for the most part, aside from the cost of the initial call. (If you're familiar with Prodigy, the prominently advertised graphical BBS of the 1990s, it's the same idea minus the graphics.)

One of the most fun things about calling BBSes with an Atari was logging in with ATASCII mode, which only 8-bit Atari computers supported, and which displayed more advanced character set animation graphics (notably, the ones you could call up from the keyboard using shortcuts). If you couldn't connect with ATASCII mode, you were running some other kind of computer, like an Apple II or a Commodore 64, so the BBS would default to the more commonly used, but less capable, ASCII mode. In one of the earlier examples of fanboyism, some snarky BBS owners would reprogram the software to read not "ASCII mode" when connecting, but "SHIT COMPUTER MODE." And there you have it.

When I first planned out this book, I had decided I was going to include a small section of famous BBSes that were dedicated to (or ran on) Atari computers. Then I realized the problem with the approach: Since most BBSes were run locally, and long-distance calls in the 1980s were quite expensive, each city had its "own" popular BBSes. The ones I knew from New York City wouldn't be at all the same as the ones known by someone who lived in San Francisco, Austin, or Chicago.

On the national level, there were also more sophisticated systems that charged you by the hour to be online, but offered news, weather, online text games, and other things you couldn't get from a regular BBS. In the early days of Atari computers, two online services were the most prominent: CompuServe and The Source. Both were information networks, although they had some interactive features as well. CompuServe was originally begun in 1969 for the government and large companies of the time.[66] The Source, a service from Reader's Digest, went online in 1979. Both services ran on large mainframe computers and had about 20,000 subscribers. They charged by the hour, and charged higher rates for evening hours and for faster (1,200bps) connections.

With both services, you could get news from the *Washington Post* or *New York Times*, shop online for mail-order delivery, chat with other users in real time, post and read messages, get stock market information, and check airline schedules. Both also offered expensive online games at an astounding $5 to $20 per hour.

Accessing the Internet—the actual Internet, not locally run and maintained BBSes—was less common if you were a hobbyist, as the Internet was primarily the domain of academia and the U.S. military at the time. In the Atari 8-bit's heyday, there was no World Wide Web; most of the Internet was text-based. I still remember my first forays into the "real" Internet, via a New York City–based service called The Big Electric Cat. It offered an Internet portal, which then brought you to Usenet, the original global discussion system that has since fallen out of favor in lieu of website forums and social media sites like Reddit and Facebook.

Allow me to quote the embarrassing contents of my first Usenet post, from August 7, 1987, which still lives buried in newsgroup archives for comp.sys.atari.st:

> *I have a question to ask. Is there any way I can deARC a file from a RAM disk into the drive, or from the drive into the RAM disk? Many files are way too big for my puny little SF 354, and getting my 300K RAM disk put into operation seems to be the only alternative. I know this is a simple minded question when compared to the complicated and knowledgeable minds of the ST users I'm writing to, but I really need the answer. Thank you for your time, whoever reads and replies to this message.*

Oh, to be 13 again. I became more active on the Internet beginning in the early 1990s, once I went to college and was able to access it from the desk in my dorm room at 19,200bps with a serial connection. And comp.sys.atari.8bit became the go-to place during the late 1980s and early 1990s for anyone talking 8-bit Atari computers.

---

66. *Antic*, June 1982, p. 11

Running Your Own Atari BBS

Many Atari owners eventually got the itch to run their own BBS—and quickly learned Atari hardware wasn't enough. Right off the bat you needed a third-party modem, because none of the Atari products had the essential auto-answer capability. And this, in turn, usually meant you had to buy the 850 interface, or a similar product, to connect the modem to the 800. You also needed a dedicated phone line; otherwise you'd have to share your regular line with voice calls, and this meant people calling you would be treated to an incredibly loud, warbling screech in the earpiece, as your modem tried desperately to handshake with your aunt's ear.

In an ideal case, you'd have two or more phone lines, although it required your BBS software to support multiple simultaneous connections. And then you'd need supporting equipment: extra modems, a special interface, more storage for larger message bases and download areas... It added up quickly.

Next, you needed some kind of BBS software. In 1984, my dad and I purchased a copy of Matthew Singer's FoReM XL BBS software, a BASIC XL–enabled version of Singer's earlier FoReM 26M with more features. Other BBSes ran various versions of Fast AMIS and Carnival. I used FoReM XL to set up and launch The Wizard's Chamber, my 11-year-old self's dream bulletin board, with a medieval fantasy theme hewing closely to my burgeoning interest in Dungeons & Dragons. I ran the BBS for about three years, which for me was from fourth through seventh grade. I eventually picked up about 500 users, although roughly 200 were what I considered active and called in at least on occasion, if not every day.

Here's how it worked: The 800 had the BASIC XL cartridge loaded; from there, I booted into FoReM XL from disk. I had the 800, the 850 interface, a Hayes Smartmodem 300, and two Indus GT disk drives, one for the system and message bases, and one for downloadable software and room for uploads. I used a Commodore 1702 monitor for the display. I later expanded the system by adding a third Indus GT drive and upgrading to a Hayes Smartmodem 1200. Few people called in at 1,200bps, though, for the three years I ran the BBS. It was an interesting occasion to see the red High Speed LED light up on the modem's front panel. And of course, the entire time I ran the BBS in ATASCII mode, complete with little character animations only other Atari users got to see when they first connected.

Running the BBS was a blast. I loved when people pressed 'Y' to "Chat with Sysop," which meant they wanted to talk to me. Each morning, I'd come down before school, or on the weekend, before breakfast, to look at the dot matrix printout to see caller activity from the night before. I knew it was a good night immediately if there was a stream of paper that reached from the printer on the desk down to the brown shag carpet in our den. If there was little or no printout, that meant trouble. I'd be disappointed if few people called, or if (as happened frustratingly often) the 850 interface had locked up, freezing the BBS and preventing it from taking callers. This required re-booting everything, and meant I missed out on possible new callers as well as old hands (and made the BBS look somewhat unreliable, which sadly it was). Since the BBS occupied my 800 the entire time, we eventually bought another second-hand 800 and Commodore 1702 monitor I could use for playing games or typing up homework in AtariWriter.

At this point, the stage was set for Atari. The 400 and 800 had launched; there was a strong lineup of peripherals, software, and games; and the company had the first real gaming PC, thanks to its four-chip architecture. As the early 1980s progressed, the Atari 8-bit line would enter its golden age. At the same time, new threats in the marketplace would begin to appear.

4 | Tramiel Trauma

This is where things began to fall apart for Atari. By that, I don't mean the platform—fans like me enjoyed using 8-bit Atari computers well into the mid and late 1980s, and the third-party market thrived. But Atari itself began to slide, for several key reasons. First and foremost: It never quite figured out how to follow up the 400 and 800 with something better, although it tried many times. While later machines had plenty of virtues to recommend them and are worth discussing for our purposes, none of them were enough to save the company. The level of incompetence was breathtaking, as we'll see shortly.

The overall climate for video games itself also began to go seriously downhill in 1982, leading to the famed Great Video Game Crash of 1983. People still debate the causes of this period today. In a nutshell, video games had become so popular that hundreds of third-party manufacturers rushed in and completely saturated the market with product—leading to consumer apathy, in many cases a loss in quality, and as a result, a huge recession in the video game industry. Atari was at the center of this, and while the crash affected the VCS and the coin-op business the most, there was plenty of collateral damage to the computer line. I don't remember this being something you could tell was happening by walking into electronics stores, but I didn't do that often enough on my own until I got a bit older.

Mainly, though, competition from other manufacturers threatened Atari's computer lineup. The 6502-based Commodore VIC-20 arrived in 1981 and undercut the 400's price by a considerable amount. The VIC-20 only supported 22 columns of text—even fewer than the 40-column display used on the 400 and 800—but its low price and colorful graphics drove some 600,000 sales.[67] Then, in 1982, the Commodore 64 arrived and presented Atari with its biggest challenge on the home computing front yet. The C64 included 64KB of memory, cost just $595, and featured hardware sprite animation like the 400 and 800. A price cut alone wasn't going to stave off the competition for long.

Atari did counter the emerging threats with a series of new machines, known as the XL and later XE lines; I'll get into those in this and the next chapter. But unfortunately, the company blew its chance. Atari vastly complicated its product lineup without adding enough differentiation between the machines or giving anyone who owned a 400 or 800 reason to upgrade. This was clear early on. "The overnight switch from the 400 and 800 to the XL series may confuse some potential buyers. It isn't always easy to figure out which machines have which features—and Atari's dismal naming system doesn't exactly endow each model with a distinctive personality," read an article in the December 1983 issue of *Electronic Games* magazine. While the machines sold well, this is more or less exactly what happened.

The interesting thing is, many Atari fans "came in" via these new machines, because they cost less and were roughly as functional as the original 400 and 800. And by that point, the third-party software lineup had become huge. Your memories of Atari 8-bit computers may well lie with a newer XL or XE machine, and that's fine! It was only bad for Atari, in that it wasn't enough to propel the platform ahead of the competition. To make matters worse, the XL lineup started with an actual dud—at least in sales, if not ambition.

Atari 1200XL

The ill-fated 1200XL ($899) debuted at an Atari press conference in December, 1982.[68] It was a crisply tailored 64KB machine that looked the part of the future. It had a completely different design motif than

---

67. arstechnica.com/features/2005/12/total-share/
68. Atari 8-bit FAQ

the angular 400 and organic 800, opting instead for brown-and-beige coloring, a sleeker profile with chunky venting around the top edges, and no cartridge doors or memory compartments to open or close. The cartridge slot—just one—was relegated to the left side of the machine, and the machine had just two joystick ports instead of four like the Atari 800. The joystick ports sat at an angle, and were easier to access. Underneath the hood, a single motherboard combined the functions of the multiple boards found in the 400. Upgraded chroma circuitry brought improvements in color saturation, while POKEY got an audio-amplifier bandwidth upgrade.[69]

Figure 4.1: The Atari 1200XL. Credit: Daniel Schwen

The front panel featured several external hardware enhancements, including two LED indicators for disabling the keyboard and activating an international character set. The keyboard output click sounds through the television or computer monitor, instead of internally via a tiny speaker in the machine, the first Atari computer to do so. The keyboard itself was superb, with a beautiful look and feel for typing out long programs. The 1200XL included four programmable function keys, which the 400 and 800 had lacked, and it came with a new

---

69. *Antic*, Feb/Mar 1983, p. 11

Help key and an interesting self-test mode for the hardware; not necessary, but useful to have. And if the display wasn't needed, you could turn it off to improve the compute speed of your code.

Atari released a North American version of the 1200XL with NTSC support only, and began shipping the machine in March 1983.[70] But aside from the RAM upgrade to 64KB, the 1200XL was otherwise no faster or more powerful than the 800. In fact, certain things about it were downright odd. The 1200XL had no Memo Pad mode; instead, it powered up to a special demonstration mode. More important, the 1200XL introduced a few compatibility problems with existing software, thanks to its new 16KB operating system, and some differences in programming thanks to the slightly revised 6502C processor (now dubbed SALLY). In addition, the SIO ports didn't have the +12 volt power line hooked up internally on pin 10, making them incompatible with some SIO-based peripherals on the market at the time.[71] The 1200XL also lacked a separate chroma video signal.[72]

If the machine had been significantly more powerful than the 400 and 800, then 1200XL owners probably would have tolerated some incompatibilities, but this wasn't the case. Its introduction also drove Atari fans at the time to run and find leftover 800s, rather than buy this model, which is never a good sign. I remember my dad bought one for his office, only to exchange it within a week after running into problems with it. The 1200XL only spent about eight months on the market—the shortest tenure of all Atari 8-bit computer systems.

Like the 400 and 800, the 1200XL was at first manufactured in the U.S., but later in its short production run, assembly shifted to Taiwan. From this point forward, all future Atari computers were manufactured overseas.[73] AtariAge forum member Karl Heller analyzed serial numbers and estimated that Atari produced roughly 100,000 1200XL machines, with about three-quarters of them in the U.S.[74] Today, the 1200XL is remembered as a beautiful and well-made computer. It's also highly prized, at least for the dedicated. Many collectors opt to

70. Atari.com, 1972-1984 page.
71. computingvoyage.com/1411/the-atari-1200xl-computer/
72. Atari 8-bit FAQ
73. Ibid
74. www.atariage.com/forums/index.php?showtopic=107234

get one of these and then upgrade it so it's more capable, and compatible with a wider range of Atari software.

Atari 5200 SuperSystem

Next, Atari finally unveiled a long-awaited successor to the VCS. The company first demonstrated the machine, code-named "Video System X," at the 1982 Winter CES. Over the next six months, Atari changed the name twice, first to 5200 Home Entertainment System, and then to 5200 SuperSystem by the time it went on sale that June. While the 5200 wasn't strictly a home computer, in that there were no keyboard attachments or storage available, it *was* the 400 inside the sleek black enclosure, albeit with a few minor tweaks.

Figure 4.2: The Atari 5200 SuperSystem, with one of its infamous analog joysticks.
Credit: Evan Amos.

It didn't matter, because the 5200 was mostly a failure. The enclosure design was striking upon its introduction. It was a giant wedge shape, mostly black textured plastic with a faux-aluminum strip in the middle of the front panel. The 5200 was intended to compete against the older Intellivision, not the newer ColecoVision as often thought, and was just late in doing so.[75] The reason was the controller design; the Intellivision had a 16-position disc ideal for playing all kinds of games, whereas Atari joysticks only operated in eight directions. The 5200 solved this problem with a new, speed-sensitive, 360-degree

---

[75] www.atarimuseum.com/videogames/consoles/5200/A5200.html

controller. It reportedly took nine revisions, including thickening the rubber base and shortening the joystick, before Atari was satisfied with the design. The controllers also included full numeric keypads and Start, Pause, and Reset buttons. Unfortunately, the controllers didn't self-center, which made it difficult to play many arcade game conversions, and the sticks themselves were prone to failure. People also complained about the rubber surrounds degrading—even Atari's own website notes that they were prone to do so within just a few hours of play—but this never happened with my system.

Another downside: Out of the box, the 5200 wasn't backward-compatible with the huge library of VCS game cartridges—at least not until later, when the company released a giant optional adapter you needed to plug into the 5200's cartridge slot. Atari also purposely made the 5200 incompatible with the 400. From an external stand-point, the cartridge housings were much larger. And a few internal quirks ensured code written for the 400 and 800 wouldn't just run on the 5200 without additional modifications.

Nonetheless, Atari often tweaked the 5200 versions of 400 and 800 games to improve on the original releases. The Pac-Man and Ms. Pac-Man cartridges, for example, contained the missing cartoons that appeared between every few levels. Centipede on the 5200 was excel-lent—almost indistinguishable from the arcade, aside from the obvi-ous orientation switch from portrait to landscape for home televi-sions.

You could also do a couple of near-magical things with the 5200 controller setup. Some games came with a plastic dual-joystick holder you could stick both 5200 controllers in, and then use them together with games supporting it. I'll go into this in more depth in Chapter 6, as I describe each game in detail, but suffice to say this made playing titles like Robotron: 2084 and Space Dungeon absolutely awesome, and I killed many an evening on these titles. Nothing else at the time replicated the arcade experience so closely. Even today, you'd have to buy an X-Arcade Tankstick (which I, um, may have also done) and play Robotron in an emulator to get the same dual-joystick effect.

In addition, Atari sold a full-featured trackball console for the 5200, complete with numeric keypads and extra buttons. Using this for arcade game home conversions like Centipede and Missile Com-mand was the way to go. The ball was smaller than the one Missile Command had in the arcade, but it certainly did the trick. Unlike the unreliable stick controllers, the trackball was a solid unit, if not up to today's X-Arcade–level professional standards. Finally, you could also use the trackball for Pole Position in lieu of a genuine steering wheel controller, although I never found this to be as accurate as using the analog joysticks.

Late as it was, the 5200 faced intense competition from both Coleco and Mattel. Atari briefly considered adding a keyboard attachment option,[76] but that would have turned the 5200 into a 400, and the company didn't want to compete with itself. It also began work on a new joystick design, but it didn't get to finish: The Great Video Game Crash of 1983 was the final nail in the coffin for the machine. Production officially ended in February 1984,[77] with approximately one million units sold.[78] Today, the 5200 is remembered as an excellent game console, and it's pretty easy to find on eBay. Just make sure you can secure some working joysticks for it before getting involved with one now.

Atari 600XL and 800XL

The 5200 game console wasn't a massive success, and the 1200XL home computer turned into a debacle, so Atari tried again. As part of its "Next Generation" line of computers unveiled at the 1983 Summer CES, the company announced the more sensible 600XL and 800XL to replace the 400 and 800, respectively. The 16KB 600XL ($199), produced through most of 1984, [79] was especially appealing thanks to its shallow depth. The 62-key keyboard was springier and quieter than the one on the 800, with a different feel and no more internal speaker click. It goes without saying that the design was a tremendous improvement over the 400's flat membrane keyboard. The two LED indicator lights and four programmable function keys from the 1200XL were gone; instead, the 600XL returned to having four main function keys and an additional Help key.

The 600XL included a faster Parallel Bus Interface (PBI) port in addition to SIO. The system contained 16KB of memory, just like

---

76. Atari - Cartridge Console history page
77. Atari 8-bit FAQ
78. *Washington Post*, May 22, 1984, C3; via Atari 8-bit FAQ
79. Atari 8-bit FAQ

later versions of the 400, and a rare, Atari-manufactured expansion called the 1064 Memory Module could bring this up to 64KB. The external memory module was an oversized brick, styled to look like the white portion of the 600XL, and it plugged into the PBI port on the back. (Later on, internal memory upgrade products appeared for the 600XL to boost its memory but maintain the system's svelte profile.)

Figure 4.3: The Atari 600XL. Credit: Evan Amos

Most important, the 600XL included built-in BASIC, bringing the total ROM up from 10KB to 24KB. Having BASIC built into the computer was one of the best features of the XL line, and probably should have been there from the beginning. Some programs required you disable it, by holding down the Option key while turning on the computer, to free up memory for certain games and programs. The 600XL and 800XL contained BASIC revision B, which corrected a bug that rendered the original BASIC cartridge unable to delete a block of memory whose size was a multiple of 256 bytes. Unfortunately, Atari subsequently introduced a new problem that locked up the computer when you inserted program lines, as outlined in the Reader Feedback section of the July 1986 issue of *Compute!* magazine.

While the 600XL was a solid entry-level 8-bit computer, the 800XL ($299) was the new flagship workhorse of Atari's home computer lineup, thanks to its expanded 64KB of memory. It was a little bit larger, and also added a composite video port. The 800XL soldiered on well into 1985, without the 600XL. It was a little tricky to access the extra 16KB of RAM after the initial 48KB, incidentally; you needed to bank-select it while programming, which ate up a few bytes of memory in the regular 48KB space. I don't remember wanting any 64KB programs at the time, so I happily kept using my 800. My dad later picked up an 800XL for his office. I got to play games on it and his Rana Systems 1000 drive, which read older disks my own Indus GT drives couldn't, whenever I visited him at work.

Figure 4.4: The Atari 800XL. Credit: Evan Amos

Despite the 600XL and 800XL's relatively short time on the market, there were distinct differences in keyboard feel depending on the production run. Some machines felt fine to type on, if mushier and less springy than the 800 keyboard, while others were prone to jamming and felt terrible. I remember having two different 800XLs at one point. One had wider letters in the silver Atari 800XL logo on the top left panel, and the other had a slightly taller, thinner font. The second one had a poor keyboard, while the first one had a sublime one. In fact, in 2007 AtariAge forum member Beetle discovered five separate 800XL keyboard types.[80]

The 600XL and 800XL were fairly nice machines and quite successful, if not different enough to impel 400 and 800 owners to upgrade. Now this is the part where things went downhill. Atari 1200XL owners had it worse, but it turned out that for a fair number of programs, you still needed to load a special disk for the program to work on a 600XL or 800XL. To remedy the problem, Atari developed The Translator, a $9.95 disk that disabled the XL's built-in OS and loaded in the original 800's instead.

---

80. atariage.com/forums/topic/105170-600800xl-keyboard-variants/

Figure 4.5: An Atari press photo from 1982 showing the Atari 1200XL personal computer and 1025 80-column dot-matrix printer.

Atari also updated many of its most popular peripherals in time for the release of the 1200XL, to match the beige, dark brown, and chrome style of the new line. That meant a new numbering scheme—and of course Atari bungled it. If the XL computers were the 1200XL, the 600XL, and the 800XL, why were the peripherals all in the 1,000 range, given that the 400 and 800 peripherals all had matching numbering schemes? The reason was an internal timing snafu. The 1200XL was originally going to be called the Atari 1000 Home Computer, but the peripheral model numbers were designated before the 1000 became the 1200XL.[81] Not only that, but Atari changed its graphics design several times throughout the life of the 8-bit line, and it didn't always correspond to the changes in the core systems.

With that, let's take a quick trip through the lineup of XL peripherals that made it to market. The boxy 1010 Program Recorder, an

---

81. *Atari Inc. Business Is Fun*, page 694.

update to the 410, looked the part, with its slotted edges and smoothly integrated cassette controls. The 1010's two SIO ports meant you could place it anywhere inside of a chain of peripherals, instead of having just one hardwired SIO cable the way the 410 did. Otherwise, in terms of functionality and performance, the 1010 was the same.

Atari also released three new printers. The 1020 Color Plotter featured a friction-fed design, and delivered ALPS-powered, four-color plotting for smooth, finely drawn charts and graphics with water-soluble ink. It printed 20-, 40-, and 80-column text at 10 characters per second on tiny 4.5-inch wide paper, and connected directly to an Atari 8-bit computer's SIO port. Other manufacturers, including Commodore and Tandy/Radio-Shack, manufactured their own plotters using the same ALPS mechanism as the one in the 1020. It quickly became nearly impossible to buy extra paper for this printer, adding to its appeal.

The 80-column 1025 was a modest upgrade over the 825, and a repackaged version of the Okidata ML80.[82] It printed at 40 characters per second, which was quite slow for a mainstream dot matrix printer at that time. The 1025 featured three modes: a standard 80-column-width, a condensed 132-column width, and a bold, wide 40-column style. The 80-column 1027, meanwhile, was one of the first home computer printers to provide letter-quality print, which was almost unheard of in the early 1980s. But it was agonizingly slow, taking minutes at a time to print out each page of text. Atari claimed a 20-characters-per-second speed, but it seemed like less than half that in real life. And it was almost unbearably loud. At full bore, the printer sounded like it would launch its mechanism straight into a nearby wall at any moment. The 1027's enclosure also made it look like a wide-carriage printer, even though the 1027 only took standard letter paper.

The 1030 modem was my own personal introduction to the online world. Like its 835 forebear, the 1030 was a direct-connect model designed for the Atari computer's built-in SIO ports. But the 1030 was still limited to 300bps, still couldn't upload or download files, and still lacked the auto-answer function necessary for running a BBS. Despite its issues, the 1030 had no problem dialing up any number of home- and business-level BBSes of the time. My dad and I quickly

---

82. Atari 8-bit FAQ

swapped it out later in 1984 for the aforementioned Hayes Smart-modem, once we decided to give running our own BBS a try.

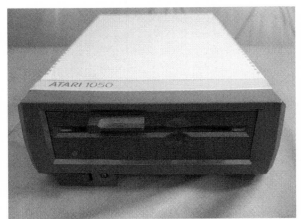

Figure 4.6: A Happy-enhanced Atari 1050 disk drive I own.

Finally, and most significantly, the 1050 disk drive replaced the 810 in the fall of 1983 after a four-year run, and was considerably smaller and sleeker.[83] The drive featured what Atari called Dual Density, which increased how much data you could store on the disk: 127KB instead of 88KB. Anyone capable of walking upright could figure out that 1.45 times the density shouldn't be called Dual Density, and ultimately, the company began to call this Enhanced Density instead. To support the new format, Atari sold the 1050 bundled with DOS 3.0, which—here we go again—was incompatible in some ways with the earlier DOS 2.0S. Later the company rectified the problem with DOS 2.5[84]—backwards in version number, but newer nonetheless. (With product marketing like this, how could Atari have failed? I guess we'll never know.) Regardless, Enhanced Density never gained much traction, since third-party drives had already offered full double density (176KB per side) at similar prices.

The 1050 disk drive was otherwise identical in performance to the 810. 1050s are still desirable today, especially since they're compatible with third-party enhancements like the 1050 Doubler and the Happy 1050.

83. Atari 8-bit FAQ
84. Ibid

The Touch Tablet, like the third-party KoalaPad, was a precursor to today's Wacom drawing tablets. It measured 7.8 by 9.4 by 1 inches, roughly the size of a hardcover book, and contained a 6.5-by-5-inch drawing surface. It plugged into a 9-pin joystick port, came with AtariArtist, and let you draw and paint lines and shapes in 128 colors. The wired plastic pen had a red button to select items on the screen. The tablet itself also had two additional hardware buttons. The Micro Illustrator–based AtariArtist wasn't bad for its time; you could draw rays, connected lines, circles, and filled discs, as well as magnify what you're working on. There was the obvious disconnect: You were drawing on a surface, but the result appeared somewhere else—in this case, on the television screen.

Atari even made a go at consumer-level light pens, albeit with mixed results. Light pens let you draw right on the CRT screen, which was pretty futuristic technology for 1983. An early version, the beige CX70, was too cumbersome and didn't sell well. The improved CX75 Light Pen was surprisingly svelte for its time, looking and feeling approximately like a ballpoint pen. The CX75 came with Atari-Graphics, a full-featured painting program cartridge designed for the pen. In use, the Light Pen was a little tricky, and it required you to sit quite close to your television monitor, which wasn't particularly comfortable. Today, people are debating the same idea, except this time with touch-screen Windows PCs. I still don't find reaching to touch a monitor comfortable, and my back and neck muscles seem to agree.

XL Prototypes

Atari had grand plans for expanding its XL line even further than the 600XL and 800XL. Ultimately, thanks to internal company dysfunction, all were scrapped and never reached production. Here's a taste of what could have been—and what many Atari fans like me continue to dream of to this day.

Two prototype computers in particular made Atari enthusiasts drool. The 64K 1400XL ($549) achieved almost mythic status rather quickly after being announced. With its deeper housing, it was reminiscent of the beautiful 1200XL, and contained both a modem and a hardware speech synthesizer—the latter meaning programs would no longer have to blank out the video DMA each time it played back a digitized voice sample, as was the case with the popular S.A.M. and other programs. Unfortunately, the 1400XL never made it into production, despite appearing in several issues of *Antic* magazine (including December 1983, where it was featured in New Products).

Figure 4.7: The fabled Atari 1450XLD, shown here in a 1984 Atari catalog and never formally released.

The top-of-the-line 1450XLD ($999) was a hulk of a machine. Unlike most Atari computers up until this point, the 1450XLD featured a prominent riser with two drive bays. The first was filled from the factory with a double-sided, double-density floppy drive, while the second was a gaping hole (without even a cover). It would eventually contain a second drive you could add later. This was also featured in *Antic* magazine, and also never made it to the production line. Atari historian Kevin Savetz managed to see one in person, in Curt Vendel's home, during an interview for Savetz's fun memoir *Terrible Nerd*. Without this sighting, I would have gone on forever believing the 1450XLD never made it into the wild.

Then there was the 1600XL, which wasn't formally announced. By 1984, the IBM PC platform was taking off for real in businesses, and IBM had released the much-maligned PCjr in an effort to combat the 8-bit home market with a computer of its own. For a short time, Atari planned to respond in kind with a dual-processor wonder, the 1600XL. It was to contain two CPUs: the usual MOS 6502B, and a specially designed 80186-compatible chip for running IBM PC software. It never happened.

Finally, along with the 600XL and 800XL, Atari also unveiled something called the 1090 XL Expansion System, which contained five 8-bit PBI slots for future projects like 8088 and MS-DOS compatibility like the ATR8000 had offered. Atari seems to have built a handful of units that have made it into collectors' hands.

The 1984 Olympics

If you purchased an Atari computer or peripheral in 1984, you may have seen a sticker on the box: "The official home computer of the 1984 Olympics." This was thanks to several agreements Atari entered into with the Los Angeles Olympic Organizing Committee for the 1984 Summer Games. According to an article in the February 1984 issue of *Antic*, Atari contracted with the group to be the sole sponsor of home computers, arcade games, and home video games, and let Atari use the Olympic logo in its promotional materials. It also ran 25 commercials during the Winter Olympics in Sarajevo, Yugoslavia, and 60 within the Summer Olympics in L.A. Finally, Atari donated $75,000 worth of gear, including computer games and arcade games for media representatives at ABC's broadcast center.

What can I say? It was a strange time.

Enter Atari Corporation

By this point, Atari computer enthusiasts were beginning to truly worry about the company. *A.N.A.L.O.G.* magazine ran an unsigned feature in the June 1984 issue called "Darkness at Noon," which it described as "an editorial and a cautionary tale of corporate mismanagement." The article covered the aforementioned tale of several core Atari developers asking for credit and royalties on their games, only to be told by Ray Kassar that they were no more important than "towel designers" (the quote originally came from the *San Jose Mercury*). The developers left and formed Activision, which went on to capture almost 30 percent of Atari's video game market, the article said. By the end of 1983, Atari's market share had fallen from 24 percent to just 12 percent.

Another big reason for the decline was the 1200XL. It cost several hundred dollars more than the 800 and yet was a "step down," thanks to its new, not-completely-compatible OS and lack of expansion. "Word quickly spread the 1200 was the computer industry's Edsel," read the article. "Rumors of the discontinuance of the 400/800 series sent prospective Atari owners scurrying to the stores to purchase the 'old' computers before they were gone forever. Ironically, Atari's introduction of the new 1200XL resulted in increased sales of its older models!"[85]

The new XL solved some of these problems, but the magazine said it was "too little too late," since they still used a somewhat incompatible OS, and the new machines were "really old wine in new wineskins." The magazine also called out the new 1050 drive as being no faster than the 810, and the 1030 third-generation modem still couldn't upload or download files. The article went on to say the problem wasn't marketing, since it was having no problem selling the VCS system or coin-op games. Instead, the problem was management, and having to play politics at the top level to keep your job. Atari "never understood the computer," that it was just different than the game consoles proceeding it, and "almost all of top management were computer illiterates. They routinely made major software and hardware decisions about a product which they did not understand and could not use."[86]

At the 1984 Summer CES, Atari continued to hype the XL line and the upcoming 1400XL, but dropped any mention of the 1450XLD unveiled a year earlier, and also had no new models to show off.[87] It turns out there was quite a bit brewing behind the scenes. Jack Tramiel (pronounced "tra-mell"), of Commodore fame and the force behind the aforementioned Commodore PET, the VIC-20, and 64, was in talks to transition from Atari competitor to owner. On July 2, 1984, he sold off Commodore and bought Atari's consumer electronics and home computer divisions from Warner Communications.[88] Tramiel combined the two divisions, formed Atari Corporation, and installed himself as chairman. The only piece left

85. *A.N.A.L.O.G.*, June 1984, p. 8
86. *A.N.A.L.O.G.*, June 1984, p. 9
87. Atari 8-bit FAQ
88. Atarimuseum.com

was the coin-op side, which stayed separate and out of Tramiel's control.

Now at the helm of the rest of Atari, Tramiel halted production of all hardware and put it under review. The 800XL and 2600 (as it was called by this point) got the go-ahead to resume. Tramiel nixed the 600XL, confirmed the 5200's death, and shelved the already-announced 7800 (which eventually reappeared in 1986). Tramiel also shut down *Atari Connection* magazine.[89] Tramiel then aggressively cut the price of the 800XL—first from $299 to $179 in August, and then to just $119 by November, famously declaring "Business is War."[90] By this point, Atari had reportedly sold almost 500,000 units of the 800XL alone.[91] Still, the 800XL only had a couple of months left to live.

Atari 65XE and 130XE

The 1985 Winter CES marked Tramiel's first running the new Atari Corporation. Atari unveiled the 65XE, 130XE, and 16-bit 520ST home computers, along with two new printers (the XMM801 and XDM121) and the XM301 modem. These all made it into production, but Atari also announced almost a dozen additional computers and peripherals, such as the 65XEP and 65XEM, which never made it beyond CES.[92] One key piece of software did, though. A stunning GTIA-based graphics demo that featured two scenes, one of a robot walking toward the camera, and another of a spaceship flying through space, complete with four-channel music and smooth color gradients on the robot's and spaceship's metal surfaces. Enthusiasts widely shared the demo by trading disks or uploading it to bulletin boards.

A month later, a new house organ magazine, *Atari Explorer*, debuted. It existed to cheer on the XE and ST lineups.[93] The big news for 1985 was clearly the ST, though only the 520ST made it into production. Plans for a lower-cost 130ST and (announced later in the year) 260ST were eventually both dropped.

---

89. Atari 8-bit FAQ
90. Ibid
91. *Atari Explorer*, Summer 1985, p. 33 (via Atari 8-bit FAQ)
92. Atari 8-bit FAQ
93. Ibid

Figure 4.8: A screenshot of Atari's awesome graphics and sound demo for the 1985 Winter Consumer Electronics Show.

Still, the XE still made sense as a lower-cost play for the company, since the 8-bit line had such a large installed user base. The 65XE and 130XE became the official successors to the 600XL and 800XL. The lower-end 65XE came with 64KB, while the 130XE was the first Atari computer to pack 128KB—putting it right up against the popular Commodore 128. In addition to the memory upgrades, they included a new and virtually bug-free version of built-in BASIC (revision C). The 130XE also included a new FREDDIE memory management chip, which let the 6502 and ANTIC independently access RAM banks,[94] although the CPU again remained clocked at 1.79MHz. The Atari ST was faulted on its introduction for its mushy, cheap-feeling keyboard, and unfortunately the 65XE and 130XE were saddled with the same kind. The XE also had all of its chips unsocketed. (This makes it less attractive to today's modding community, incidentally, since you can't replace the chips on the board so easily.)

At CES in January 1986, Atari unveiled a new package bundle with the 1027 printer, 1050 disk drive, and five programs (Silent Butler,

94. Atari 8-bit FAQ

Star Raiders, Music Painter, Paint, and AtariWriter) for $399.[95] New starter packages debuted again at the 1986 Summer CES; they included the 1027 printer, 1050 disk drive, AtariWriter Plus, Home Filing Manager, Music Composer, Defender, and Star Raiders. The 65XE version cost $349, while the 130XE version cost $399. Another package included the 65XE, a joystick, Star Raiders, Pac-Man, Donkey Kong, and Sky Writer for just $99. While the 130XE began shipping in April 1985 for $149.95, Atari held up the release of the 65XE until early 1986, thanks to an abundance of 800XL inventory it wanted to clear out first.[96] All of these products were priced competitively, but keep in mind that by this point, the computers were packing seven-year-old hardware.

Figure 4.9: The 8-bit Atari 130XE, which featured styling similar to that of the new 16-bit ST line. Credit: Evan Amos

As a result, the tech world began to focus more on the 16-bit ST, the Amiga, the Apple IIGS, the Apple Macintosh lineup, and the rising IBM PC juggernaut. The 65XE and 130XE slipped under the radar in comparison, but were killer values if you didn't mind the dated architecture. Both could run thousands of programs, and were fully compatible with the existing 400/800 and the XL. While not everyone loved the new ST-style keyboard, the machines certainly looked slick, and the lack of a numeric keypad made for truly compact enclosures.

95. Atari 8-bit FAQ
96. Ibid

Atari also saw it fit once again to remodel its main peripherals in the style idiom of its new XE computers. The XM301 modem was another 300bps direct-connect modem. But unlike the older 835 and 1030, it drew power from the SIO port and didn't require an AC adapter. As a result, its cable was hardwired and thus the XM301 has to be placed at the end of a peripheral chain, just as the old 410 Program Recorder did. The XM301 came packaged with XE Term software, which was Atari's first terminal program to support file transfers—several years after third-party vendors had figured out how.[97] The SX212 modem appeared in November 1986 and shipped in September 1987.[98] It was Atari's first modem to support 1,200bps—several years late, in case you're picking up a theme—and offered both SIO and a standard DB-25 RS232 serial port, though it also had to be at the end of an Atari SIO chain.[99]

Atari also released two new printers. The XMM801 direct-connect dot matrix printer featured a smoked plastic cover, a wire-style chrome printer tray, and a rightmost control panel with six slanted function buttons. Underneath were the inner workings of a typical 80-column printer. It supported both friction and tractor-feed, it printed in two directions for faster speeds, and it worked with Atari-Writer and AtariWriter Plus. The XDM121 was a daisy wheel, letter-quality, 80-column printer; it also connected directly to Atari computers without needing the old 850 interface (or third-party equivalent). It featured slanted function buttons on the front panel to match XE computers.

Atari's upgraded, matching floppy drive for the XE line was the XF551, a true double-sided, double-density drive for 360KB per disk. The XF551 was also smaller and quieter than the 810 and the 1050. But despite being the company's most crucial peripheral for the XE, the XF551 was unveiled (you guessed it) late—at the 1987 Summer CES, two and a half years after the XE line debuted, and didn't ship until January 1988.[100] Oddly, you couldn't use the XF551 to format side B of older, single-density floppies. It was a safety mechanism to prevent you from overwriting double-sided 360KB disks by accident.

---

97. Atari 8-bit FAQ
98. Ibid
99. Ibid
100. Ibid

Worse, the XF551 still came with DOS 2.5, which only supported 88KB single-density and 127KB Enhanced Density disks. You needed to buy DOS XE ($10) separately to work with 360KB floppies, but Atari didn't release *that* product until January 1989. DOS-XE originally came from OSS's A-DOS, and wasn't directly compatible with DOS 2.0 or 2.5. DOS XE had a command line, but it wasn't as powerful as SpartaDOS; Atari still intended the menu system to be the primary way to control the OS.

Atari also upgraded its aging AtariWriter word processor a few times. The disk-based AtariWriter Plus was coded from scratch and included two versions: one for 48KB and 64KB computers, and one supporting the 130XE's 128KB RAM. More important, AtariWriter 80 finally shipped in the summer of 1989, and included Proofreader and Mail Merge. It also required the long-awaited XEP80, Atari's first in-house solution for an 80-column display. The XEP80 connected to the joystick port and replaced the default 40-by-24-column text mode with an industry-standard 80-by-24-column display. In fact, it did more: It created a virtual 256-by-24-column mode, and then showed you any 80 columns you wanted at a time. The module also came with a parallel port, so you could connect a regular parallel printer to the Atari. With the module connected, you couldn't use the rest of your Atari's regular graphics modes. Atari recommended a monochrome monitor for use with the XEP80, but the company didn't sell one that connected to it.[101] You can see how messy this became. While some enthusiasts stayed loyal to the 8-bit Atari, it was much easier to skip all this and upgrade to a proper 16-bit system with native 80-column support.

XE Prototypes

By this point, you may be detecting another running theme: Atari wasn't so good at follow-through, despite having some truly innovative ideas. The 65XEP debuted at the 1985 Winter Consumer Electronics Show along with the 65XE and the 130XE. It was intended to be a $400 portable system. It included a 5-inch monochrome monitor, a cartridge slot, and (get this) a 3.5-inch floppy drive, which made it more like the ST line, even though it was a 400/800-compatible 8-

---

101. Atari 8-bit FAQ

bit system. That meant that *no* off-the-shelf Atari 8-bit software would work with it. The keyboard snapped into the side of the unit. Atari designed the 65XEP to compete with the Commodore SX-64, which came out the year prior with a 5-inch color screen and a luggable handle. The 65XEP was never released.

Atari also had in the works the 65XEM, an under-$150 8-bit computer like the 65XE, but it could produce eight synthesized voices instead of four like the old POKEY chip. *InfoWorld* quoted Zeb Billings, then-president of Sight & Sound Music Software, which wrote all of the software for Casio's electronic music peripherals at the time, as saying that his company would be working with Atari on software for the XEM. "This chip is so highly advanced that if you close your eyes, you can't tell if the music is coming from a piano or the computer," Billings said. Unfortunately, the XEM never made it into production.

Atari being Atari, it also planned quite a few extra XE-themed peripherals, none of which ever saw retail shelves either. There was, however, one last gasp for the Atari 8-bit line—and strangely enough, it came in the form of another game console.

Atari XE Game System (XEGS)

By 1987, Atari was struggling with its game console lineup, too. The 5200 SuperSystem didn't do so well, and the planned 7800 launch for 1984 was shelved after the video game crash of 1983, only to be dusted off and shoved into stores in 1986 after Nintendo arrived and ate Atari's lunch. This "plan" didn't work well; while the 7800 was indeed a nice upgrade in graphics and had some good games, it was a downgrade in sound quality, and in the end wasn't competitive with the NES.

So Atari decided to try again, this time with the XE Game System, shown first at the 1987 American International Toy Fair in New York.[102] Another oddball 8-bit computer offshoot like the 5200, the XEGS, a restyled 65XE, was a blatant attempt to go after Nintendo. The $150 64KB XEGS shipped in October 1987, and came packaged with an attachable keyboard, a video light gun, a joystick, and several games: Flight Simulator II, Missile Command, and Barnyard Blaster,

---

102. Atari 8-bit FAQ

a Nintendo Duck Hunt clone with light gun support. You could also purchase an optional XE disk drive for the system, and Atari bragged that XE cartridges could store as much as 256KB.

Figure 4.10: The XEGS game system, which also came with a joystick, attachable keyboard, and light gun (not pictured). Credit: Bilby/Wikipedia

The XEGS aped the NES gamepad design and light gun strategy. While the NES was much newer than the Atari 8-bit architecture, the latter still held up well. But the games just weren't there. Few developers at this point wanted to work on an eight-year-old platform, no matter how capable it was. In all, just 32 cartridges were packaged and released for the XEGS, and most were games that were at least several years old. The XEGS did pretty well thanks to its low price; Atari sold 100,000 XEGS units for the Christmas 1987 holiday season and had trouble meeting demand, and then seemed to quickly taper off thereafter.[103] I'll cite a particular Usenet post in comp.sys.atari.8bit from 1987 from Neil Harris, then the director of marketing communications for Atari Corporation. The post is in response to an existing thread, "Is Atari killing the 8-bit?" Harris delivers a surprising burst of honesty about the XEGS and the state of Atari:

We come again to that perpetual question: is Atari intent on killing the 8-bits? One way to answer that would be to give you a tour of our warehouse. If you could see the number of 8-bit computers and software in inventory, you'd know we are highly motivated to keep the line going.

---

103. Atari 8-bit FAQ

Regarding the new XE Game System, which on the first glance is a slap in the face to those who know how powerful the 8-bitters are—this system is purely a strategic move on our part. In order to keep the 8-bit line going, we must do two things: 1. Get the computers available in more stores, and 2. Get new software developed for them. Software is not being developed by and large because of problem #1. So which stores do we go to? The mass merchants, who sold the bulk of the hundreds of thousands (not, unfortunately, millions) of Atari 8-bit computers out there, are currently retreating from the computer business. K-Mart carries NO computers. Ditto for Montgomery Wards. And for J.C. Penney's.

On the other hand, these same stores are doing a fabulous business in game systems like Nintendo, Sega, and, of course, Atari. The solution, from a business point of view, was to develop a product that would be appealing to the mass merchants (and also to the public which buys there), one that also accomplishes the corporate objective of revitalizing the 8-bit line... When someone buys the XE Game System, they get the complete package—console, keyboard, light gun, and three programs (including a new version of SubLogic's Flight Simulator including scenery, all on a single cartridge). We expect stores to do a great business in these. We'll make available the current library of cartridge software, plus we're converting some disk programs into cartridge format for this system...

So, those few of you out there who are looking at Atari management as the evil group who are plotting to quash the 8-bit line, you have it all wrong. We're trying hard to keep things moving forward. Without the distribution and the software, no amount of advertising and new hardware development could work. The XE Game System is our best hope to keep things moving.

The XEGS didn't keep things moving. But even as Atari 8-bit computers fell out of favor in the U.S., they gained traction in Europe. Atari released a specific model for the European market called the 800XE, a 65XE with PAL graphics. It was a good market performer for Atari. The company said in its December 31, 1987 annual report, "In [then] Czechoslovakia, the [then] German Democratic Republic, and Poland, the 800XE and 65XE computers have gained brand dominance and are among the most popular systems being sold in these countries."[104] Atari echoed these comments a year later, saying its XE line of 8-bit computers "is extremely popular throughout Eastern Europe, and most recently, has begun to appear on retail shelves in the [then] Soviet Union." This will all prove important later, once we get to today's Atari 8-bit modders, many of whom live in Poland.

104. Atari 8-bit FAQ

5 | Sunset in Sunnyvale

By the start of 1986, developers had begun moving away from the Atari 8-bit platform in droves. The January 28, 1985 issue of *InfoWorld* quoted Jack Tramiel as saying that by the second half of the year, Atari would be producing 200,000 16-bit 520 and 1040STs per month and 80 percent of the computers produced at Atari by then would be the ST series. The ST never took off to this extent, but the statement also told Atari 8-bit fans everything they needed to know about where the future was, even as production of the XE lineup was getting underway in earnest.

Around this time, Atari began issuing the new *Atari Explorer* magazine in earnest, and published it at whatever frequency the company felt like. Example issues: February 1985, April/May 1985, Summer 1987, January/February 1990, September 1991, and May/June 1992. Who needs publishing schedules anyway? At any rate, while there was some 8-bit coverage in *Atari Explorer*, the vast majority of it focused on the 16-bit ST line, which appeared later in 1985, during the magazine's first year.

Not only had the market begun to shift away from the 8-bit line, but Atari itself wasn't doing anything to help it along. At this point, the company was focusing on the ST—although "focus" implies competence, which I'd argue wasn't in strong supply in management at the time. Over the course of the next seven years, Atari tried a whole bunch of things, including building an unremarkable series of PC-compatible computers. Surprisingly, Atari produced XE machines for several more years, which made them the longest running of the 8-bit lines.

This brings us to a strange question: Exactly when *did* Atari stop producing 65XE, 130XE, and (for sale overseas) 800XE machines? Atarimania's History of Atari section quotes the December 31, 1989 Atari annual report as saying that "sales of its 2600 and 7800 game systems and range of older XE 8-bit computers decreased by 35 percent." In 1990, *Atari Explorer* magazine shut down, only to reappear in 1991 for some more issues. A separate *Atarian* publication in 1989 only lasted for three issues. In May 1990, Atari said at a shareholder meeting it sold 250,000 XE computers in 1989, and it sold 70,000 in Poland, making it the most popular computer in that country.[105] In May 1991, at another shareholder meeting, Atari said the XE was still in production, in contrast to a report from Canada saying the XE was being discontinued.[106] At the Chicago Computerfest in November 1991, Atari was said to bring most of its remaining 8-bit inventory to sell.

"As of Christmas 1991, Atari decided to discontinue the XEGS, 2600, and 7800 systems,[107] and the company officially ceased 8-bit platform support on January 1, 1992[108] Many Atari fan sites echo the same end-of-life dates, although at a shareholder meeting in June 1992, Atari stated the XE line was still being made, but not available in the U.S. Instead, it continued to produce 800XE models for Mexico, South America, Eastern Europe, and Germany (this from *Atari Interface* magazine, Fall 1992, p. 19).[109] Atari's Annual Report at the end of 1992 didn't even mention the XE—the first time that had happened.[110] *A.N.A.L.O.G. Computing* shut down at the end of 1989, and *Antic* magazine followed suit in the middle of 1990.

The thing is, if you bought an 800 at the beginning—maybe updating the OS ROM module and adding a GTIA chip early on, or just buying a machine manufactured in 1981 or later—you had no need to buy another one even 10 years later. If something went wrong with your computer during the 1980s, it was often less expensive to buy a

---

105. Atari 8-bit FAQ
106. Ibid
107 AtariUser magazine, July 1992, p. 22
108 Atari Classics magazine, Dec. 1992, p. 4
109. Ibid
110. Ibid

new 65XE off the shelf than repair an older 400, 800, or XL. While the XE lineup was stable, less complex internally, and relatively bug-free, it only served to prolong the inevitable.

In the end, a number of things did in the Atari 8-bit platform. The first was the confusion over how to market it and the early software lineup. It ended up becoming a killer gaming platform, but management didn't want that at first and never fully embraced the potential. As a result, there was a persistent tension between how Atari computers doubled as excellent game machines and how they couldn't possibly be serious computers *because* they were such good gaming machines. This is a fully accepted duality today, but at the time it confused some portions of the market.

The second was the introduction of the ill-fated 1200XL, which wasn't compatible enough with the earlier models and didn't offer enough new and more powerful features to compensate. This move certainly set the company back the better part of a year, until it began to right the ship with the 600XL and 800XL. You could also argue that the platform's lack of internal expansion and expensive external peripherals were a factor. SIO was brilliant, and arguably a precursor to today's USB in its simplicity and reliability (although certainly not speed), but it was also limiting in a business or otherwise professional context.

But the fourth, and arguably most important, was the way Atari kept the technical details of its products proprietary for so long. "Unfortunately, Atari neutralized their own advantage," Michael S. Tomczyk wrote in *The Home Computer Wars*. "To everyone's shock and dismay, they decided to keep secret vital technical information like memory maps and bus architectures which programmers needed to write software. They then tried to blackmail programmers by indicating they could get technical information only if they signed up to write Atari-brand software. This alienated the fiercely independent hobbyist/programmer community, and as a result many serious programmers started writing software for other machines instead. By the time Atari realized their mistake and started wooing the serious programmers, it was too late. The only programmers who remained loyal were game programmers."

In the October/November 1982 issue of *Antic*, editor/publisher Jim Capparell wrote that Atari was the number-one-selling home computer, and he predicted sales would reach half a million by the end of 1983. It's tough to confirm total sales figures, but most publications have pegged the number at two million by the end of 1985.

So after a strong start, Atari lost the plot quickly, thanks to hand-wringing in top management over whether the company just built a Real Serious Computer or a fantastic gaming machine. Then Atari shuffled the lineup several times, complicating matters. I wish I could say Atari kept improving it, and in some ways the company did. But the biggest problem was a general lack of innovation. The XL and XE lines that followed, combined with Atari's sale to Tramiel and resulting transformation, ended up doing little for the 8-bit Atari platform. It couldn't have lasted forever anyway, as the world was moving to 16-bit machines with better graphics, hard drives, and more power. But it's painful even now to realize how Atari could have beaten Apple and Commodore, and instead let an early home-court advantage in hardware and gaming prowess slip through its fingers.

Most of this stuff happened out of sight and out of mind, as far as I was concerned. The thing was, once you got your own Atari computer, chances were you weren't salivating over any newer models. They just weren't different enough. Your entry point into the Atari 8-bit lineup may well have been one of the newer machines. With the exception of the 1200XL, they were solid values and good budget buys, and let you into the same world of amazing games.

So while Atari was busy rearranging deck chairs on the S.S. Management Failure, I blissfully carried along as if nothing was going on, and played games on my computer throughout the 1980s.

With its launch in late 1979, the Atari 8-bit line began a graphical arms race in PC gaming that still rages on today.[111] Now we see it most with Nvidia and AMD graphics cards, ever-evolving drivers, state-of-the-art home consoles from Sony and Microsoft, and new and more powerful game libraries developers can harness for incredibly realistic effects, and at resolutions exceeding 1080p high definition. In the end, the Atari 8-bit line didn't die; it just faded away, as the saying goes. But no matter—as you'll see, fans like us are keeping it alive today just fine.

First, let's get to the best part of all—the games.

---

[111] www.ign.com/articles/2014/12/24/happy-35th-birthday-gaming-pc

6 | Golden Age Gaming

There's no way around it: Atari's 8-bit computer lineup was terrific for gaming. There were several thousand titles made for the platform, and of those, at least 300 to 400 were worth playing. Plus, plenty of titles appeared for other machines or in the arcade first. To narrow things down, I'll focus on the biggest and best platform exclusives, where the Atari 8-bit version was first. I'll note some key titles with interesting characteristics specific to the Atari 8-bit conversion. Some games were just fantastic to play and a huge part of the experience of owning an Atari computer, even if there *were* ports available on other platforms. Finally, I'll include just a few key games that didn't live up to the hype, and I'll explain why. Whether you have an emulator or real Atari computer handy, or you just want to remember the good times, let's go through the most significant games to grace the Atari 8-bit platform.

Culling the List

Some games by design don't offer an appreciably different experience on the Atari 8-bit than they do on other platforms. Case in point: interactive fiction, which, because of its text-based nature, works on all computing platforms. Infocom is arguably the most famous of text adventure game developers, with even its early titles consisting of sophisticated language parsers and intricate plots and maps. Infocom employees began programming games on a DEC PDP-10 mainframe at MIT, but all of the best titles made their way over to the Atari within a few years, notably between 1982 and 1986. Games like those in the Zork and Enchanter series, and The Hitchhiker's Guide to the Galaxy, are essentially novels you can play, and I played them on my own Atari 800 all the time. Infocom games were also notable for their included "feelies," or trinkets, maps, and other materials, which helped breathe life into the well-written text-based games without a computer-based visual component. If you plan on reexperiencing these games in an emulator, instead of with actual Atari hardware and software, it's worth heading over to sites like Atarimania.com to download the manuals and box art images. (In some cases it's necessary, as the materials also functioned as de facto copy protection.)

Infocom text adventures weren't even the first to reach the Atari 8-bit. Scott and Alexis Adams founded the lesser-known Adventure International, one of the earliest game development studios, in 1978. Taking its cue from the famous "first" text adventure, Colossal Cave, Adventure International released a series of adventures for various computer platforms, including the Atari 8-bit. Each one had a distinctive font on the Atari, with some of the more notable titles being The Count and Ghost Town. There were more than a dozen in all, plus some graphic adventures as well, before the company eventually folded in 1985. While the company's parser wasn't as advanced as Infocom's, Adventure International beat Infocom to market by a couple of years.

Some of Atari's own early games were mediocre; they were exceedingly basic, rushed versions of Basketball, Hangman, and other games populated early company catalogs and brochures. Most of Atari's business, educational, and home management software didn't do enough to demonstrate the wide capabilities of the platform, other than to scream "me too" next to the Apple II in the early years of the 8-bit Atari. Worse, a few major titles never made it over to the Atari 8-bit platform at all. As a certifiable role-playing game nut, I lamented the lack of Wizardry, Might and Magic, and Bard's Tale games. Origin Systems stopped its famed Ultima CRPG series on the Atari with Ultima IV: Quest of the Avatar. But there was so much gaming goodness to be had with an 400 or 800, it didn't matter. (Almost.)

Building an 8-Bit Ecosystem

While Atari refused to credit its own developers, some game programmers from this era gained fame nonetheless. Bill Budge, Bill Williams, Philip Price, and Scott Adams were four of the biggest, while programmers developing across multiple platforms like Richard Garriott and Dani Bunten also became famous to Atari users. Eventually, an entire healthy ecosystem of game software studios catered to the installed base of Atari 8-bit computer owners. Stalwarts included Lucasfilm Games, Avalon Hill, Parker Bros., Datasoft, Datamost, Electronic Arts, Epyx, First Star Software, Synapse Software, Brøderbund, and subLogic.

One of the biggest early trends was the conversion of popular arcade coin-up machines like Asteroids and Centipede. What stood out in my mind—and as a kid, what was of paramount importance—was just how close the home version could get to the arcade. This way you could play at home for free instead of begging your parents to take you to the arcade (and stuff your pockets with quarters). Gamers from the era may remember full-page ads depicting six or nine television screenshots in a grid, showing how the home conversion of, say, Q*bert or Popeye looked on various game consoles as well as Atari and Commodore computers. The worst sin of all was putting up fake screenshots in magazine advertisements. The ads didn't document the on-screen graphics, but instead showed an idealized, Platonic version with seemingly unlimited screen resolution (I'm looking at you, Activision).

The arcade conversions played significantly differently on the 400 and 800 than on the VCS. Pac-Man was solid and Missile Command was excellent, but others didn't fare as well; Space Invaders and Asteroids in particular came in for some criticism, which I'll get to. Later on, as more third-party developers began working with the platform, we started to see exclusive titles appear on the 8-bit Atari computer lineup first.

A smattering of games even support multiplayer—not just in the "your turn, then my turn" mode of early arcade games, but true two-player action. Depending on the game, it can be a split-screen competitive mode (Spy vs. Spy and Ballblazer), a four-player mode for the Atari 800's four joystick ports (M.U.L.E.), a good-versus-evil mode (Bruce Lee), or genuine two-player combat (Archon). If you got creative, you could do things like play Star Raiders with the joystick and then assign your best friend as the wingman to control the keyboard.

Figure 6.1: An ad for Frogger showing how it looked on nine different competing systems of the time. The Atari 8-bit usually came out on top in these.

Which Version Was First?

Timing the releases also gets a bit tricky. A developer could program the game on the Atari 8-bit first—usually because that was the computer they already owned—and then port it to other platforms. Or, as was often the case, a developer targeted the Apple II first, and then ported it to the Atari—games with limited color palettes and sound capability were often created this way. One of the maddening things about being an Atari computer owner was waiting for ports of popular games from other platforms, which became more and more common as the Apple II and especially Commodore 64 continued to outsell the Atari lineup. Usually the most popular titles appeared on those platforms first, and show up on the Atari later. It became a chicken-and-egg problem; as other platforms began to take hold and Atari couldn't effectively compete, larger developers began to plan their roadmaps with the Atari as a second or third consideration.

Even so, by the time the XL line was in full swing in 1983, there were many more software developers on board for writing and porting games for the 800. And once Atari let up on its restrictive third-party development policies, it opened up the doors for a true golden age in Atari software. These games weren't just for owners of the newest 8-bit Atari computers, though. Many (upgraded) 400 and 800 owners could also take advantage of these titles, as none of them required more than 48KB, though some required a disk drive.

Finally, all dates given for games are for when they arrived on the Atari 8-bit computer platform, not when they were first released in arcades or on another computer platform. For example, Taito released Space Invaders in 1978 as a stand-up arcade game, but the Atari 400/800 cartridge version arrived in 1980, so it's marked as a 1980 release.

A.E. (Brøderbund, 1982)

Anyone reading Atari magazines circa 1982 or 1983 will likely remember the full-page color ads for A.E. The Eugene, Oregon–based Brøderbund Software was known early on for its excellent games, and was reported to search overseas to find the best programmers. "'The Japanese are by far the best at this. It's their attention to detail,' said [cofounder] Gary Carlston—and their dedication to perfection. Carlston had to fish the code for the game A.E. (Japanese for stingrays) out of [programmers] Jun Wada's and Makoto Horai's wastepaper basket. They didn't think it was good enough to sell. It is currently one of Brøderbund's top sales performers."[112]

This Brøderbund game is a distant cousin of Galaxian and Galaga. You play by fighting off successive waves of space aliens, which swirl around in changing formations. You could see the Apple II roots in the basic color palette, rendered on the Atari 8-bit thanks to artifacting. Even so, the beautiful space backgrounds for the game were truly otherworldly if you were coming from a VCS or even some early arcade machines. The Atari version has much better audio, with polyphonic music and more robust sound effects during gameplay.

From floppy disk, it takes a while to start playing; you have to load the entire first disk and then flip it over before you can begin, thanks to all the graphics data. Strangely enough, although A.E. was a 48KB disk-based game, Atari apparently considered porting it to a 16KB version and releasing it as a cartridge for the 5200 SuperSystem. It

---

112. *InfoWorld*, April 4, 1983, p. 4

made it so far as a full-blown prototype, but it was done two years late and after the Great Video Game Crash of 1983 and was never released.[113]

Figure 6.2: A.E. is an early vertical shooter that features stunning background graphics on the Atari 8-bit.

Agent USA (Scholastic, 1984)

"Somewhere in America, this dangerous FuzzBomb™ is on the loose!" (I have no idea if the word FuzzBomb is trademarked, but it sure looks like it needs one.) So goes the beginning of Agent USA, a terrific romp through America in the guise of a sci-fi B-movie. The FuzzBomb is turning people into wandering balls of fuzz (FuzzBodies), which are traveling by train and contaminating the whole country.

You must ride the nation's train system from city to city, gathering clues to the FuzzBomb's location based on how the disease is spreading. Along the way, you learn about U.S. cities, state capitals, time zones, and the nation's overall geography. But Agent USA doesn't feel at all like an educational game—which is a compliment. The bigger cities have higher-speed rocket trains. You can get free tickets for

---

113. www.atariprotos.com/5200/software/ae/ae.htm

train rides at booths, and in state capitals you can get info about which cities have fuzzed people in them. To collect a ticket, though, you have to type the full name of the city, which helps you learn its name.

To defuzz people, you use crystals; you start the game with 10, but can get more by dropping a few and letting them multiply. When FuzzBodies touch the crystals, they're cured; regular people just steal them. It takes 100 crystals to kill the FuzzBomb. You have to figure out where it is currently, go there, and not touch any of the fuzzed people until you get to it or they'll deplete your crystal supply. As is often the case, the Atari 8-bit version has a funky sound track. The humans, such as they were, are little black hats with smoothly animated legs. You have a white hat. Uh, get to it.

Alley Cat (Synapse Software, 1983)

This exclusive Atari 8-bit title—which was later ported to MS-DOS in a horrendous cyan-and-magenta CGA-compatible version—is one of my favorite games. John Harris started work on it, but handed the project to Bill Williams after being unhappy with his one-screen prototype version.[114] Williams first developed Salmon Run (see below), then Alley Cat and Necromancer for the Atari 800—three of the platform's best original games—and then some Amiga games including Sinbad and the Throne of the Falcon for Cinemaware.

At any rate, as Freddy the Cat, you must navigate five different rooms, each of which serves as a discrete minigame. One room contains a fishbowl on a table; you must jump in, swim around, and catch the fish without touching any of the electric eels. Another room contains a birdcage you have to knock off the table so you can free and catch the bird it contains.

In the kitchen, you have to catch the mice that appear in a giant block of Swiss cheese. Then head to the living room to find a fun-to-climb bookcase, on top of which are three ferns you must knock over while avoiding a giant spider. The fifth room contains sleeping dogs; you have to eat the food in the dishes without waking the dogs. There's also a bonus round in which you must reach your valentine

---

114. www.dadgum.com/halcyon/BOOK/HARRIS.HTM

kitty date while avoiding Cupid's arrows, which pierce the hearts forming the platforms you walk on, making you fall.

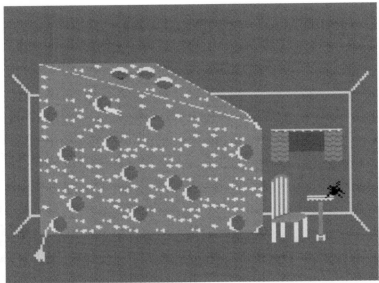

Figure 6.3: Alley Cat worked perfectly on my original Atari 800, but it requires a Translator disk on XL and XE machines.

Tons of clever touches abound. In the kitchen, for example, by running back and forth, you leave paw prints on the floor, which a *Fantasia*-style animated broom has to clean up first before coming back after you. The main screen features a series of garbage cans and clotheslines you must jump on to reach one of the rooms (which the game selects at random).

Alternate Reality: The City (Datasoft, 1985) and The Dungeon (1987)

One of the best and most distinctive games ever to be developed for the 8-bit is Alternate Reality: The City. It was intended to be the first in a six-part series by Philip Price: The City, the Arena, The Palace, The Wilderness, Revelations, and Destiny. Sadly, only the first two games were ever written and released—and they were originally supposed to form the first game together. Datasoft forced an early release, and so split the first game in the series in half.[115]

As a result, Alternate Reality: The City is barely half a game in the traditional sense, although it's not obvious at first. The game starts with you being kidnapped, brought aboard a spaceship, and taken from present-day Earth to (you guessed it) an alternate reality. From there, you create a character, begin exploring the city, get jobs to earn money, defeat monsters, sleep at inns, and level up. It's addictive and fun for quite some hours or even days—and the environment is certainly immersive. But as it eventually becomes clear, once you explore the entire map of the city, there's no real goal or even plot. The City was intended as a roaming area to bridge the other chapters, and only one of the other chapters made it to market (and I'll get to it below).

Figure 6.4: An intro screen from the amazing Alternate Reality: The City.

Despite all of this, Alternate Reality: The City is beyond compelling in its atmosphere and realism. It featured sophisticated 3D texture-mapped graphics, sound, and music for the time, all of which take full advantage of what the Atari 8-bit platform has to offer. No other version comes, not even on 16-bit machines, and the Commo-

---

115. www.dadgum.com/halcyon/BOOK/PRICE.HTM

dore 64 port is downright pathetic. The game also keeps track of your character's well-being, which includes hunger, exhaustion, and whether you're drunk or poisoned. To this day, I still remember the main song, complete with lyrics. I play it from time to time just to hear and see it run. Also enjoyable is the 16-bit Atari ST version, which lets you join guilds and offers a tiny bit more of a sense of accomplishment. Composer Gary Gilbertson redid the three-voice versions of his songs so they make the most of the Atari ST's less-powerful sound chip.

The Dungeon, meanwhile, is a classic dungeon crawl in a three-dimensional perspective. Inside the dungeon, you can buy weapons and other provisions, and you'll encounter fountains, wizards, secret doors, and plenty of monsters in your travels. While exploring, you need to eat food and drink water to stay alive. You need a compass to navigate, and you'll find keys, gems, and jewels as part of your quest.

The four levels contained in The Dungeon were supposed to be the sewers under The City. Philip Price ended up leaving the game industry in the middle of The Dungeon's development; two other programmers finished the game for Datasoft. While The City was a true breakthrough and technical achievement in 1985, The Dungeon already looked a bit dated by the time it hit the market. A review in *Dragon* magazine criticized both games for their excessive disk swapping, especially when just trying to save your game and then continue playing. You needed a separate blank disk just to save your character data, and it had to be a different disk than the one for your character in The City. (The same 1988 *Dragon* review also criticized the Mac version for not letting you copy it to a hard drive, but Atari 8-bit users didn't expect this sort of luxury.) The same year, FTL Games released the real-time Dungeon Master on the Atari ST, with a larger view and party of four characters to control, and dungeon exploration was never the same again.

Archon: The Light and the Dark (Electronic Arts, 1983)

Archon is a game of violent chess—and I mean that as a compliment. Each side has a leader: the Wizard on the Light side, and the Sorceress on the Dark side. The game takes place on a nine-by-nine-square grid with alternating colors. It otherwise looks like a chessboard, albeit with so-called power points at the top, bottom, left, right, and center. And, as in chess, each piece has different abilities. Your goal is to either capture the five power points on the board, or defeat all of the opponent's pieces in real-time combat.

Figure 6.5: The classic Archon: The Light and the Dark.

Both of these paths to victory are trickier than they sound. Whenever two pieces occupy the same space, one side fights the other to the death. The color of the square affects how much energy each side has. So if a Light piece battles a Dark opponent on a Dark square, the light side will have fewer hit points than usual and the dark side will have more. The total also changes depending on the kind of piece it is; some just naturally have more stamina. This makes it tough to defeat a side on its native color squares (white or black).

The other complex issue is time. Time continuously progresses in the game, and shifts between day and night. This affects roughly half the squares on the board, including all of the middle squares in a cross pattern. Three of the five power points are located on these changing squares. By the time you maneuver enough pieces to capture most of the squares, the colors will turn against you—a perfect opportunity for your opponent to attack and defeat you.

Archon: The Light and the Dark continues to play well today. First developed for the Atari 8-bit by Free Fall Associates, it became one of the first games published by Electronic Arts. It offers a perfect balance of strategy, speed, and polish. And there's no mistaking the opening music riff, with its rising introductory fanfare and bombastic theme. Several later versions of Archon attempted to update the original game, notably in 1994 with Archon Ultra (with mixed results) and in 2010 with Archon Classic (much more successfully) for the PC. There was also a short-lived iOS version.

Archon II: Adept (Electronic Arts, 1984)

Archon II: Adept changes up the main board layout and mechanics. This time around, instead of a chess-style design, the game is arranged in bands around the four elements of air, earth, fire, and water. You control one of four wizards (adepts) on each side, either Order or Chaos. The five power points are still vital to the game, maybe even more so, since there's a greater emphasis on spell casting—you are no longer limited to one of each spell. You spend much of the game summoning various kinds of elementals and demons to fight the other side, including kraken, juggernauts, wraiths, and gorgons. There are five ways to win instead of two, including triggering an Apocalypse with a final battle in the void.

It may be a stretch to call Archon II: Adept better than its predecessor—tougher would be a more accurate word. But it's definitely worth playing, and some even prefer it to the original. Oddly, the Commodore 64 lost its graphical advantage over the 400/800 version; the two looked pretty much identical this time around. I've always found this game exceedingly difficult to play, and in a good way. Today it's interesting to look back on just how innovative this sequel was, in a world where "sequel" usually means "more of the same." Archon II: Adept takes some of the best elements of the first game and brings the storyline to a grander, almost epic scale—even if it's not as tightly honed as the original.

Asteroids (Atari, 1981)

In the early 1980s, you couldn't have a home computer platform without some version of Asteroids, and Atari needed to move heaven and earth to build up the Atari 8-bit's cartridge library in the beginning. Yet even this brain-dead-obvious choice for a port of an *existing*

1979 Atari coin-op took more than a year to arrive on the 400 and 800. Unfortunately, management really was convinced the 800 should be a home computer first and a game system second; it took the wild success of Star Raiders, which I'll get to below, to get Atari to reconsider its plan for the computer lineup and put conversions like Asteroids back on the schedule.

For the three people still on the planet who haven't played this phenomenal classic arcade game, you control a tiny ship in an asteroid field. You must clear each screen of asteroids without crashing into any of them, and destroy the small and large UFOs that appear at regular intervals to attack you. You can jump into hyperspace as a last resort to prevent a collision, but there's no guarantee you won't reappear in the path of a different asteroid and die anyway. The physics of your ship's thruster and bullets felt as real when the game was released as anything you'll play today.

Although this 8-bit Atari conversion is passable, it's not exciting. The main problem with it, as with any Asteroids clone, is replicating the arcade version's spotless, tack-sharp vector graphics. The 8-bit Atari does a bit better than the lower-resolution VCS in this regard, breaking up the asteroids into multiple smaller pieces when you shoot them. But its pale-blue asteroids are weird; whoever decided to use different colors for the VCS version to make up for the lower resolution was onto something. The Atari 8-bit loses out on the overall gameplay balance, though. For some strange reason, you can't fire straight to the left or right; no matter what you do, the bullets always veer a little bit to the above or below.

Also of note is one interesting gameplay variation: Up to four people can play at once, against each other or the asteroids, thanks to the 400 and 800's four joystick ports.

Astro Chase (First Star Software, 1982)

Astro Chase, with its smooth scrolling and attractive launch sequence screen, was one of the first third-party games to show what the 8-bit Atari was capable of. It was the first major release from the prolific (and still-in-business!) First Star Software studio, and developed by the first winner of Atari's Star Awards for the Atari Program Exchange. Parker Brothers picked up the rights to port the game for a then-astounding $250,000 advance. The game also won awards from *Electronics Games*, *Creative Computing*, and *Computer Games* magazines.

This game puts you in charge of defending Earth (of course) from an alien attack (of course). You can move and fire in any of eight directions on the 2D space landscape. More important, you can fire in a direction independently of movement. This usually requires two separate joysticks, as in games like Robotron: 2084 or Space Dungeon, but Astro Chase makes it work. There are 34 levels; your goal is to destroy all 16 megamines while fighting eight different types of enemy spacecraft. The playfield is many screens wide. Four energy generators mark the furthermost corners of space, along with shield depots across the top, sides, and bottom.

Like many games for the Atari, Astro Chase came on both cassette and disk; both versions required 32KB to play. This shut out Atari 400 owners, at least before memory upgrades became available. Today, the game looks dated. The sound is weak for an Atari 8-bit title, and though moving your ship in eight directions on a wide playfield was clearly a novel feat originally, the controls feel stiff. The aforementioned launch sequence seems a little lame now, too. For a similar game, I'd recommend Sinistar or Zone Ranger over this one if you're playing today, but Astro Chase certainly earned its place in Atari 8-bit lore.

Attack of the Mutant Camels (Llamasoft, 1983)

This horizontally scrolling shooter is essentially a clone of Star Wars: The Empire Strikes back for the VCS, except with giant camels instead of AT-ATs. Talk about a weird pedigree: It's the work of Jeff Minter, the famed game developer who designed Tempest 2000 and Defender 2000 for Atari's Jaguar console in the early 1990s, and later, a Tempest clone called Space Giraffe for the Xbox 360.

There's an actual plot, but it's too complex and unrelated to the actual gameplay to bother with. Here's what happens: During each wave, several giant camels march slowly and to the right toward your home base. Your spaceship can destroy the camels, but it takes roughly a hundred shots to kill each one. If a camel reaches your home base, it's game over. The physics work the same way as in The Empire Strikes Back. It's tough to keep your spacecraft in one spot, so you'll find yourself constantly overshooting the camel target and doubling back until you get better at it. The camels also shoot multi-colored bullets at you. Like I said: Star Wars: The Empire Strikes Back with giant camels.

It's unclear whether Minter developed the game for the 800 or the C64 first. Either way, the 800 version is superior, thanks to its more detailed, graded backgrounds; psychedelic moving playfield lines with rapidly changing colors; and detailed, distant mountain ranges. In 2012, the Smithsonian featured this game among others in its (now ended) "The Art of Video Games" exhibit. It's a hard game and definitely worth a look today, despite its ultimately repetitive play, and it's another example of a title that just looks and plays better on Atari 8-bit computers.

Aztec (Datamost, 1982)

An interesting and innovative take on 1981's *Raiders of the Lost Ark* craze, Aztec puts you in control of an Indiana Jones–type character who must avoid snakes, giant crocodiles, traps, and guards while searching for a jade idol in the recently discovered (and reportedly cursed) Tomb of Quetzalcoatl. You have a machete, a pistol, and dynamite sticks with which to make progress in the catacombs.

To do so, you can walk, run, jump, stop, crawl, or climb. Sometimes you'll come upon a rubbish pile, which you can search for items, or a box you can open. The dynamite works as you'd expect: You set it, and then have to walk quickly away before it goes off or else you'll be killed in the blast. You must keep track of your character's remaining strength, bullets, and sticks of dynamite while you play. Technically, the game is a platformer, but it's more strategic and deliberate. You have to figure out how to proceed, rather than just blindly move and jump around.

Aztec was originally an Apple II release, as is obvious by the restricted color palette, slower pace of gameplay, spare sound effects, and lack of player-missile graphics. On the plus side, the graphics themselves are high-resolution, you can choose from one of eight difficulty levels, you can save your game in progress, and most important, the dungeon is randomized from one of 32 designs each time you play. The game originally came on disk and required at least 24KB—an unusual configuration, but one you could have had if you had bought a 16KB Atari 800 and then purchased just one CX852 8KB memory cartridge.

Ballblazer (Lucasfilm Games, 1984)

Ballblazer is a standout showcase for the Atari 8-bit's graphics and sound capabilities. The game is an intense futuristic version of soccer. It takes place between two "rotofoils," or pods, on a checkered field. You control one rotofoil, and your opponent controls the other. When you gain possession of the ball, it hovers in a field in front of your craft. You must head to the goal and shoot the ball through it to score a point. The other player, meanwhile, automatically turns to face wherever the ball is, and can hone in on your position and try to fling the ball away. The goalposts move closer together as the game progresses, which makes scoring points even tougher.

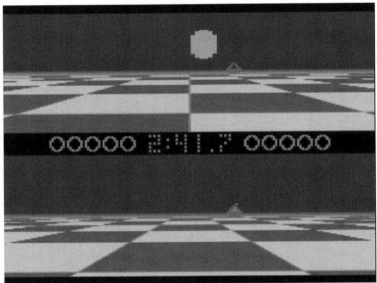

Figure 6.6: Lucasfilm Games' split-screen, fast-paced Ballblazer.

Lucasfilm Games officially unveiled Ballblazer on May 8, 1984, concurrently with Rescue on Fractalus![116]. The two games were the studio's first foray into computer gaming, originally announced as a collaboration between Lucasfilm Ltd. and Atari Inc. (Lucasfilm

---

116. Atari.com, 1972-1984 page

Games later became LucasArts Entertainment.) In the wake of the tremendous success of the *Star Wars* movies and *Raiders of the Lost Ark,* Lucasfilm set out to make a giant impression with Ballblazer—and succeeded by any measure. Ballblazer made the cover of *Antic*'s August 1984 issue, and quickly defined a kind of next generation for 8-bit games. The release roughly coincided with the arrival of Atari's XL computer lineup, just before Jack Tramiel bought the company in July 1984.

Ballblazer also contains one of the earliest examples of in-game algorithmically generated music. It varies in a structured, semi-random fashion as time goes on. "One reviewer, an eminent jazz player, said it sounded like John Coltrane did it," said Peter Langston, Ballblazer group lead at Lucasfilm Games and composer of the theme music, in the *Antic* cover story. "I think that's my best compliment so far." Either way, Ballblazer wouldn't have gone on to become much if it weren't a good game; it's quite addictive to play, and still holds up today. (Note: You may have seen this game titled Ballblaster; that was what it was called in its development phase. Pirated versions floated around ahead of and after the official version's release.)

Bandits (Sirius Software, 1982)

Bandits is a vertical space shooter with superlative graphics, sound, and animation. It also offers a twist: You have to shoot down the alien ships that are trying to capture your lunar base's fruit, which is on the right side of the screen. There are 28 levels in all, each with different groups of aliens and goods to protect. You also have special bombs at your disposal. Every few waves, you battle larger carrier craft, which drop difficult-to-avoid nusiants (bouncing balloon-type aliens). Your ship has a shield, but you can only use it for seconds at a time before it's depleted.

You can tell right from the beginning, with its bouncing truck and rocket liftoff animation, that Bandits was lovingly crafted. The spitty sound effects, from your laser gun to the aliens appearing and disappearing, are a big portion of the experience. A part of me still can't believe Bandits was a 1982 release. It was part of the first wave of third-party games for the 400 and 800. The only downside at the time (which affected a large portion of disk-based games) was the length of the load times, though once you got going it wasn't too bad per screen.

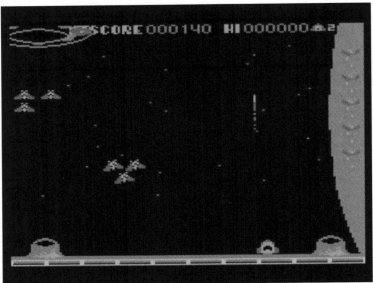

Figure 6.7: Bandits is one of the most smoothly animated games to grace the Atari 8-bit platform.

The 48KB game was written in assembly language, and the packaging proudly lists the programmer's names (Tony and Benny Ngo). Bandits exhibited polish and sophistication absent from many games at the time, and as a result became more than the sum of its parts. It's one of my favorite games for the 800, and barely shows its roots as an Apple II title.

B.C.'s Quest for Tires (Sierra On-Line, 1983)

This humorous game, essentially a prehistoric Moon Patrol, puts you in control of a caveman dude named Thor on a unicycle. The game is based off of the *B.C.* comic strip, which ran from 1958 to 2007. The title of the game is a play on the movie *Quest for Fire*, which came out in 1981 and was also set in ancient times.

The goal of B.C.'s Quest for Tires is to rescue Cute Chick from a hungry dinosaur. (I am not making this up, and Cute Chick is indeed capitalized in both the original strip and the video game.) To do so,

Thor has to jump over logs, rocks, and holes; dodge ash spewing from a volcano; and avoid "the troublesome Fat Broad," in what is clearly a nod to political correctness. Sometimes, Thor has to jump onto the backs of turtles to get across a river, while another caveman swings a club at Thor and says, "Jump, Sucker!" (in a cartoon balloon, at least.)

You control Thor on the wheel (which he invented!) by pushing the stick left or right to move him toward either side of the screen, up to jump, and down to duck. Hold the button and you can increase or decrease Thor's speed; you'll need this to gain enough momentum for to jump over cliffs. You get five wheels, and a speedometer on screen shows you how fast you're going. No explanation is ever given for how the wheel you're riding propels itself.

Sierra On-Line developed B.C.'s Quest for Tires for personal computers—it was never an arcade game—and it eventually came out for lots of platforms. The Atari 8-bit version was notable both for its pace and hilarious sound effects. Despite this, the best-known version is probably the port for the ColecoVision game console, where it regularly turns up on lists of "best ColecoVision games."

Beamrider (Activision, 1983)

In Activision's Beamrider, a force field surrounds Earth somewhere above its atmosphere, and you must find a way to break it to save humanity. You control a craft, which rides an ever-moving set of laser beams that construct the force field. You can jump left or right to avoid obstacles from one beam to the other while shooting a variety of alien ships. An intro screen at the beginning of each sector prepares you for the battle ahead; you get three torpedoes and unlimited laser firing. Your goal is to break the force field sector by sector by destroying 15 enemy ships in each one. The ships sometimes shoot at you, and on later levels you have to avoid falling meteors on the beams. At the end of each sector, a large Sentinel spaceship flies across the horizon line. If you have a remaining torpedo and shoot it, you get bonus points before moving on to the next level.

Beamrider is most recognized for its pulsing square-wave sound effects and minimalist, *Tron*-style graphics. If you squint, the graphics are even reminiscent of the arcade game Tempest. Activision programmer Dave Rolfe originally developed the game for the Mattel

Intellivision, and then ported it to other platforms. Like many Atari 8-bit translations, Beamrider looked and played in a more sophisticated fashion, with most of the difference in the sound design and added little graphic details compared with the VCS version.

In 2013, Google's DeepMind division published a study claiming its AI technology learned to play some Atari VCS games, achieving "close to human performance" on Beamrider and "better than human" performance on Breakout and Enduro.[117] It's interesting to consider the somewhat mindless, reflex-based play a game like Beamrider champions. You could argue the Atari 8-bit computer lineup was ideally suited to it.

Berzerk (Atari, 1983 prototype)

A stellar conversion of the arcade shoot-'em-up, the Atari 8-bit Berzerk delivers all of the level-building tension and plodding robots of the original. Your goal is to clear each board (or maze) of enemy robots. On the first board, the robots can't shoot. On the second board, they can shoot one bullet at a time. On the third board, they can shoot two bullets. Things become progressively more difficult the longer you play and the further you get, and eventually the robots shoot faster, too. Fortunately for you, the robots aren't particularly bright, and are prone to walking into the electrified walls or shooting each either when pursuing you. You can't walk into the electrified walls either, incidentally.

If you take too long to clear a board, the dreaded Evil Otto bounces onto the screen and comes after you. The 400/800 version even includes the digitized voices of the arcade cabinet—"Got the humanoid, got the intruder!"—and sounded clear and distinct. If you leave the board without clearing the robots, Evil Otto calls you a chicken. The only difference is that, unlike the arcade cabinet, the computer version freezes the action momentarily whenever the voices speaks.

For whatever reason, Atari never released this game on the 400/800, even though its employees finished a completed prototype; it's surmised that Atari wanted to give the 5200 some exclusive car-

---

117. www.usatoday.com/story/tech/2014/01/27/google-deepmind-artificial-intelligence/4943049/

tridges and canned it at the last minute.[118] It's also reported that the prototype version doesn't work on XL or XE computers, and thus requires the Translator disk (or an appropriately loaded 400/800 OS in another fashion) to run.[119] Berzerk has continued to influence popular culture, with references popping up on *The Simpsons*, *Futurama*, and *My Name Is Earl*. It's also rumored to be the first game to coincide with the death of a player, an 18-year-old with a reportedly weakened heart, in October 1982.[120]

Black Lamp (Firebird, 1989)

This open-world platform game delivers the kind of play you'd expect from a Nintendo Entertainment System (NES) or even a 16-bit Sega Genesis cartridge. You're in control of Jack the Jolly Jester, who must explore the kingdom of Allegoria (yep) and find nine lamps in different colors, while fighting eagles, witches, and other denizens. Each time you find a lamp, you must bring it back to a special rack before you can start searching for the next one. A dragon guards the ninth lamp; kill the dragon and rescue the last lamp, and you win the game.

Many Atari 8-bit owners never got to see Black Lamp, because 1989 was late in the platform's life cycle—a full 10 years after the 400 and 800 were unveiled, and right around the time the PC was getting its first VGA cards and sound boards, and pulling ahead in computer gaming. I certainly hadn't seen Black Lamp until I started doing research for this book; I'm glad I found it.

Black Lamp is also notable because it was developed for the 16-bit Atari ST (and Amiga) *first*, and then ported over to the Atari 8-bit. There aren't many other examples of this phenomenon. Nevertheless, Black Lamp is certainly worth a look today for its polish and sophistication. Perhaps in retrospect, and thanks to emulators, it's often cited as one of the best games available on the platform now, despite the game's high level of difficulty.

---

118. www.atariprotos.com/8bit/software/berzerk/berzerk.htm
119. Ibid
120. home.hiwaay.net/~lkseitz/cvg/death.html

Blue Max (Synapse Software, 1983)

This action game by Bob Polin puts you in control of a Sopwith Camel propeller plane, complete with altitude, speed, and weapon readouts. The game is set in Europe during World War I; your job while flying for the Royal Air Force is to destroy Axis airfields, bridges, and fighters. Presented in a scrolling three-quarter overhead view, the game delivers smooth shoot-'em-up action and strategy, and is kind of a cross between Zaxxon and River Raid in the objectives and on-screen graphics. During gameplay, you fly both high- and low-altitude bombing runs, and even lower (25-foot) strafing missions. You can set the joystick in either regular or reverse configuration (the latter so it behaves like a real airplane stick). You have specific goals for each mission, both on the way to and over the enemy's capital cities.

Figure 6.8: A solid technical achievement for its day, Blue Max features three-quarter-view diagonal scrolling.

You can turn gravity on and off, and choose one of three levels of difficulty. Damage indicators let you know if there are problems with the plane's fuel tank, bombs, engine, or machine gun, all of which will affect gameplay until you land at a base and get repairs.

Screenshots don't do this game justice. It's in the smooth animation, excellent sound effects, and overall game balance and sophistication where Blue Max shines. A review in *Antic* magazine called the game challenging without being frustrating, and it provided a reasonably realistic sensation of flying a biplane: "All you need is the wind blowing in your face and this can be simulated with the use of a fan."[121] A sequel set in the future, Blue Max 2001, wasn't as warmly received and didn't sell well. My recommendation: Skip it and stick to the excellent original.

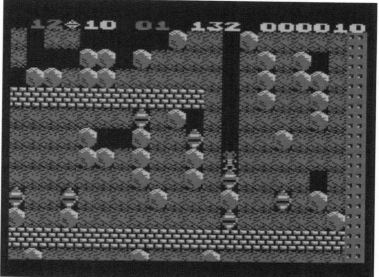

Figure 6.9: Boulder Dash, from First Star Software, which is still in business in 2017.

Boulder Dash (First Star Software, 1984)

In Boulder Dash, you control Rockford as he digs through caves to collect gems and diamonds. When you dig under rocks, they fall to open up new pathways. You must avoid getting crushed or straying too close to a resulting explosion. The game features 16 caves, each of which consists of several screens you walk or dig through. Each cave is successively tougher to solve than the last, and introduces

---

121. *Antic*, October 1983, p. 92

more challenges, such as butterflies you have to crush with rocks to get jewels, or fireflies you must avoid.

Boulder Dash is tremendous fun. Rockford's impatient foot tapping and arms folding whenever you took too long to do something never gets old. This game eventually made it to all of the popular platforms of the day. In 2014, the company released a 30th anniversary version for Android and iOS with vastly updated graphics and sound effects. Sticklers like me will always want the Atari joystick in hand instead of a touch screen, but that's a topic for another day.

Electronic Arts and Activision may have become tremendous publishing houses over the past few decades, but few original Atari 8-bit developers like First Star Software are still around today. Boulder Dash remains one of the most popular Atari 8-bit games, thanks to its original and engrossing gameplay, with well over 15,000 downloads at the time of this writing on Atarimania.com alone. It's still one of the best games ever made for Atari computers, and the theme song ranks right up there with the start of Archon: The Light and the Dark and M.U.L.E. for its distinctiveness. The game's atmospheric pings and boulder crash sound effects are also quite memorable.

Bristles (First Star Software, 1983)

This deceptively simple 32KB Atari 8-bit original makes you a painter. As Peter—or one of seven other characters—you must paint each level completely before moving to the next one, while avoiding the Bucket Chucker, flying Half-Pints, and dumb Buckets. To complete each board, you have to navigate a series of elevators and stairs, and be careful not to step into an empty elevator shaft. You begin each game with 10 brushes, and there's a timer you race against while completing reach room. The controls are simple: You paint automatically, so all you have to control is the direction and jumping. You can only jump while moving; you can't just stand in one place, which may seem confusing at first.

You also have to clean up after the super's daughter, who likes walking around and putting giant handprints everywhere in the fresh paint. I mean giant—the handprints end up almost as large as she is, which never made any sense to me. You can stop her by picking up a candy cane on the board and giving it to her; she then begins flashing different colors while you get back to work. The problem is that while you're carrying the candy cane, you can't paint either, so you must deliver it quickly.

Fernando Herrera, the developer behind Astro Chase, created Bristles. You can play as either a boy or a girl; this was significant for 1983, and the back of the game box prominently advertised this feature. The game contains eight different boards and six levels of difficulty, and up to four people can play at once. The background music features catchy renditions of portions of *The Nutcracker* by Tchaikovsky, and the game cues up different sections or motifs depending on what happens on screen. Just a few weeks prior to writing this section of the book, my wife and I painted our daughter's bedroom in real life. I can verify that playing Bristles requires a lot less cleanup work.

Figure 6.10: Datasoft's Bruce Lee. The ninja on the bottom of the screen is a giant pain.

Bruce Lee (Datasoft, 1983)

Chances are if you had an Atari computer in the 1980s, you know this game—especially if you were a fan of martial arts movies in the 1970s and 1980s. Bruce Lee, developed by Ron Fortier, is a platformer and adventure game at heart, but there's also plenty of fighting. *Your Sinclair* magazine called it the first combination of a platformer and "beat-em-up" game,[122] and I believe it's correct; all of the other examples that I can think of came out at least a year or two later.

Your goal as the famous martial artist is to get through all 20 screens, collecting lanterns along the way and opening secret doors, in order to reach infinite wealth and the secret of immortality. Two incredibly annoying enemies are on your case at all times: a staff-equipped ninja who is always in the way, and a large green sumo warrior who's tougher to defeat and tries to karate chop or kick you. Both enemies are easy to dispense with, but it's always temporary; they soon reappear again at the top the screen. The joystick and button combine to let you run, jump, punch, kick, climb ladders, and duck.

Interestingly, in addition to the usual one- and two-player alternating modes, a second person can play the sumo warrior just to beat up on the first player. Bruce Lee is quite polished, especially with regard to animation, though the graphics themselves and the sonic soundscape are sparse if distinctive on both counts. I can still hear the sumo warrior yelling (or is it yawning?) in my head. Bruce Lee remains one of the highest-rated Atari 8-bit games on Atarimania and still plays well. The game was later ported to the Commodore 64 and some other platforms.

Captain Beeble (Inhome Software, 1983)

Another Atari 8-bit exclusive and not particularly well known, this original Canadian game by Bob Connell was one of my early favorites. You fly around caverns with a jetpack, shooting mutant bugs and avoiding moving blockades while keeping an eye on your fuel, which essentially acts as a timer. You also have to contend with a somewhat weak force of gravity constantly pulling you down. You must increase the world's supply of Borinium by searching through the caverns to find a crystal "in a precarious state of imbalance"—once you get it, you only have moments to fly it back to the CPU (Crystal Processing Unit, of course) at the start of the level.

---

122. *Your Sinclair*, May 1990;
www.ysrnry.co.uk/articles/completeguidetobeatemups.htm

Captain Beeble is a tricky game, thanks to realistic thrust physics similar to what you'll find in Asteroids. To do well, you have to allow for the relatively slow acceleration of the jetpack, while simultaneously accelerating to a fast enough speed to make it through portions of the tunnel before one of the moving walls smashes into you. The longer you play, the harder it gets, with narrower passageways to fly through, an increasing number of mutant bugs, and poisonous walls you can't touch.

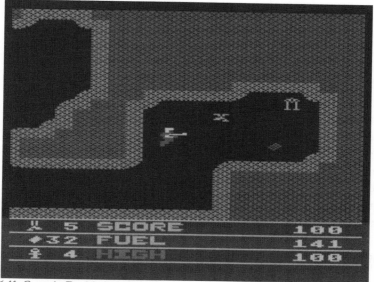

Figure 6.11: Captain Beeble is polished action adventure game that could pass for an NES title if it had slightly higher-resolution graphics.

The program feels all of a piece, with graphics, sound, and gameplay polish, and still holds up today. Even the intro screen is charming: It displays lots of the mutant bugs crawling around. (What? That's not charming?) There's the sound of a drumbeat reminiscent of the march of aliens in Space Invaders. Captain Beeble was a notable feat of programming for a single developer. It was available solely as a 16KB cartridge and didn't receive wide distribution in the U.S. market. Like most Atari games, it made its way around warez bulletin boards more easily. Inhome Software produced a number of other educational and game titles in 1982 and 1983; probably the best known is the also-fun-to-play Hard Hat Willy.

Caverns of Khafka (Cosmi Corporation, 1983)

This complex platformer crams a lot of action onto the screen, thanks to the use of smaller player graphics. Your goal is to search for the treasure of Pharaoh Khafka, plowing through many different caverns to reach the Grand Gallery and the Kings Chamber. Along the way, you have to contend with insects, boulders, electrified walls you can't touch, and pools of acid while finding keys to unlock still more passages. Your score is based in the dollar value of the treasure you pick up—and make no mistake, there's lots of it to get.

The game's collision detection is bizarre—though not inconsistent, so you can get used to it. But your character can get away with certain seemingly dangerous moves, while others that don't look any riskier kill him immediately. Otherwise, precious little information about this game exists today, though you can easily still play it in an emulator or via flash storage on an actual Atari computer, like all of the games in this chapter. Back in elementary school, I played this game a lot. It was quite difficult, and it doesn't seem to have been super-popular. But it's a solid example of the kind of original platformer you'd only find in the 1980s.

One bit of trivia: While Robert Bonifacio programmed the original game on an Atari computer for Cosmi, studio musician and game designer Paul Norman decided to remake the game when he ported it to the Commodore 64 for Cosmi. Instead of the frenetic original platformer, he coded a more cerebral, movie-like graphic adventure. It plodded along at a slower pace, but with larger, more detailed graphics; it's a completely different experience. Cosmi the company still exists today, albeit under the radar—it acquired ValuSoft in 2012 and sells productivity, home, utility, and game software under the name ValuSoft Cosmi. For the 800, Bonifacio also developed Aztec Challenge, Richard Petty's Talladega, and Super Huey.

Caverns of Mars (APX, 1981)

Caverns of Mars was written by a 17-year-old named Greg Christensen and sold on the Atari Program Exchange (APX). As you'll recall, the APX program initially ran against the wishes of Atari management, which was still thinking it should control all hardware and software developed for the Atari 8-bit platform. Caverns of Mars is a simple, vertically scrolling space shooter. Aside from the vertical part, it's quite similar to the popular side-scrolling arcade game Scramble.

Christensen coded the game in assembly language. Caverns of Mars is difficult, yet addictive. There are four skill levels. Your goal is to fly through the caverns to reach the Martian fusion bomb, activate it, and then fly all the way back out in a matter of seconds before the bomb explodes and takes the planet with it. You get five lives, you have a limited amount of fuel, and your craft can't touch the walls. Along the way, you'll encounter several kinds of hostile rockets, space mines, and laser gates. You can also pick up extra fuel to stay alive longer.

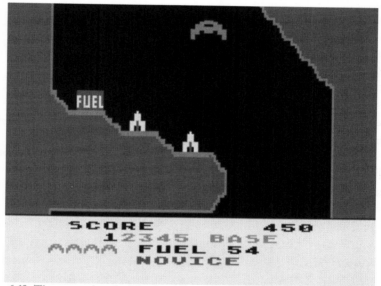

Figure 6.12: The crown jewel of the Atari Program Exchange, Caverns of Mars is a fun vertical scrolling shooter written by a then-17-year-old.

Today, Caverns of Mars is known both as a fun game and probably the most significant early APX release. It proved the effectiveness of the program. The following year, 1982, Atari itself began to distribute the game as one of its own boxed products, which was the first time this had ever happened. Atari invited Christensen to work on a cartridge port, but he declined, since he had just entered college at the time.[123] Atari sold versions of the game in both black and lined silver boxes for the next several years. During his first year in college, Christensen received an $18,000 royalty check, and it's estimated he went on to receive roughly $100,000 from this game alone,[124] in addition to the $3,000 he won for it first being accepted into the APX program.

Christensen went on to program a sequel to Caverns of Mars, called Caverns of Mars II, which does scroll left to right like Scramble did. It features oversized player-missile graphics. Rockets launch at you from the ground as you fly. This game was never officially released, as such; although it was also completed in 1981 shortly after the original Caverns of Mars, it didn't get distribution until *Antic* Magazine picked up the remains of APX several years later. It was sold as Mars Mission II.[125] Even so, thanks to rampant piracy on the 8-bit Atari platform, many people remember it as Caverns of Mars II nonetheless.

Centipede (Atari, 1981)

A home version of one of the best arcade games of the time was bound to be successful, and the 800 version of Centipede largely fit the bill at first. It's only an average port, using character-set-based graphics. But it contains all of the elements from the original arcade cabinet, and has the same sense of pace and urgency.

The game is set in an enchanted mushroom patch. Your goal is to attack the incoming centipedes, segment by segment, as you also battle a jumping spider, falling fleas (starting in the second round), and a poisonous scorpion (which begins appearing after you score 6,000 points). The scorpion poisons mushrooms as it crosses the screen. When the centipede touches one, it mutates, makes a beeline for the bottom of the screen, and gets in your way, and it even starts regenerating new segments.

The later 5200 version is clearly superior. It features proper multicolored mushrooms with outlines, a larger spider, improved sound

---

123. *The Creative Atari*;
.atariarchives.org/creativeatari/Dog_Daze_and_Caverns_of_Mars.php
124. *Video Games* magazine, December 1982;
www.atarihq.com/othersec/library/apx.html
125. www.atarimania.com/game-atari-400-800-xl-xe-mars-mission-ii_6813.html

effects, and just an overall more colorful and exciting presentation. Even the font used for the current and high scores looks nicer. At least for a short period, Atari wanted the 5200 versions of games to be better than their 400/800 counterparts, even though the underlying hardware was more or less the same.[126] This 5200 version of Centipede made its way over to Atari 8-bit computers anyway. Thanks to a famous software pirate named Glenn the 5200 Man—known by his signature on "crack" screens—most 5200 games ended up ported over to the Atari 8-bit computer lineup.

Playing Centipede with a joystick is fine, but you need a trackball to get the most out it. The console-style model for the 5200 was excellent, and brought the arcade experience home. But several third-party models also did the trick for the 400 and 800, as did Atari's own CX22 Trak-Ball. No matter which version you play, it will still be fun. Centipede was an original arcade coin-op and a centerpiece to the home arcade experience at the time.

Atari released a sequel, Millipede, in 1983, a year after it debuted in arcades. In addition to spiders, and instead of scorpions and fleas, Millipede pits you and your garden against bees, dragonflies, inchworms, mosquitoes, and earwigs, and there are DDT bombs you can shoot and destroy all nearby enemies. The DDT bombs are fun to shoot, and Millipede is a good distraction, though I always preferred the original game.

Choplifter (Brøderbund Software, 1982)

Dan Gorlin developed Choplifter for the Apple II first, but it's an astoundingly fun game to play on the 800. If you squint, it's a Defender clone, but it also captures the post-Vietnam and Iran hostage crisis malaise on the minds of Americans at the time. Your role in the fictional Bungeling Empire is to pilot a helicopter, rescue 64 hostages on the ground from enemy tank fire, and then return them safely to a local U.S. Postal Service base. There are four barracks, each containing 16 hostages. The worst thing is that if you aren't fast enough, one of the enemy tanks will fire on the barracks and kill all the remaining hostages in it.

126. www.atariprotos.com/5200/software/centipede/centipede.htm

How did a U.S. helicopter get to the Bungeling Empire in the first place? From the packaging: "You have smuggled an entire helicopter into the post office by disguising it as a mail sorting machine. There, while you reassembled your chopper, you have carefully planned to rescue the 64 hostages and bring them back to the post office." I'm pretty sure my local post office will not accommodate this sort of thing.

The first Choplifter conversions across 8-bit platforms were similar. The Atari obviously had its own character set for the title screen and on-screen text and numerals, but otherwise looked like an Apple II game with its restricted color palette and lack of player-missile graphics. Notably, Sega released this game several years later in a coin-op arcade version. More often the opposite occurs, where a game is first released in the arcade and then manufacturers make home versions thanks to its popularity. Atari also updated the graphics when it released a dedicated XEGS cartridge later on. This version contains brighter color choices, although I have to admit I'm partial to the original. I still play it, too.

Clowns and Balloons (Datasoft, 1982)

This silly-looking Breakout clone puts you in control of a pair of janitors holding a trampoline at the bottom of the screen. A monkey at the top of the screen sits on a high wire and blows up balloons to make your life difficult. You must bounce a clown up and down to burst all of the stuck balloons near the ceiling. The more he jumps on the trampoline, the more momentum he gets. You have to clear the balloon rows in order, or else the out-of-order row reappears and you have to clear it all again. If you succeed, you join the monkey on the tightrope, and it tips its hat to you before you begin the next level. Why you don't just strangle the monkey while you're up there is never explained.

The game works with a joystick or paddle controllers. As with Breakout, the angle and speed the clown lands on the trampoline affects the way he launches off again the next time. Since the balloons move, there's an added challenge compared with Breakout, and that combined with the physics makes the game quite challenging and addictive. The whole thing fits in 16KB, like many early 400/800 releases, so it could fit on either cassette or disk.

"The game took me about four months to program," former Datasoft developer Frank Cohen told Atarimania.com in 2007. "The last month was bug fixing and that was really painful. I had a hundred bugs to fix. One of the minor ones was I got the text wrong for the bonus round. When the game displays 'Bonus Round' it would print 'Butus Crewt' on the screen. I was working with Mark Rielly, Ron Rosen, William Robinson, and others at the time. They started asking me when Butus Crewt was going to be done! I was all of 21 at the time." Thanks, Frank, for making my childhood just a bit more fun than it would have been without this game.

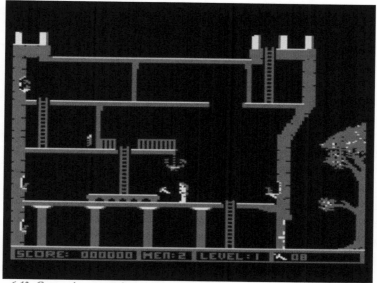

Figure 6.13: Conan is a complex, seven-screen adventure puzzle game with great music.

Conan (Datasoft, 1984)

Conan is a sophisticated platform adventure game. It was originally developed for the Apple II, and then made its way over to the Atari shortly thereafter. Conan barely has a plot—fight dragons and floating eyeballs, get treasure, use gems and keys to progress forward— but its boards and action are beautifully detailed, especially for a 1984 game. You have to navigate ladders, lava pits, floating ledges, and trapdoors along the way. The good news: Falling doesn't hurt or kill you, and you can tumble and leap around, as well as toss your magical sword at enemies. The four-voice music, which plays before and during the game in the Atari version, sounds fantastic. Compared with the near-silent Apple II version, it's no contest.

A few downsides: From disk, it took several minutes to load each of the seven boards once you were done with the last one. "Better take along some coffee on Conan's quest," said the *Antic* magazine review at the time,[127] and the writer wasn't kidding. My friend Carlo and I would go do something else for a few minutes—race matchbox cars? Play with Legos? Figure out where my grandmother hid the chocolate chip cookies?—while we waited; minutes feel like years when you're a teenager. Today, each board loads instantly when you can just play Conan off an SD card or an emulator.

Conan also lacks polish, with less-than-perfect collision detection, though it doesn't appreciably get in the way of gameplay. The same *Antic* review listed Whistler's Brother and Montezuma's Revenge (both covered below) as two games with crisper movement; this may be true, I suppose. I also noticed some slowdown whenever there were a lot of objects on screen. Regardless, it just wasn't the 1980s without Conan the Barbarian looming over you in some fashion, and this game was just the ticket.

Crystal Castles (Atari Prototype, 1984)

Crystal Castles was one of Atari's more unique and solid coin-op offerings when it debuted in arcades in 1983. The company released a 5200 cartridge in 1984, and a prototype 8-bit computer version leaked around the same time. I got a copy as a kid in 1984 and played it constantly on my 800.

The premise: As Bentley Bear, you must collect the many sparkling gems in a series of M.C. Escher–like multilevel mazes filled with elevators and secret passages. You have to clear each screen, Pac-Man style, while avoiding animated trees, gem eaters, crystal balls, ghosts, skeletons, and occasionally, the Witch Berthilda with a steaming cauldron. A magic hat confers temporary invincibility to help you. There are also some hidden warps, which let you skip to later levels. Pots of honey are good for bonus points.

---

127. *Antic*, April 1985, p. 85

The 5200 conversion is quite accurate and plays just as fast as the real thing; the only noticeable differences are the slightly muted colors, and the less-detailed bear and monsters. The sound effects and music are superlative, as befits anything running on the Atari 8-bit architecture.

In the end, Crystal Castles did eventually arrive officially. Atari didn't release the game for its computer lineup until 1988 as an XE cartridge—way too late, given the game itself was five years old by then, and the NES had already been out for several years. The XE version includes some changes and tweaks, which added missing sound effects and music in places, and some minor improvements to the way the various characters in the game are drawn. I remember spending many hours playing this game on the 800, and to this day I gravitate to Crystal Castles machines in any retro arcade I happen to come across.

Dandy (APX, 1983)

This 26-level dungeon crawl, written by then-MIT-student John Palevich for the Atari Program Exchange, lets you and up to three friends cooperate (four joystick ports!) to kill monsters, eat food to restore health, and collect treasure. You lose some health each time your character collides with a monster, so stocking up on extra food is paramount. You need to find keys to unlock certain doors, and to get to the next level you need to find the descending staircase. Smart bombs let you blow up all of the monsters in the immediate vicinity. There are four levels of difficulty to play, and you can create your own dungeon maps from within the program. (In fact, you can find additional dungeon packs floating around the Web.)

Today, the graphics, sound effects, and map design all seem primitive; this was clearly a homebrew effort. But if you thought from the description above Dandy sounds a lot like the arcade game Gauntlet, you are correct. Aside from being a fun game to play despite its limitations, Dandy has historical significance: At the 2012 Game Developers Conference, Gauntlet developer Ed Logg said Dandy was the direct inspiration for the hit arcade game two years later. Atari remade Dandy in 1988 as an XE cartridge called Dark Chambers that featured improved graphics and sound effects. But Dark Chambers also had fewer enemies on screen at any one time, and only support for two players instead of four, since the XE line of computers and the XE Game Console all had just two joystick ports.

Decathlon (Activision, 1984)

Olympic-style video games were a running theme around the 1984 Olympics, and I'd argue that Decathlon was a lot better (if harder) than Atari's Track & Field conversion. Unfortunately, this game is an example where the Commodore 64 version was better. For whatever reason, the 800 port didn't take much advantage of the more power-ful hardware. The result was a near-VCS-version clone with (still silent) crowds in the stands and more descriptive on-screen text, but that lacked the extra player detail and sound design of the C64 conversion.

The game features 10 events: the 100-meter dash, 400-meter race, 1,500-meter race, long jump, high jump, shot put, hurdles, discus throw, pole vault, and javelin throw. You can race against another player simultaneously when applicable, or take turns otherwise. In any of the versions, my biggest memory about the game, aside from the addictive gameplay, is how destructive it was for Atari joysticks. You had to move them back and forth so hard and so fast to score high, it's a wonder any CX40s still survive in the wild today. I remember trying to figure out how to take care I didn't push the joysticks too hard, while simultaneously working the living heck out of them; it was a tricky balance to get right if you didn't want to ask your parents to buy new joysticks every few weeks.

Based on the insane control scheme, and how most people today are playing emulators with gamepads or the computer keyboard, playing Decathlon the way it was originally intended is nearly impossible. And if you *are* using a real Atari computer—I'll get to all of this later in the book, about the best ways to play Atari games today—you may not want to shred your joysticks for this purpose.

Defender (Atari, 1982)

It's tough to overstate the importance of the Williams Electronics coin-op game Defender. The plot of this horizontally scrolling space shooter is simple: Aliens have swarmed over your planet and are try-ing to capture all the humanoids. Whenever they're successful, and bring one to the top of the screen, it changes to a mutant alien, which is then extra-difficult to kill. You must shoot all the aliens and protect the humanoids, sometimes catching them in midair and returning them to the planet's surface.

Along the way, your ship must fight off baiters, swarmers, bombers, and pods. You start the game with three lives and three smart bombs, and you can use hyperspace to jump to a new (and unfortunately sometimes even more dangerous) spot than you were previously. A scanner view on top of the screen shows where you, the aliens, and the humanoids are located. You start the game with 10 humanoids, and if you lose them all, the planet explodes; you get all 10 humanoids back again every fifth wave. The included manual was packed with tips, including flying low, not using your thrusters too much, and reversing direction twice in succession to confuse the aliens.

The Atari 8-bit version looks and plays well, if a tad more slowly than the tremendously difficult arcade version, and is more faithful than the one the VCS saw. Worthy of note today are the beautiful laser shots from your spaceship, the detailed aliens, the sparkling particle-effect explosions, and the trademark Williams-style square-wave sound beginning each level. Atari's 8-bit Defender port offers a nice contrast to the decidedly more strategic and involved Star Raiders. After the disappointing Asteroids and downright odd Space Invaders, Defender joined Missile Command, Donkey Kong, and Pac-Man as one of Atari's best coin-op conversions for the 400 and 800.

Dimension X (Synapse Software, 1984)

This three-dimensional, first-person space shooter, like Ballblazer, was developed by Steve Hales for the Atari 8-bit. The game conveys a serious sense of speed thanks to the scrolling checkered landscape. Synapse called it "Altered Perspective Scrolling," which meant "cool scrolling." You control a cyclo-skimmer on a desert planet in a forgotten corner of the star cluster Jaraloba. The game combines 3D combat with a Star Raiders–like sector map, which lets you travel to different quadrants in search of the invading Rigillian enemy you must defeat.

Dimension X offers three difficulty settings and three levels of shield strength, for nine possible combinations. The game consists of two sections: the aforementioned desert, and underground passages. In the desert, you must watch the radar scanner and communications monitor, and keep an eye on your fuel and shield status. If your ship takes on damage, some of the systems will stop working and the game becomes harder. The passageways let you travel between sectors, and are stocked with electrified gates you can maneuver around with your cyclo-skimmer's tunnel tracking system.

Synapse Software advertised Dimension X for months ahead of release in various Atari magazines. Hales was already known for his excellent work with Fort Apocalypse (covered below) and Slime. So expectations for Dimension X were running high. Unfortunately, Dimension X represents a missed opportunity; the whole thing just doesn't come together as an addictive game. A June 1984 *A.N.A.L.O.G.* magazine review called the final game "disappointing," thanks in part to the seemingly unfinished and opaque passageways sequence, and in part to unfulfilled promises from the packaging. The game is missing the promised tanks, missile-launching silos, and detailed spaceships, and there's no separate-screen 64-sector map showing enemy locations and the fuel necessary to reach them.

Figure 6.14: A later ad for Dimension X that dialed back the broken promises.

The game also features a horrific form of copy protection: "A foolish protection scheme built into the program causes the game disk to try to write to itself," reviewer Robert T. Martin wrote. "It can't complete the task, the program boots fine. However—if you, like several thousand disk drive owners (myself included), have installed a switch to disable the write-protect mechanism, and the switch is engaged, Dimension X will write to itself and *reformat the entire disk, wiping out the program!*" (Emphasis in the original.) And to think we complain today about always-on DRM in PC games. Still, Dimension X is worthy of inclusion here thanks to its graphical feats.

Donkey Kong (Atari, 1983)

Any home computer and game console worth its salt in 1983 had a version of Donkey Kong, which was one of the first platform-based and most popular arcade games at the time—and it brought the character Mario to the world. As Mario, you have to rescue Pauline, the damsel in distress, from Donkey Kong, a giant ape who kidnapped her and brought her to the top of an under-construction building. On the first board, you must jump over barrels Donkey Kong rolls down the girders at you, or pound away at them with the magic hammer—though you can't climb ladders whenever you have the hammer. Successive stages put Mario in a variety of construction-related scenarios, removing rivets and climbing elevators.

The 800 has the best home version of Donkey Kong, complete with all four boards (including the "conveyor belt") and even the "How high can you go?" intro screen. Plus, the gameplay balance is superb. Coin-op ports for the 400 and 800 didn't get better than this.

If you're a Donkey Kong fan, chances are you also love Donkey Kong Jr. The 800 version contains all four of its coin-op boards, too: Vine, Chain, Jump Board, and Hideout. I spent untold hours playing this game as well, climbing jungle vines, avoiding Snapjaws, and unlocking padlocks in order to rescue "papa." The graphics, sound effects, and music all combine to make an incredibly addictive game and an experience pretty close to the arcade. Both Donkey Kong and Donkey Kong Jr. introduced an entire generation to several of Nintendo's most famous characters.

Draconus (Cognito, 1988)

Many Atari gamers never heard of Draconus, although if you're active on current Atari forums, you've almost certainly come across it and may even already be a fan. As with Black Lamp, by the end of the 1980s newer Atari 8-bit games were sliding under the radar in the U.S. Gamers had gravitated to the NES, the 8-bit Sega Master System, and the 16-bit Sega Genesis on the console side, and to more advanced computer platforms like the Atari ST, Amiga, and increasingly, the PC.

Even so, Atari 8-bit computers were still selling well in Europe. The U.K.-based Zeppelin Games developed and released Draconus, a side-scrolling adventure platformer and essentially a Metroid clone in gothic clothes. You can almost tell the game needs an NES-like controller with two buttons, because the controls are a bit difficult to master. You jump by pushing up on the stick. To punch, you press the button down and then push right or left (depending on where you were facing). To breathe fire, you hold the button down and push up; this function would have ideally been assigned to a second fire button.

Nonetheless, Draconus plays smoothly and has excellent graphics and music for an Atari 8-bit game. The graphics are nicely shaded, the animation is nigh on perfect, and the programmers even managed to get halfway-realistic drum sounds in the soundtrack using the POKEY chip (most Atari games have various takes on white noise to achieve the same effect). It's quite a big adventure, and there are many screens to explore and underground denizens to fight. This game is a solid example of the most the 8-bit Atari computer was able to achieve; you'd need to move to a 16-bit console to see appreciable upgrades in graphics, audio, and animation.

The Dreadnaught Factor (Activision, 1984)

This overhead space shoot-'em-up puts you in control of a tiny aircraft, which flies over giant Star-Destroyer-like ships descending on your home planet. You get 10 lives, and there are seven difficulty levels to choose from. You take down each dreadnaught by shooting up its cannons and bunkers, the four main engines on its back, all of the vents on its surface, and anything else not completely nailed down.

The trick is, you can't fly backward. While you can slow your flight to a crawl, you're incessantly advancing upwards. This means that if you miss some of the targets, you'll have to fly back around and start over, where you'll be in empty space once more, until you start to hear the telltale engine sound of the giant ship. The plus side is you can fly over targets without crashing into them. The downside? Each time you make a full pass, the dreadnaughts get a little closer to your home planet. Each dreadnaught slows down as you destroy its engines one by one.

The Dreadnaught Factor is an interesting take on the space genre; the only other port was for the Intellivision, and it was far worse (and even scrolled horizontally instead of vertically, which was just weird). The game doesn't look or sound exceptional, but the gameplay keeps you coming back. By this time in the Atari 8-bit's cycle, space games had been done to death, and reviews at the time were mixed, with *Antic* magazine in particular saying the game's "kill or be killed" concept wasn't as original as other Activision games.

Dropzone (Mindscape, 1984)

Dropzone is easily one of the best Atari 8-bit games ever made. Developed by Archer MacLean, it's an original Atari platform title that MacLean later ported to the Commodore 64. Essentially, Dropzone amplifies the side-scrolling, hostage-rescuing concept of Defender. In this game, the hostages are scientists on a base being overrun by hostile aliens. Dropzone features excellent graphics and super-smooth animation, with lots of little details; for example, the astronaut main character claps quickly each time you successfully finish a wave.

Dropzone is still mostly a clone of Defender otherwise. The game is set in 2085, after only a small number of people survived the robot wars in our Solar System. Dropzone apparently includes 99 levels; I never made it this far and had to look up the number. The original Atari game runs faster than the Commodore 64 version.

MacLean has said he's a fan of Eugene Jarvis games like Defender and Robotron: 2084, and he took inspiration from the former as well as Stargate, Scramble, Galaxian, and other space games when developing Dropzone. "In 1981 I got hold of an Atari 800, a Star Raiders cartridge, and a joystick. I remember being absolutely hooked on this for weeks at a time," he said.

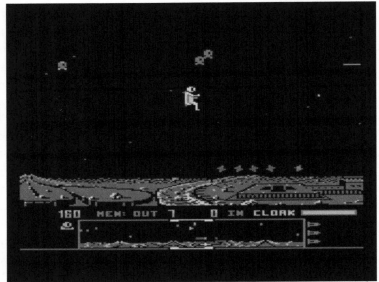

Figure 6.15: A Defender clone turned up to 11, Dropzone features smooth animation and slick gameplay.

"I realized straight away there must be some real clever hardware inside the Atari 800," he continued. "It could not have been done with just software. But Atari remained very tight lipped about what exactly was inside their machine. My lucky break was to obtain a bible written by Chris Crawford on how to access the hardware bits. Once I read it there was no turning back. For the next year or two I became obsessed with pushing the machine to the limits."[128]

Well done, sir—looks like you did the job just fine.

Eastern Front (1941) (APX, 1981)

Chris Crawford's original claim to fame, Eastern Front (1941) is a tactical strategic war game for the 800. It simulates the German invasion of Russia in World War II; you controlled the Germans, while the computer managed the Russian side. The game drew from paper-and-pencil war games popular throughout the 1960s and 1970s. Crawford claims it was the first computer strategy game to feature a scrolling map of the playing field. Changing seasons, troop morale, and fatigue all figure into your strategy as well.

---

128. www.dadgum.com/halcyon/BOOK/MACLEAN.HTM

Eastern Front (1941) was originally an APX release, although Atari eventually packaged it and sold it as part of it main lineup, just as happened with Caverns of Mars. Crawford remembers how wonderful it was to see software for the first time (in August 1980) with a huge map and smooth scrolling. "I realized this opened up a world of possibilities for wargames," he wrote in *Chris Crawford on Game Design*. "No longer would we have to squeeze the entire map onto a single 320x192 screen; now we could have huge maps... It may be difficult for designers brought up with modern PCs to appreciate just how exciting this was. We had been confined to single-screen, low-resolution displays; the best we could do to add more information was to jump from one display to the next. The smooth scrolling map was absolutely revolutionary!"[129]

Crawford said this was around the time that Atari charged him with setting up a group to approach third-party software developers with documentation for the 8-bit platform, and he used the scrolling map demo to convert Apple II diehards. "Programmers' eyes would bug out when they saw that," Crawford wrote in the book. And yet, not many of them were interested in the Atari—which led Crawford to develop Eastern Front (1941). "Very well, I decided, if nobody else will accept this challenge, then I shall have to do it myself." He said later that while the game is remembered primarily for the scrolling map, he can't take credit for it, because it was already "built into the hardware." He did take credit for all the AI in the game.

The Eidolon (Lucasfilm Games, 1985)

In this ambitious first-person Lucasfilm game, you learn about an ancient 19th-century machine that supposedly lets you "teleport and transform enchanted creatures" and even control the flow of time. You're not told who invented the contraption and what happened to this person. When you find the machine and attempt to operate it, you're immediately transported to underground caverns. To win, you must find and kill dragons on 10 different levels. The game featured fractal graphics and required 64KB, putting it out of reach of early 400 and 800 systems.

---

129. *Chris Crawford on Game Design*, p. 246

Most of the game is a mystery. The documentation is purposefully vague, and part of the game is figuring out exactly what is going on and what you must do to make progress. Developing the game was even tougher. To create The Eidolon, Lucasfilm Games created a utility program called Animated Cel Editor (or A.C.E.), which let the company design a huge number of oversized animated creatures to populate the underground world, according to a December 1985 *Antic* profile of the game. The tool utilized some of the methods classic animators used in cartoons, at a time when this level of sophistication in computer game design wasn't commonplace the way it is today.

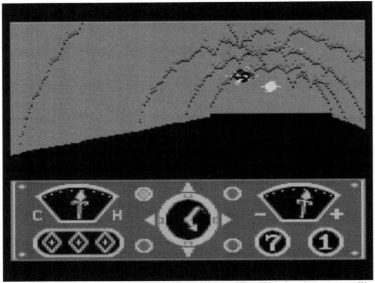

Figure 6.16: A second-wave Lucasfilm Games title, The Eidolon is a compelling time-travel adventure game.

The Eidolon was Lucasfilm's second pair of killer Atari 8-bit games along with Koronis Rift (see below), after releasing Rescue on Fractalus! and Ballblazer. Some people consider The Eidolon more of a tech demo than a real game, as tends to happen when the technology involved threatens to overpower balancing gameplay. But the steampunk atmosphere and excellent sound design themselves were worth the price of entry, and there's still enough there for an engaging experience. To this day, The Eidolon is one of the highest-rated (and most frequently downloaded) games on Atarimania.

Encounter! (Synapse Software, 1983)

This exclusive Atari 8-bit game developed by Paul Woakes takes place in a three-dimensional field with a series of kamikaze aliens. You sit inside a tank, but while there are some similarities, this is no Battlezone. The game moves more quickly, and includes both filled-in obstacles instead of wireframe graphics, and a larger series of in-game objects.

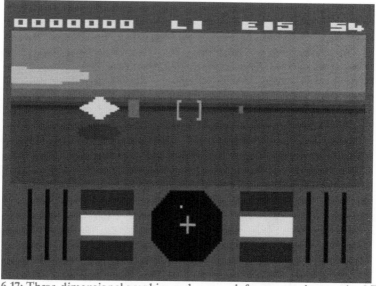

Figure 6.17: Three-dimensional graphics and a smooth frame rate characterized Encounter!, a futuristic tank battle game.

An oversized radar screen in the center of your dashboard tells you where the aliens are. There are two main kinds: saucers, which hover over the ground and fire at you, and become increasingly sophisticated in their attacks as you progress in level; and drone missiles, which sound a low pitch as they approach and are tough to hit without backing up while firing. These also gain increasingly complex patterns of movement on higher levels. Whenever you're hit, you lose a shield, and you also get extras as the game progresses; lose them all and your tank will be destroyed.

Destroy all the enemies on a level, and a gate appears. You must pass through it to reach the next level. The tunnel sequence itself contains spheres you must avoid. If you don't, you lose a shield and drop back a level. Nothing is a cakewalk in this game.

As was somewhat unusual for the time, Encounter! came in both 16KB (cartridge) and 32KB (disk) versions. The game features three difficulty levels. Regardless of the version, it's super-stressful to play. Even though static screenshots of it look simplistic today, as is often the case, Encounter! was quite a technical achievement and something uniquely suited to the Atari 8-bit's architecture. If you want to play Battlezone, skip the official one and play this instead—you'll be glad you did.

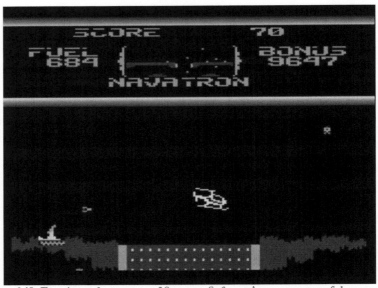

Figure 6.18: Fort Apocalypse, one of Synapse Software's most successful games.

Fort Apocalypse (Synapse Software, 1982)

Fort Apocalypse, developed by Steve Hales, is an excellent if difficult side-scrolling helicopter rescue game that takes elements from both Scramble and Choplifter. Instead of rescuing hostages in the field and returning them to base, as in Choplifter, you fly deep underground "inside the granite mantle of the Earth" (as the box says). Your "rocket copter" can shoot straight or drop bombs. You have to rescue eight prisoners from the Draconis caves and another eight from the Crystalline Caves before heading into Fort Apocalypse itself to destroy it.

There are enemy helicopters, missile drones, Kralthan tanks, and impact shields to contend with. You have a horizontal radar screen on top similar to what you get in Defender. Fort Apocalypse is another Atari 8-bit original, though it was later ported to the Commodore 64. It's a good early example of what the platform was capable of once Atari loosened its ill-advised tight grip on software development. Fort Apocalypse is highly polished, and having to watch your fuel lends a real sense of urgency to the proceedings. Some people prefer Fort Apocalypse to Choplifter, but the games are sufficiently different that it's worth playing both today.

"I spent maybe six months total on 'Fort,'" said Hales in an interview in *Halcyon Days: Interviews with Classic Computer and Video Game Programmers.* "It was my third commercial title, and it came very quickly. I liken it to writing a book. You get into a groove and it just flows. The hardest part was the AI for the enemy RoboChoppers. It's not very good, but it works okay. The other hard part was tuning the game for play. The very first version we had shown at CES in 1983 was very hard to play. The first level was different, and we changed it after too many people complained."[130]

The most heartbreaking part is the game only contains the aforementioned two levels—and there could have been much more. "Originally I had planned for fifty levels," Hales said. "But since we wanted to put it onto a cartridge instead of disk, I only had room for two. I spent almost two weeks working on compression methods, but could only get two levels. The ROM was only 16K, and I believe there were only a few bytes left."[131] Anyone else up for an expansion pack?

130. www.dadgum.com/halcyon/BOOK/HALES.HTM
131. Ibid

Frogger (Parker Brothers, 1982)

Famed programmer John Harris developed the Atari 8-bit version of this popular arcade game, and he did a stellar job. Several versions of it were floating around. Including cartridge, 5200, and disk, the latter of which had more of the music and more detailed graphics. To program the game, Harris used an 800 with 48KB plus an AXLON 128KB upgrade, Dave Small's LE Systems high-speed floppy disk interface, and an Austin-80 80-column display board.[132]

In case you've been living under a rock since 1980, here's the plot of Frogger: Get a bunch of frogs across a road and stream without being run over or sinking. You have to hitchhike on the backs of crocodiles and turtles, as well as hop between logs, to cross the river. As mentioned earlier, Parker Brothers was known for running full-page ads in magazines showing the various platforms of the day and how each game looked; usually the ads contained nine screens showing the VCS, the ColecoVision, and so on. The Atari 8-bit version often prevailed in these ads, and this was certainly the case with Frogger.

Frogger's soundtrack cycles between a number of different songs as you play, ensuring against monotony—and then eventually becoming monotonous as a whole, because there's no break in the music, ever. To this day, whenever I mention old Atari games (or arcade games in general), it's more likely than not that at least one person in the room will ask about Frogger. So many people remember it, and hey, if you're a native New Yorker like me, you knew how to play it in real life just trying to get across the street in Manhattan. The less common and more complex sequel, Frogger II: Threeedeep!, uses three screens instead of one and is a unique challenge all its own.

Galaxian (Atari, 1982)

One of the earlier arcade games Atari itself brought to the 400 and 800, Galaxian makes good use of the wider, horizontally oriented aspect ratio of home television sets. Galaxian is a kind of step up from Space Invaders. Enemies break off from the main group and dive-bomb your ship, and you can shoot enemies in combos for addi-

---

132. www.dadgum.com/halcyon/BOOK/HARRIS.HTM

tional points. The Commander ships (yellow) direct the proceedings; those are worth the most points if they're in flight.

Unlike with Space Invaders, the Atari 8-bit version of Galaxian looks and plays a lot like the arcade version. The game contains 11 levels of difficulty—having lots of levels of difficulty was a big thing for early Atari games, and it gave the company something to sell on the boxes. You get three ships to start with and a fourth at 5,000 points. Still, the colorful graphics, detailed sound effects, and smooth animation made the game a solid early demo for the platform, and a worthy purchase for anyone disappointed by the odd Space Invaders cartridge.

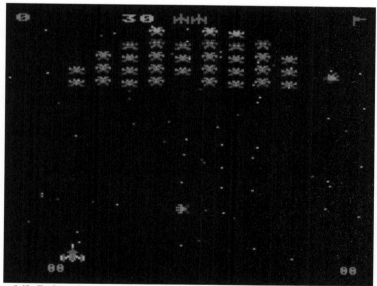

Figure 6.19: Before there was Galaga in the arcades, there was Galaxian, and this almost pitch-perfect port is a stellar early Atari 400/800 cartridge.

As golden age arcade enthusiasts know, Galaxian paved the way for Galaga, one of the most popular games of all time, although Galaga never saw a proper Atari 8-bit conversion. Still, of the hordes of Space Invaders clones to grace the Atari 8-bit platform, Galaxian was one of the best. An honorable mention here goes to Galactic Chase by Stedek Software; it's considerably rarer and plays at a slower pace, but it is closer to the original game in other respects. Some Atari enthusiasts prefer Galactic Chase, as various forum threads indicate. But coming at that one fresh while researching this book—I hadn't played it as a kid—I still prefer Atari's original conversion now for its speed and smooth animation.

Ghost Chaser (Fanda, 1984)

Despite the title, this game was nothing like Ghostbusters (below). Instead, Frank Cohen's Ghost Chaser is a horror-themed adventure game and a platformer put together, with colorful graphics, a fun soundtrack, and a dose of whimsy to boot. Your mission is to expunge Fairport Manor of ghosts, and takes place across 16 rooms, many of which are locked and require keys to access. The instructions are simple: Find and collect the eight keys needed to open the ghost chamber, watch out for obstacles, and "avoid anything that moves."

In this game, just about everything moves. You must avoid trap doors in the floor, and even just jumping over them is tricky. You can walk, crouch (by pushing down on the joystick), or jump (by pushing up). As you progress, you find bullets you can then shoot using the joystick button. Sometimes when a ghost passes through you, you just get the chills and don't die. Sometimes you die anyway. Ghost Chaser isn't forgiving; if you try it today, plan on dying a lot. One commenter on Atarimania said the controls on the emulated version are even tougher than when using an actual Atari computer, but I do remember having the toughest time with this game as a kid as well. Booting it up again today seems to confirm the impression.

Like many Atari 8-bit and Commodore 64 games, Ghost Chaser features smooth sprite animation, a memorable theme song, and is almost as polished as any good Nintendo console game to appear a few years later. Cohen developed several other titles for the Atari 8-bit, all of which have similar art design and gameplay mechanics, such as Cohen's Towers, Ollie's Follies, and the aforementioned Clowns and Balloons. To this day, I still remember the theme song to Ghost Chaser.

Ghostbusters (Activision, 1985)

Ghostbusters was a cultural milestone when it was released in 1984, and remains one of my favorite movies of all time. David Crane's eponymous home computer game, which debuted the following year, is quite enjoyable. Your job is to rid the city of ghosts, sweeping the streets of them with a vacuum on your car and capturing them in front of building facades. Ultimately, you have to confront the dreaded Marshmallow Man at the Temple of Zuul. The game gives you $10,000 in cash to start equipping your team and vehicle; you'll need things like ghost traps and bait to complete your mission.

The Atari version isn't quite as fetching as the Commodore 64's, lacking outlines around the car and the in-game characters. But it's still quite good, and I spent many an evening after school piloting the giant station wagon on the screen around the city, earning money to add features to the car, and capturing slimers in traps in front of buildings. A map of the city shows you where paranormal activity is taking place, so you always know where to go next.

The game also contains a four-voice synthesized version of the movie's title song, which sounds better on Atari's POKEY than the Commodore's three-voice chip. Following the karaoke-style bouncing ball over the on-screen lyrics is a kick, too. The music plays incessantly during the game; this kind of thing never bothers me, because I love game audio so much, but it puts many players off. Later versions of the Atari 8-bit version include a nifty "Ghostbusters!" speech sample, which plays on startup. I had both copies, and remember being thrilled to hear the version with the added speech, even though this is the only difference between them. Whenever your computer talked in the 1980s, no matter how, it was considered groundbreaking.

The Goonies (Datasoft, 1985)

A tie in with the cult-classic Steven Spielberg and Warner Bros. movie of the same title, The Goonies puts you in charge of two of the characters on each board—Mikey, Brand, Chuck, Mouth, Data, Andy, or Stef. Your group finds a treasure map. You must get through each level while avoiding the denizens of the underworld. The eventual goal is to find One-Eyed Willy's Pirate Ship, get the treasure, and use it to save your parents' homes from foreclosure. The game is known as being one of the first to get a movie tie-in that appeared in the same year the movie itself debuted in theaters (and, miraculously, the game was excellent).

The game looks like a platformer, but it's more of a puzzler, as you have to figure out how to best use the two characters on-screen to solve each of the eight boards. The game randomly selects different pairs of characters on each screen. You switch back and forth between the characters by pressing the joystick button. You literally have to use both characters on each of the eight screens, or else you won't be able to make progress. For example, on the first screen in the restaurant, one character must operate a machine to spill counterfeit cash out the top-story window and distract Mama Fratelli (who runs outside to catch it) while the other character runs to the water cooler Mama had been blocking access to. On any of the eight screens, if one character dies, you have to start over even if the other is still alive.

The game features excellent multi-voice renditions of music from the movie's original soundtrack. The graphics are good, if not spectacular. Each of the characters look noticeably different on screen, and the game is well balanced and quite difficult. Interestingly, a bunch of fans ("The Sloth Team") got together and made an updated version in 2014, with improved graphics, for Windows and Linux machines.

Gorf (Roklan Software, 1982)

By the early 1980s, it seemed as if there were a million Space Invaders clones out there. Just a few added something to the genre; Galaxian and (later) Galaga were two examples, and Gorf is a solid third. This faithful conversion of the Midway arcade game consists of four main missions you can play at six different difficulty levels. (Gorf reportedly stands for Galactic Orbiting Robot Force.)

The first mission, Astro Battles, is basically Space Invaders, albeit with a giant force field over the center of the screen instead of three bunkers to hide behind. But from there, things get more complex. Laser Attack features two clusters of enemy ships; each one has a special craft that shoots an antiparticle beam at you. Space Warp pits you against circling TIE-fighter-like enemies in a quasi-3D perspective, putting you behind your own ship. Flag Ship [sic] is a bit reminiscent of the end stage in Phoenix. You attack the main enemy flagship by penetrating the large force field arc and aiming for the ship's power reactor vent. Once you go through all the stages, the game starts over at a higher difficulty level.

The coin-op version also has a stage called Galaxians, which was essentially a miniature version of Midway's Galaxian; it presumably didn't make it into the ports thanks to copyright issues. For its part, Roklan Software developed Gorf as well as Deluxe Invaders and Wizard of Wor (the latter is also covered below). The game translated well to the Atari 8-bit, but memory constraints prevented most of the home ports from containing the synthesized speech that made the original distinctive. For historical purposes, it's worth checking out Gorf to get a taste of what early 1980s space shooters were like, but none of the minigames measure up to a full-blown, more focused title like Galaxian.[133]

Gossip (APX, 1983)

This is a strange social simulation by Chris Crawford, and rose out of his work in Atari Research under Dr. Alan Kay.[134] It's an example of the kind of experimentation that used to take place in the game industry (and that we see again today with indie games on PCs and mobile devices). The screen contains up to eight characters; one calls another on the phone and then gossips about some of the others. The simulated people then reinforce their own opinions based on what the other person thinks, or change their opinion of the caller if they disagree.

I do remember playing this game as a kid and getting lost in the odd social interactions for a few hours. But without a main goal, there isn't much more to do. Crawford later bundled the engine underneath Gossip as part of the game Excalibur, and he says there's some debate as to whether the game was even officially released by APX,[135] or if it just made its way into the piracy wild like so many other Atari programs. "Gossip had the bad luck to be published in 1983, just as Atari was beginning its death spiral," Crawford said in *Chris Crawford on Game Design*, in what I think was a reference to the Great Video Game Crash of 1983 and not the ultimate death of Ata-

---

133. *1001 Video Games You Must Play Before You Die*, p. 48
134. *Chris Crawford on Game Design*, p. 259
135. *Chris Crawford on Game Design*, p. 267

ri itself, though it's possible he was already calling it for Atari then. "With all the chaos of the layoffs, jobs like publishing games proceeded at a snail's pace and without much in the way of verve and élan. There is some question as to whether it ever appeared in the sales catalog; I myself don't know. I don't even know its sales figures; it seemed every time I called someone to ask, that person had been laid off. I'm sure it sold poorly; few people recall the game."

Regardless, Gossip is an interesting glimpse into what would later become "software toys" like SimCity. Crawford said he is proud of the game and called it "the first computer game about people instead of things."[136]

Figure 6.20: The Great American Cross-Country Road Race is a race car game blown up to national size, with a campaign-style component, police chases, and necessary fill-ups at gas stations.

The Great American Cross-Country Road Race (Activision, 1985)

This one takes the basic gameplay of Activision's Enduro for the VCS and turns it into a full-fledged adventure for the Atari 8-bit lineup (and later, Apple II and Commodore 64). This is one of the

136. *Chris Crawford on Game Design*, p. 267

best games to grace the Atari 8-bit platform. It lets you drive across the country through 25 major cities and 3,000 miles in a variety of routes, while dealing with all manner of weather and road conditions. At the start of each race, you see a map of the U.S. showing the next segment. As you race, you can see the skyline of each city approaching on the horizon.

The Great American Cross-Country Road Race, designed by Alex DeMeo, also retains Enduro's day and night racing, which makes it unusually fun and realistic for its time. The dashboard combines analog and digital gauges, and includes a speedometer, tachometer, a fuel gauge (this is crucial in gameplay), an odometer and timer, and even a radar detector to warn you of upcoming speed traps. Naturally, you must avoid getting speeding tickets. If you blow past a cop car and got one, the officer may ask you "Where's the fire?", among other sarcastic comments.

The actual gameplay bears little resemblance to driving a real car, but most arcade-style racers didn't at the time—at least until 1988's Hard Drivin', which came complete with a steering wheel, shifter, and clutch pedal. Never mind—The Great American Cross-Country Road Race is no racing sim. It's about as close as you could get to the speed, feel, and overall atmosphere of 24-hour road racing at the time. And the campaign-style play provides a good backdrop for what is an incredibly addictive racing game you can play for hours without getting tired.

Gyruss (Parker Brothers, 1984)

This frenetic arcade port remains one of my favorite games to play on the 800. The game is often referred to as "Galaga in 3D," and the description isn't far off. It's a quasi-three-dimensional shooter, in which you rotate around the edges of the screen using the joystick, and firing inward toward alien ships, satellites, laser beam generators, and meteors that swirl and swarm at the center. You exterminate aliens in two to three stages each, plus bonus rounds, as you tour the outer reaches of the Solar System in an attempt to return to Earth. Some enemies power up your laser gun so you can shoot from both sides of your ship simultaneously.

Your first goal is to reach Neptune, then Uranus, and so on, until you make it home to Earth. Each time you reach a planet, there's a bonus round where you try and shoot all of the enemies as they appear in groups, before they even make it all the way onto the screen in formation (because it's tougher to hit them all once they do). If you kill all 40 enemies, you'll get 10,000 bonus points.

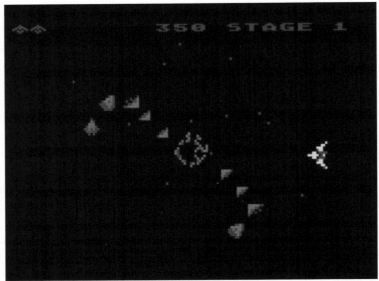

Figure 6.21: A screenshot from Gyruss, a game I played constantly. And still play today.

While the Atari 8-bit conversion of Gyruss isn't identical to the arcade, it's quite close, and just as fast. I've played this game for countless hours. The soundtrack, which is sped-up Bach (Toccata and Fugue in D minor), almost makes the game on its own. Once you've seen it, you'll never forget the TV commercial with the guy playing it in his living room and his recliner rotating in the air 360 degrees to follow the on-screen action. Little-known fact: The Konami arcade game was designer Yoshiki Okamoto's second; the first was the classic Time Pilot (of which there never was a proper Atari 8-bit conversion).

Jawbreaker (On-Line Systems, 1981)

This game started life as a Pac-Man clone programmed by John Harris, except you were in a candy factory and you controlled a set of choppers (as in teeth). You must eat all of the candy before one of the "bratty kids" got a hold of you. Aside from how Jawbreaker was derivative of Pac-Man, the game itself was a 400/800 original and one of the first games to hit the platform by a third-party developer. It also spawned the considerably different and cartoon-like Jawbreaker II in 1982, which featured larger sprites and a simplified maze, but with funny tooth-brushing animations.

Atari had sought an injunction against On-Line Systems (which later became Sierra On-Line and then Sierra Entertainment), because Atari had acquired the home rights to Pac-Man.[137] On-Line Systems cofounder Ken Williams saw both sides of the issue, saying "I don't think Jawbreaker is a rip-off of Pac-Man. And I definitely won't take Atari's word for it. If a judge tells me it's a rip-off, I'll gladly take it off the market." When a judge found no reason to grant Atari's request for the injunction, Williams wasn't entirely in a victorious mood and said, "If this opens the door to other programmers ripping off my software, what happened here was a bad thing."[138]

In a later interview, Harris clarified why he preferred programming for Atari computers. "When comparing the hardware and operating system of the Atari 800 and Apple II computers, there is virtually nothing about the Apple that isn't done much better or faster on the Atari and yet it is the Apple II that got most of the respect and success," Harris said. "This is of course entirely the fault of Atari Corporation, who didn't have the slightest clue about marketing. They once told a company who wanted to convert their successful business programs to the Atari that their products were simply not wanted on the Atari computer. 'It will ruin its game machine image,' they said. Can you believe that?"[139] Unfortunately, in hindsight, we can, John. But you were right.

Joust (Atari, 1983)

Atari's 400/800 port of the Williams Electronics classic Joust is just as addictive as the arcade original. In this bizarre take on science fiction, you ride an alien ostrich and have to fight the Buzzard-Riders.

---

137. *Softline*, 1982, p. 18
138. Ibid
139. www.dadgum.com/halcyon/BOOK/HARRIS.HTM

You fight them by approaching them head-on, flapping your ostrich's wings to get just high enough to be over your opponent's lance. The red Bounders are the easiest ones to beat, the gray Hunters ride higher and faster, and the blue Shadow Lords are the toughest.

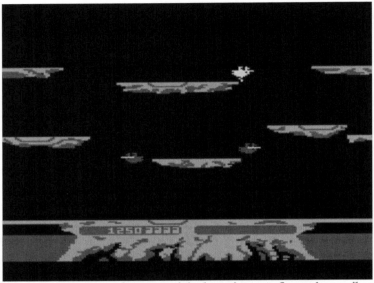

Figure 6.22: A fine home port of a great, original arcade game, Joust plays well on the Atari 400/800.

As you beat each rider, you have to remember to also go after the egg, which bounces to a stop and eventually hatches another buzzard. Spend too long on a board and the terrifying pterodactyl comes out looking to eat anyone and everyone in its path (usually you first). Every fifth board is an Egg Wave; get as many as you can before they hatch and get riders. Survival Waves net you a 3,000-point bonus if you make it through without being dismounted. As the game progresses, the board adjusts. The third wave sees the lava pits open up, while the fourth wave introduces the Troll, who grabs at you from the pits with its hand as you fly by. Other times, one of the remaining rocky platforms disappears before the wave starts.

The 8-bit conversion of Joust loses some detail in the translation: Birds are only one color including the rider, except for the white "lance," and the animations are simpler—when an egg hatches, it sprouts bird and rider fully formed, rather than just a rider who would then wait for a new bird to arrive. But the game features all of the right screens, including the Egg Wave and the pterodactyl, and it plays just as smoothly and quickly as the real thing.

Jr. Pac-Man (Atari Prototype, 1984)

This prototype game never reached the retail market, but pirated copies made it out into the wild nonetheless. And it's a shame it was never released, because it plays well. It looks similar to Ms. Pac-Man at first, with dots, power pellets (albeit six instead of four on some screens), monsters, and filled-in maze walls. The main gameplay difference is that the boards are larger left to right—usually two screens total in size—and they scroll as you eat up all the dots. It's quite a challenge to complete each level, especially since there's no overall Defender-style radar at the top of the screen to show you where you are, and what's left to complete.

Another key difference is the presence of larger dots, which are worth more points, but take longer to "eat," slowing you down. The prizes roam similar to the way they did in Ms. Pac-Man, but here they also devour the power pellets, which makes it tougher to get through each maze. The prototype version doesn't contain the arcade cabinet's intermission scenes, but it's not clear if it's because of memory limitations or because they just weren't completed in time.

Unfortunately, as is often the case with games developed around this time, Atari canned the 8-bit and 5200 releases of Jr. Pac-Man thanks to Tramiel's takeover of the company and the continued collapse of the video game market in general.[140] According to AtariProtos.com, the game was basically finished, except for one bug, which crashed the game if a prize was eating a power pellet right at the same time as when you died (the pellet then gets stuck on the screen and can never be eaten).

Today, it's worth getting a hold of this prototype and playing it. Jr. Pac-Man demonstrates some pretty advanced multiscreen scrolling without having any effect on the on-screen characters and animation. It's also just plain fun, which is the biggest reason of all to snag a copy.

---

140. www.atariprotos.com/8bit/software/jrpacman/jrpacman.htm

Karateka (Brøderbund, 1984)

Jordan Mechner is best known for creating the Prince of Persia series, but Karateka was his first published masterpiece. Karateka puts you in control of a martial arts expert in feudal Japan who has to rescue Princess Mariko from the evil warlord Akuma inside his castle fortress. You fight enemies one at a time with your hands and feet, which becomes progressively more difficult as you approach and finally enter the fortress. If you die, you must start over from the beginning.

Critics praised the game for its cinematic presentation at a time when this concept was still in short supply, thanks to the limitations of available technology. Mechner, who developed Karateka in two years on an Apple II while he was in college, wrote on his website he adapted silent film techniques he learned from cinema history classes at Yale, including rotoscoping, cross-cutting, and tracking shots.

The game eventually hit number one in U.S. sales on the *Billboard* charts in April 1985,[141] and had already sold 500,000 units across platforms by the end of 1984 alone.[142] The Atari version in particular has excellent four-channel sound. Mechner himself praised it in a 2013 Reddit AMA: "[Brøderbund developer] Robert Cook's conversions for the Commodore 64 and Atari 400/800 were definitely the best ports, and actually improved on the Apple II in certain ways, especially sound and music. My dad re-orchestrated the entire music score to take advantage of the better sound capability, and Robert tore his hair out trying to get it all to play correctly." Mechner has since remade the game for Android and iOS devices with updated art.[143]

I found this game exceedingly difficult to play, and yet I kept trying, because it was so good. You can easily draw a line from this game to the first Prince of Persia in 1989.

---

141. www.jordanmechner.com/projects/karateka/

142. venturebeat.com/2012/11/07/jordan-mechner-launches-karateka-remake-on-digital-gaming-platforms/

143.www.reddit.com/r/IAmA/comments/14e6p3/im_jordan_mechner_creator_o f_prince_of_persia_and/c7c9lsk?context=3

Figure 6.23: A follow-up to Rescue on Fractalus and Ballblazer, Koronis Rift further pushes the boundaries of Atari 8-bit hardware.

Koronis Rift (Lucasfilm Games, 1985)

Lucasfilm Games followed up Rescue on Fractalus! and Ballblazer with Koronis Rift. This innovative science fiction adventure game puts you in the role of a technology scavenger. It's the year 2049; you must explore a remote backwater planet and search abandoned spaceship hulks, left by The Ancients, for many different kinds of weapons and shields, all while sneaking around and avoiding alien saucer guards. Your ultimate goal is to assemble the weapons and use them to attack the aliens' base and destroy them permanently.

The first-person view places you at the controls of a surface rover. Whenever you find a spaceship hulk, you can send out a droid to pick it apart. "On a primary level, it's a standard shoot-'em-up," said Noah Falstein, project leader and main designer, in an interview in the December 1985 issue of *Antic*. "Someone who likes that sort of thing can jump in there, blow up anything that moves and have a good time." But as the article noted, beneath the surface is a multilayered strategy game, where colors and shapes clue you in to the different weapons systems. For example, a particular color laser may only be good against one type of alien saucer.[144]

The graphics make good use of the Atari 8-bit's GTIA chip's shading. Take a look at the Psytek Science Droid, which helps you analyze and take apart the gear you scavenged. As your craft roves around on the planet's surface, you'll see the background fade in as you approach and it becomes the foreground. "I think our stuff looks the best on the Atari, but they're fairly close on the Commodore, although the graphics are certainly slower," said Rescue on Fractalus! project lead David Fox in an interview in the February 1986 issue of *ZZAP! 64*. "We've been able to come across on both machines. There are some things you can do on the Atari that you just can't match, like the shading—if you take a look at Koronis Rift on the Atari... with [Koronis] Rift the Commodore version and the Atari version were both developed in parallel and we tried to make each version look the best we could within each machine's capabilities."

One last bit of trivia: A Lucasfilm employee by the name Ron Gilbert was responsible for the C64 port. You may know him from Maniac Mansion and The Secret of Monkey Island.

Livewire (A.N.A.L.O.G. Computing, 1983)

This little-known Tempest clone is a solid game to begin with—a shooter that places you on a quasi-three-dimensional battlefield, with the goal of clearing as many enemies and screens as you can. It's simple and fun, if not as richly designed or challenging as the original Tempest. But I'm including it here for a broader discussion of the oddities of Atari and its place in the broader arcade game market. Atari never released a home version of Tempest, even though it was one of the company's own most popular coin-op games. Unfinished prototypes of VCS and 5200 (and therefore 8-bit computer) versions were floating around Atari, and the 5200 version was roughly 90 percent completed before it was abandoned.[145] Usually whenever this happened, the reason given was the project was cut either because of

---

145. www.atariprotos.com/5200/software/tempest/tempest.htm

the Great Video Game Crash of 1983, or because Tramiel canceled it after he took over in late 1984.

In this particular case, as developer Tom Hudson tells it, Livewire got started almost on a dare at *A.N.A.L.O.G. Computing* magazine. "There was something very appealing in [Tempest's] basic wireframe forms and the 3-D effect of zooming down the tube," Hudson wrote. "I liked the game so much that I bought one while at *A.N.A.L.O.G.* and kept it at the *A.N.A.L.O.G.* offices on Free Play for all of us to play. I have a smaller 'cabaret'-style case Tempest in my office right now. Like I said, we loved that game."[146] It turned out while at the West Coast Computer Faire in San Francisco in 1983, an attendee went back and forth between the *A.N.A.L.O.G.* and *Antic* booths about doing a Tempest game, and the *Antic* folks had said it was impossible to do on an Atari computer.

Hudson took this as a challenge, and sure enough, a clone of Tempest called Livewire showed up as a machine language game in *A.N.A.L.O.G.*'s July 1983 issue; you could type the program in yourself. There were four listings, which is one of the things that made *A.N.A.L.O.G.* such a solid magazine. The first was a BASIC program, which would create the machine language data for the cassette and disk versions. You added Listing 2 if you were making a 410 cassette version, or Listing 3 if you were making a disk drive version. The fourth listing was the actual source code for Macro Assembler; you didn't need to type it in, the magazine emphasized, but it was "provided for those readers interested in seeing how the program works." As for the game itself, while it's not as detailed as Tempest, it will nonetheless scratch the itch for that kind of game and is a good quick distraction.

Lode Runner (Brøderbund, 1983)

The popular game Lode Runner, developed by Doug Smith, is a fiendishly difficult combination of platformer and puzzler. As a galactic commando, you have to figure out how to get to all of the gold cubes on a given board while avoiding the Bungeling Empire's enemy guards. The AI is fierce; the guards immediately shift movement to follow you across overhead tightropes and up and down ladders.

---

146. analog.klanky.com/funstuff.htm

With your laser pistol, you can drill passageways in the brick ground, which the guards can fall into and get trapped, or you can use to make a fast escape below. The laser pistol doesn't shoot otherwise; all it does is drill holes.

Complicating things, the hole seals instantly and becomes ineffective if a guard reaches it before you finish drilling. Worse, the holes all eventually refill. You can even fall in one with more brick underneath, get stuck, and then get sealed up, Edgar Allan Poe–style (my favorite). The controls in Lode Runner are simple: The joystick lets you move left and right, and you can climb ladders up or down. If you reach an overhead rope, you instantly shift to climbing across it automatically. The button activates the drill; you press it and push left or right to drill a hole in the ground in the appropriate direction. The game comes with an insane 150 levels, plus a level editor for creating your own.

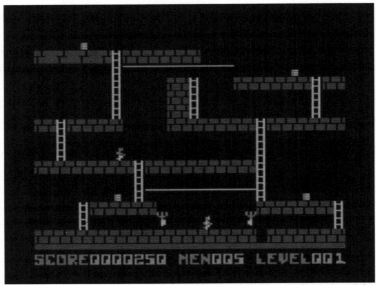

Figure 6.24: Lode Runner offers many levels of tough action and puzzle solving.

Lode Runner saw immense popularity in its day. While the 8-bit Atari version was one of the first ports, it eventually ended up on more than a dozen platforms, and even made it into an arcade cabinet with some gameplay tweaks. *Computer Gaming World* magazine ran a contest in the August 1984 issue to see who could build the best levels. Brøderbund also released a 50-level version of the game called Championship Lode Runner in 1985, which is even harder than the original. And in 1987, Atari turned the disk-based Lode Runner into a cartridge version for the XE Game System.

Mario Bros. (Atari, 1983 and 1988)

This game puts you in control of Mario and Luigi. Your goal is to clear the screen of turtles and other pests by various means, such as flipping turtles (called Shellcreepers) onto their shells—either by bumping them from below or using the POW button at the center of the screen, both of which stunned them. At the same time, you must collect coins and avoid the floating fireballs. Sometimes all the pests disappear and you're faced with a coin phase; you have to collect as many as possible in a short period of time.

I almost left Mario Bros. out of this book. The original 1983 conversion for the 5200 is enjoyable—and made it over to the 8-bit in an unreleased prototype distributed by Glenn the 5200 man—but, like that system's Asteroids port, nothing special. Mario Bros. is a decent game, but doesn't show off the Atari computer's potential in any way. But Atari commissioned Sculpture Software to redo the game for the XE Game System in 1988. I hadn't realized this until recently, since when I was younger, I never owned an XEGS and had moved on from the 800 to the 16-bit ST by then.

It turns out the XE cartridge is spectacular—so colorful, smooth, and detailed, you could easily mistake it for a proper NES cartridge. This, along with later games like Draconus and Zybex, is a good example of how much developers were able to squeeze out of the Atari 8-bit computer's architecture even nine years after its introduction. This version is definitely the way to go if you're playing today. It's funny to think that this game originally led to the groundbreaking Super Mario Bros. on the NES. It's so different, and so much smaller in scope, although the coin-op Donkey Kong introduced Mario to the world in 1981.

Master of the Lamps (Activision, 1985)

Master of the Lamps makes you a prince and lets you fly through time and space on a magic carpet. It's another beautiful game that demonstrates how programmers had learned how to take advantage of the Atari 8-bit's then-six-year-old hardware. Your goal is to rebuild three magic lamps, recapture the three evil genies, and complete the game. You need seven pieces to rebuild each lamp. For each piece, you have to follow and navigate through tunnel rings, and then summon a genie to solve a musical puzzle, which employs memory, notes, and color.

There are three modes: Seven Trials (beginner), Throne Quest (standard), and Magic Carpet (for flying practice). The Seven Trials game means you need to just complete one lamp. The Throne Quest involves all three lamps, so you need to fly through a total of 21 tunnels. The first seven dens give you the color and tone in each puzzle (the colors disappear after just a moment), the second set of dens gives you just the disappearing colors, and the third set of dens gives you just the tones, so you have to do it all by ear.

Like Karateka, Koronis Rift, and others, Master of the Lamps is as much an experience as a game. The Atari 8-bit version shines thanks to its four-voice POKEY chip and punchy soundtrack. The three-dimensional effect of flying through the expanding rings is smooth, fast, and convincing. The game itself doesn't have as much substance as it should, and gets repetitive quickly. But it's still a fun romp, and the flying becomes quite difficult as you progress.

At the time of this writing, the Wikipedia entry for Master of the Lamps calls it one of the first music video games, albeit without a citation. That's probably true, although I don't know of any of the current crop of music games (Amplitude, Guitar Hero, and so on) citing Master of the Lamps as an influence. It certainly paved the way for music-based adventure games like Lucasfilm Games's Loom.

Miner 2049er (Big Five Software, 1982)

An exclusive (at first) Atari game and one of the more famous to grace the platform, Miner 2049er took early advantage of the 8-bit Atari's player-missile graphics and four-channel sound. You're Bounty Bob, searching through abandoned uranium mines and "claiming" each part of them by running over the ground, all while avoiding various obstacles—not to mention radioactive enemies. Whenever you walk over a section of the mine, it changes color; you complete the level by changing the color of all of the platforms.

The game is a simple platformer at its core, but still more sophisticated than Donkey Kong or, say, Dig Dug. This was Big Five's first native 8-bit game; it was known as a TRS-80 developer before then. "Miner 2049er is written entirely in machine language by the president of Big Five, Bill Hogue," wrote *The Creative Atari* in 1983. "The whole program is crammed into a huge 16K ROM cartridge... Whereas Donkey Kong has only four screens, Miner has a stupefying ten separate boards, each with a different scenario." What can I say? It was a different time. These things were impressive. At any rate, the manual helpfully contained descriptions of each of the 10 boards and explained what you had to do to complete each one.

The sequel, Bounty Bob Strikes Back!, landed in 1985. It's a devilishly hard platformer game with 25 levels, instead of 10 as in the original game. The other notable change is the move to platforms with a three-dimensional look to them. Bounty Bob Strikes Back! was one of the most popular games available for the Atari 800, and is still frequently downloaded in ROM form off of Atarimania.com. Many gamers around the Internet still play this (and the original Miner 2049er) even today. It's tough to argue with this kind of longevity.

Missile Command (Atari, 1981)

The 1980 coin-op game Missile Command was certainly a product of its time—and a centerpiece of Atari's arcade and home lineups for years. Missile Command presents the player with a geopolitical nightmare: incoming intercontinental ballistic missiles (ICBMs) you must destroy using three missile batteries stationed at the bottom of the screen, before the missiles obliterate your six cities. You control an on-screen crosshair using a giant trackball; your task is to observe the missile trails and aim for where each missile was headed, so by the time your own missile arrives and explodes, it collides with the "tip" of the trail (meaning the incoming ICBM itself) and destroys it.

You can also destroy several ICBMs at once with this method, or do what what's called a "barrage" or "spray" tactic, where you shoot several missiles in a row at the beginning of each wave. This creates a line of explosions, which stops an entire group of incoming ICBMs. Each wave usually contains two main stages (called 1-1 and 1-2, 2-1 and 2-2, and so on). Often you'll see a wave stage begin with a plane or other vehicle flying across the screen; you'll want to destroy it before it launches some missiles of its own, which have less distance to travel before hitting one of your cities.

Beginning in wave 3-2, you'll start to see smart bombs, which trickle down the screen and around any of your exploding missiles. To destroy them, you must be right on target, or else the smart bomb will see it coming and dodge it. Naturally, the game gets tougher as you progress from wave to wave. To this day, just seeing the black sky change for the first time to blue starting at wave 4-1 makes the hair raise on my arms: "Oh no, now I'm really in for it." There's no way to win other than by beating the high score; things just get worse and worse until you lose all six cities, at which point the game flashes a disturbing "The End" screen, which then explodes itself.

Atari turned out an early and stellar conversion of Missile Command for its 8-bit computer platform, unlike the stripped-down VCS cartridge. You can play this game surprisingly well with the joystick. But for the true connoisseur's arcade-like experience, you'll probably need the CX22 Trackball controller. The computer version contains all three missile batteries, unlike the VCS version; the center one always fires the fastest. When Atari released its XE Game System in 1987, it made Missile Command the pack-in game (actually built-in; it's what fires up if you turn on the machine without a cartridge inserted).

Montezuma's Revenge (Parker Bros., 1983)

One of the best 400/800 games of all time in my opinion, Montezuma's Revenge is challenging, fun, and exceedingly polished. It can easily pass for something on the NES—except the game beat the NES to market by a few years, and was done on the Atari. I learned while researching this book that "Montezuma's Revenge" also means something entirely different; I'll leave it as an exercise for the reader to find out what.

Montezuma's Revenge is set in 100 underground tombs underneath the Mexican emperor's fortress. The tombs mix Aztec, Incan, and Mayan design, with light pastel colors, oversized sprites, and beautifully animated graphics. You have to collect jewels, pick up keys to unlock doors, and find torches, swords, and amulets, not to mention avoid or confront a host of underground denizens—each time you touch one, you "use up" a sword. There are chains, laser walls, lava pits, conveyer belts, and disappearing bridges to contend with. Some of the rooms are even invisible, making navigating the platforms exceptionally difficult without a hard-to-find torch.

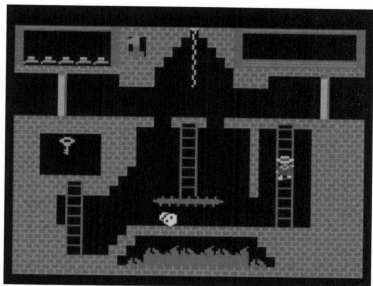

Figure 6.25: One of the first screens in Montezuma's Revenge.

Montezuma's Revenge was developed by Robert Jaeger; he formed his own company, Utopia Software, at age 14, dropped out of high school at 16, and programmed Montezuma's Revenge on an Atari 8-bit computer at 17. His initial version of the game required too much memory for a 16KB cartridge, so Parker Bros. condensed it as part of the release. Unfortunately, this version is missing some of the original's endearing qualities, such as the simple background music theme, the fancy title screen that draws out the word "Revenge" in script, and the intermission screen, which plays quickly each time you lose a life. Unfortunately, while more detailed and polished, the prototype program is unfinished and impossible to complete, as I found out the hard way as a kid. Plus, as was often the case in the 1980s, there's no save option. Once you lose the game, you have to start over from the beginning.

Moon Patrol (Atari, 1983)

This game put you on the lunar surface, in charge of cleaning out Sector Nine of "thug" alien craft. Your rover acts as a patrol car, and features a laser cannon and antigravity jump capability. You need both to deal with all manner of obstacles, including rocks, craters, landmines, tanks, and alien ships. Pushing the joystick right increases your speed, while pulling it "back" (really to the left) slows you down. There are two main courses, each with 26 segments grouped into five sections.

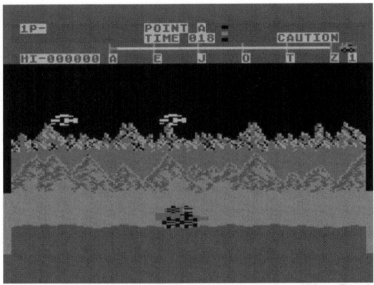

Figure 6.26: One of my favorite arcade games, the home version of Moon Patrol is a blast to play on the Atari 8-bit platform.

The gameplay is relentless; you must jump over obstacles while shooting alien ships above you, and reach lettered marker points for each segment (A, B, C, D, and so on), all while ensuring your lunar buggy doesn't fall into a ditch. The faster you complete a section, the more points you get. The game has a pattern to the obstacles you can learn over time, for both the beginner and championship courses. But even when you know the patterns backward and forward, the game is still a challenge, particularly when you're being shot at and the bullets form new craters right in front of your vehicle as you drive. Some of the rocks roll toward you as well.

The 400/800 port of Moon Patrol isn't quite as good-looking as its original counterpart. The most notable difference is the appearance of the purple rover. It looks considerably more pixelated and less cartoon-like, and only has two wheels instead of three. But despite this and some other minor graphical downgrades, the conversion was arguably the best of the home systems. More important, it kept the coin-op game's groundbreaking parallax scrolling and trademark musical intro motif intact.

Mountain King (CBS Electronics, 1983)

Your goal in this stellar and original platformer is to run rampant around a diamond mine, collecting diamonds until you have enough to retrieve the golden crown and run it to the top of the mountain. Along the way, you must avoid getting stuck in a spiderweb, or you'll be eaten alive once the spider returns. You also can't touch any of the open flames on the board or you'll burn alive. Get enough diamonds, and next you must locate the Flame Spirit by finding the source of music playing. This reveals the entrance to the Temple Chamber, which contains the crown. Once you carry the Flame Spirit to the Temple Chamber and retrieve the crown, the game starts a second timer and plays a polyphonic, frenetic version of Edvard Grieg's "In the Hall of the Mountain King" as you race to the top of the mountain. It isn't stressful *at all*. Fail, and you die. Succeed, and you get to do it all over again.

I'm not making Mountain King sound fun, and the graphics, with their muted brown, black, and blue palette, don't do the game justice either. But trust me: It's addictive. The entire game is fast-paced and smoothly animated, with lots of bats flying through the passages, wispy flames, and sparkling diamonds. And the careful use of sound to clue you in to the location of the Flame Spirit, or scare you to death when the ultra-fast spider appears, elevates the game to an even higher plateau. Hearing the Atari's POKEY chip at full song was a reward in and of itself, the same way a beautiful graphics scene was, if not even more. I learned to play "In the Hall of the Mountain King" on the piano (well, the basic two-handed melody, at least) all because of this game.

Mr. Do! (Datasoft, 1984)

At first glance, Mr. Do! looks a lot like Dig Dug, but Mr. Do! is easily the better game. Your goal is to guide a clown and pick cherries out of a field, ideally in groups of eight at a time for bonus points, all while avoiding the Boss's henchmen. You can squish the henchmen by digging underneath an apple at just the right time while they're chasing you, or you can shoot them with your powerball (which returns to you like a boomerang). A bonus monster periodically appears with a letter from the word EXTRA. If you collect all five letters, you get a bonus screen and extra points.

The garden screens themselves usually contain a word or number as part of the whimsical design, such as the numbers two through nine, and the first board contains the word "Do" backwards. There are 99 screens in all. The 800's home port of Mr. Do! is the best, even beating out the (admittedly more vibrant, if less detailed) ColecoVision version. It even includes the cartoons between some levels, and its main board had the same vertical orientation as the arcade's, compared with the ColecoVision's stretched-out horizontal boards.

Mr. Do! was a popular arcade game in its day. When I finally encountered one of these cabinets for the first time—in the lobby of a roller rink in Sheepshead Bay, Brooklyn, as part of an elementary school class trip—I remember a) doing pretty well, given all my practice on the home version, and b) did I mention people went to roller rinks all the time in the 1980s? A sequel called Mr. Do's Castle made it to the 5200, and a pirated rip circulated around Atari BBSes; it's a completely different game and is also worth playing.

Mr. Robot and His Robot Factory (Datamost, 1984)

This innovative platformer, developed by Ron Rosen for Datamost, recalls Donkey Kong and Donkey Kong Jr., and yet looks and plays differently. You're a humanoid; you must navigate 22 levels of conveyer belts, ladders, and platforms and collect power pills. The whole time, you must avoid an array of floating fireball enemies, which stalk you and deplete your energy reserves on contact. Pulsing energizer squares give you a temporary force field you can use to destroy the alien fireballs.

You can also slide down poles and bounce on trampolines, and there are bombs you trigger as you walk over them, and magnets, which enable you to jump farther than normal. Transporters take you from place to place as well. You must make use of any or all of these techniques to complete some of the levels. You die if you fall more than a short distance.

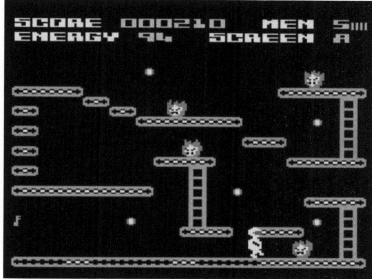

Figure 6.27: A supremely colorful platformer that took full advantage of the Atari's graphics capabilities, Mr. Robot even came with a level editor.

The game also comes with an easy-to-use level editor (the Robot Factory). You use the joystick to select and position objects on the screen, and then "paint" the length of tread or platform until you stamp it out with the joystick button and complete it. I remember spending many afternoons designing new levels and getting the game balance just right (or at least trying to).

Mr. Robot and His Robot Factory is nicely finished in an array of pastel colors and was also smoothly animated. The game has a particularly distinctive "computerized" font for the scoreboard, screen counter, and energy level at the top of each board. Datamost ported the game to the Apple II and Commodore 64 after seeing success on the Atari 8-bit platform, though only the Atari version had four-voice music from Gary Gilbertson using Philip Price's Advanced Music

Processor[147] (which would factor into the development of the Alternate Reality series later on).

Ms. Pac-Man (Atari, 1983)

Anyone who has played Pac-Man probably knows all about Ms. Pac-Man already. The game features a female protagonist, four mazes instead of one, and fruit that moves around the board (with the distinctive "voot voot voot" sound you can probably still hear in your head) instead of staying in one spot. The fruit even traversed the warp tunnels on occasion, and all of the main sound effects are different, including one that plays whenever you gobble a power pellet and the ghosts turn blue, the death sound for Ms. Pac-Man herself, and of course the iconic theme song.

After Atari's disastrous regular Pac-Man port on the VCS, it got this one right, so it's no surprise the Atari 8-bit computer version is excellent as well. The game came out in a lined silver box, just in time for the XL lineup announcement. The 800 version of Ms. Pac-Man features all four colorful boards from the arcade with solid-color maze walls as well as the dancing fruit, and the game animates smoothly throughout. You can choose the starting board via the fruit icon from the title screen, and two players can take turns as in the arcade.

Atari made sure to trumpet how its 8-bit port contained the intermissions, unlike the Pac-Man cartridge. The instructions proudly proclaim: "There will be three brief cartoon breaks immediately following the strawberry, apple, and second random fruit mazes." It still isn't arcade-perfect—no Atari 8-bit games were—but it's close enough to be enjoyable and challenging. The Atari 8-bit version is stretched a bit horizontally when compared with the arcade, but it's closer to square and not as bad as the original Pac-Man in this regard.

M.U.L.E. (Electronic Arts, 1983)

Dani Bunten's M.U.L.E. (which stood for Multiple-Use Labor Element) is a multiplayer strategic battle of planetary mining, supply and demand economics, and resource development I've yet to see

---

147. www.dadgum.com/halcyon/BOOK/PRICE.HTM

equaled. It supports all four of the 800's joystick inputs, and if other human players aren't available, the game supplies smart AI-infused computer opponents instead.

You start a game of M.U.L.E. on the planet Irata (Atari spelled backwards) by choosing from one of nine races and four different colors; you begin with $1,000 in cash and $300 in goods. As each turn passes, each M.U.L.E. gets one free piece of land they can claim as the cursor passes over it. The land may be plain or have mountains or river terrain. You can grab a M.U.L.E., bring him into town, and outfit him for mining, energy production, or farming. As the game progresses, players compete with each other for resources, sometimes trading when it's advantageous to both sides, and occasionally creating shortages to inconvenience other players. Sometimes unexpected events occur—say, your M.U.L.E. runs off, or there's a meteorite crash.

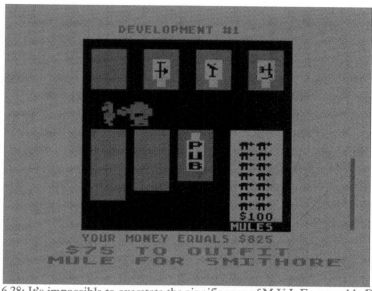

Figure 6.28: It's impossible to overstate the significance of M.U.L.E., arguably Dani Bunten's magnum opus for the Atari 8-bit.

M.U.L.E. has near-perfect game balance. You can play it over and over again and never discover all of the intricacies underneath the surface. It also has a robust theme song I've heard used as a ringtone, complete with a funky bassline and stomping drum track, and to this day I can get it stuck in my head. The attract mode shows the main character dancing to the theme song. If you haven't already played M.U.L.E., you have to try it to experience brilliant game design using a bare minimum of graphical resources. It's one of the first titles to come to mind whenever someone mentions Atari 8-bit computer games—and with good reason.

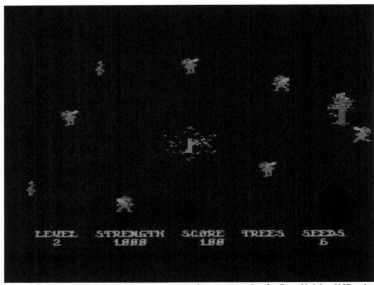

Figure 6.29: Necromancer is a three-stage action game that's fiendishly difficult and completely original.

Necromancer (Synapse Software, 1982)

Another Bill Williams masterpiece, Necromancer is a strange and original Atari 8-bit game that takes place inside a magical forest ruled by an evil wizard. In the first act, you (the druid Illuminar) must fly a magic wisp around the board to plant seeds. The goal is to grow as many trees as you can while protecting them from troglodytes (which shrink the trees by walking over them) and poisonous spiders (which can kill the trees outright). In the second act, you must use the trees you grew to destroy spider larvae, while planting new trees in the vaults that contain the larvae, all while avoiding a magical hand descending from the ceiling. The third and final act pits you against the necromancer himself in his lair full of gravestones. You must walk over the stones to prevent the necromancer from appearing, and when he does appear, you must avoid his fire trails.

The controls change from screen to screen; for example, on the first board, the fire button plants a seed, but on the second board, you need to hold down the fire button to move. This can make it tricky to get the hang of the game at first. The graphics, sound effects, and music are all inspired and quite unlike any I've encountered before or since. The music even features dynamics, with softer and louder sections, at a time when computers usually didn't have more than one voice to play tunes with. It's compelling and worth playing today, and shines as an early example of the platform's power for gaming. It's one of the best games to originate on the Atari 8-bit.

Night Mission Pinball (subLogic, 1982)

"Take a break… with Night Mission Pinball." So goes the clever pun in the long-running ad for this game in *Antic* magazine. Despite the screenshots you may see around the Web, this game is in color and uses artifacting for the graphics. The table features five bumpers, seven targets, nine rollovers, and two spinners, and you control just the bottom two bumpers. The game includes support for up to four players. There are 10 preset modes of play, and there are also 40 different parameters you can adjust in an editor and save in up to 100 additional slots. So while you can't make entirely new tables, you can certainly change up the mechanics of play.

This was the first computer pinball game to look and feel realistic to me. The ball physics are spot on, and the graphics and sound were quite advanced for the time, especially considering that this was one of the earlier Atari 8-bit titles to become available. It also held up well next to the Commodore 64 version, and positively destroyed the CGA, pink-and-cyan DOS version.

Night Mission Pinball and Pinball Construction Set were the two best pinball games to grace Atari 8-bit computers. Coming off of Video Pinball for the VCS, Night Mission Pinball was a revelation, and the sentimental value of playing it today is there. But it's safe to say that pinball simulation has advanced since the Atari 8-bit's day. You'll be forgiven if you'd rather play Pinball Arcade or Pinball FX2 from Steam.

N.Y.C. The Big Apple (Synapse Software, 1984)

Back in the day, I couldn't stop playing this game. I'm a native New Yorker, which may have had something to do with it. Anyway, your goal is to visit 12 tourist attractions around the city—which is laid out nothing like the real thing in the game, and is randomized each time—and complete minigames in each location. The attractions include famous ones like the Empire State Building and the United Nations, and more pedestrian stops like the Post Office and the Automat.

The minigames are fun, and are essentially platformers. For example, at the Post Office, you have to grab a letter, put it on a stamp pad, wait for the stamp, take the letter back, climb the ladder, and toss it into a mailbox, all while avoiding runaway mail carts and a random dog. You can also accidentally get "stamped" by the stamping machine, or fall off a ladder. In the Subway, you have to catch a token while avoiding bullets (it was the 1980s). Playing N.Y.C. is basically this, times 12.

You drive around the city to each location, and have to avoid getting towed, which any New Yorker will tell you is almost impossible in real life. Whenever you're towed, you have to pay a fine and pick the car up from the Lot. You can also buy gas and store the car in the Garage. The bank and subway are always open, but the others are only open at certain times; you're notified of this, and can drive to a location when you find out it's open. If you get hit by a car while walking, you pay a visit to the Hospital and fork over additional cash. The graphics are unremarkable, but driving around is fun, and the city is chock full of sound effects like running cars, horns, accidents, and more horns. You have seven in-game days to complete all of the tasks and get to City Hall. Good luck with that.

One-On-One (Electronic Arts, 1983)

The Atari wasn't known for its sports games—the Intellivision had a near-monopoly on the best ones, thanks to its omnidirectional controllers and keypads. One-On-One is different. Instead of pitting two basketball teams against each other, it puts you and another player in control of two of the biggest stars of the era: Julius Erving and Larry Bird. The scene is an empty half-court with a single hoop. You compete for getting the most points, or the most points within a given time.

This alone is enough for some serious gameplay. But once in a long while, if you time it *just* right and are super lucky, you can shatter the backboard with a stunning dunk. My friend Carlo and I saw this happen maybe twice, and we played it all the time. When you did it, a janitor would come out and sweep up all the glass. In addition, the game attempted to simulate the two players' actual playing styles, and if something cool happened, you'd get to see an instant replay.

This version didn't cater to the Atari's strengths, with little sound and not much to animate on screen, but it was still quite addictive. Perhaps thanks to the decidedly 1970s and 1980s stars, One-On-One is largely forgotten today. But it's easily the best basketball simulation available for the Atari 8-bit platform, and positively destroyed the feeble (although more team-oriented) Basketball game Atari sold in cartridge form. Thanks to its popularity, Atari rereleased it in cartridge form for the XE Game System in 1987. A sequel, Jordan vs. Bird: One on One, came out in 1988 for the Commodore 64 and some consoles, but it didn't make it to the Atari 8-bit platform.

Pac-Man (Atari, 1981)

What could I possibly add about this game that no one else has already said? The Atari 8-bit conversion of Pac-Man differs from the 1980 arcade machine notably in its landscape, rather than portrait, orientation. One of the bonus fruits, which appear in the center of the maze and mark the level number—the pineapple—is replaced with the Atari logo. It lacks the arcade version's in-game cartoons every two or three boards. And a few other details are missing, such as the whites in each ghost's eyes.

Otherwise, the Atari 8-bit Pac-Man captures all of the original's addictive qualities. This was one of the first cartridges I got for the Atari 800, and I played it constantly. It was such a huge leap over the rushed, disappointing VCS version that I couldn't get over it. A 5200 version of the game remedied the lack of in-game cartoons, adding ones to match the arcade's; this version soon made its way into piracy circles on the 400/800 and was widely distributed.

Atari promoted this game heavily in its various 8-bit computer brochures for the next couple of years. The company sold it first in the black box and then the XL-style silver lined box. The artwork on the boxes and in the manuals for the 8-bit version was different than on other platforms. Atari seems to have done its own, and also added in some strategy tips, which was another unusual move at the time. Atari didn't sell an XE version; my hunch is that by this point, Atari wanted to put the "pre-crash" era behind it, and practically no other game from the early 1980s loomed as large as this one.

The Pharaoh's Curse (Synapse Software, 1983)

Another innovative title from Synapse Software, Pharaoh's Curse is an adventure platformer. It puts you inside a tomb in search of long-lost treasure. (How long was it lost? The box says 3,000 years, but the manual says 43 centuries, so the jury is still out.) The game starts with you entering the tomb from above. As you explore, you must avoid or otherwise temporarily disable the crypt's mummy. The Winged Avenger can carry you unexpectedly to different parts of the tomb—if you've played Adventure on the VCS, you know exactly what this is like—and traps are laid everywhere. You'll need to find keys to unlock secret passages containing treasure; you're looking for 16 treasures in all.

There are three difficulty levels, and you get to the harder two by learning and then typing in a secret word at the start of the game. The controls are simple: You walk by pushing right or left, jumped by pushing up, climb magic ropes by pushing up, and shot your pistol by pressing the joystick button. You can fall as far as you want; often an Atari platformer's difficulty level is correlated to whether you could fall safely, and if so, how far. Sometimes you'll find a crown, which gives you life, or an arrow, which kills you.

Keep in mind that games like this had little precedent. While today it's easy to think of hundreds of platform-style games, particularly after the NES came out in 1985, early platform-style games like Donkey Kong didn't have an adventure aspect to them spanning dozens of screens and with involved goals. So a game like Pharaoh's Curse was uniquely suited to taking advantage of the Atari 8-bit computer's extra memory and graphics architecture.

Pitfall II: Lost Caverns (Activision, 1984)

The original Pitfall! is one of the best games on the VCS; the Atari 8-bit version is almost identical, aside from a bit more graphics detail. Pitfall II: Lost Caverns, also developed by David Crane, far surpasses the original in complexity, with many underground screens, water you swim through, and multilevel platform-based challenges, all while remaining just as fun.

The plot, such as it is: You, Pitfall Harry, must find your niece Rhonda, her cat Quickclaw, and the Raj diamond. Along the way, you must battle eels, frogs, and bats in addition to scorpions and crocodiles. And as in the first Pitfall!, you must grab gold bars along the way, each of which is worth 5,000 points. You lose a few points whenever you fall too far, and you lose lots of points if you touch a bat or other enemy. The four-voice music in particular is memorable, especially when you "die" and are transported back to the last checkpoint you reached.

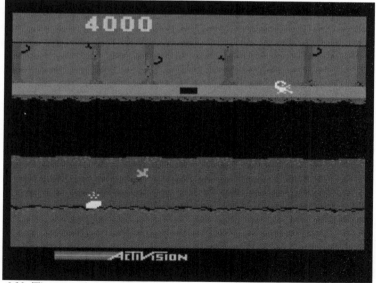

Figure 6.30: The sequel to a wildly popular Atari 2600 game, Pitfall 2: Lost Caverns really shone on the Atari 8-bit, complete with underwater levels and a full musical soundtrack.

When I was eight years old, I got to meet David Crane. I idolized him as the programmer behind Dragster, Laser Blast, Grand Prix,

Kaboom!, and other games I didn't even know he worked on (thanks to Atari's no-credit policies). Apparently one of my dad's close colleagues in the kitchen renovation business knew Crane; they arranged a dinner where they surprised me with meeting him. Then we went to an arcade afterwards and Crane let me win at a cocktail-cabinet Centipede. This was easily one of the best days of my childhood. I can't remember if this happened before or after he released Pitfall!, but it was the same year, and I received a shrink-wrapped copy of Pitfall! for my birthday along with a matching green Activision backpack.

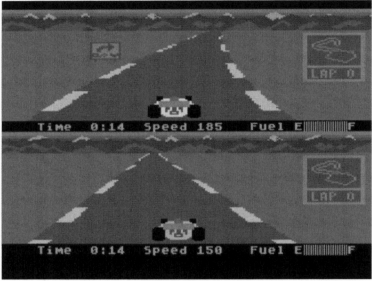

Figure 6.31: Pitstop II brought the pit crew made famous in the original version to a new split-screen, three-dimensional racer.

Pitstop II (Epyx, 1984)

Pitstop is a fun vertical racing game, similar to Turbo in the arcade. Pitstop II advanced the genre: It was the first game to allow split-screen 3D racing. Pitstop II comes with six tracks, including famous ones like Watkins Glen and Sebring, and lets you choose three, six, or nine laps to race—the last of which is plenty when you're 11 years old and have the attention span of a caffeinated gnat. I still remember getting out of school three hours early one Friday because of a snowstorm; I trudged home a few blocks in the snow, sat down at the

Atari, and played nine-lap games of Pitstop II all afternoon while sipping hot chocolate. It was like I won the lottery.

As with the original Pitstop game, you spend a lot of time worrying about tire wear and fuel. As your tires turned from black to dark blue to light blue, you must plan your next pit stop (hence the title of the game). The pit stops are almost minigames themselves, and how long you spend in the pits changing tires and fueling up affects how long it takes you to complete the race. Fueling up just requires walking the right guy over to the car with the pump, but getting the tire changers into position is more difficult.

While the split-screen view was innovative at the time, it's split-screen even when you play by yourself; the other half just shows what one of the computer-controlled players sees, which is pretty useless. While driving, a diagram on the right side of the screen shows where you were on the track. All in all, it's a fun game with more depth and strategy than Pole Position along with the unique (for the time) two-player view.

Pole Position (Atari, 1982)

This cartridge was one of the first games to come with Atari's silver label. It's a nice conversion of the arcade car racing game. The Atari 8-bit version of Pole Position plays smoothly, with what was then a fast frame rate. The game itself is simplistic. You must first complete a qualifying run in less than 73 seconds. This scores you a position in the actual race based on how fast you ran the qualifying lap.

Perhaps Atari's shrewdest move with this game was to make the acceleration automatic. This way the joystick lets you shift up and down gears, steer, and brake (with the fire button). If you enter a turn too fast, you scrub off speed and slide to the outside; there's no oversteer modeling. You can also play this game with a trackball, although in my opinion it's not much closer to a steering wheel than the joystick is.

A few nits: The official version lacks the arcade's synthesized "Prepare to Qualify" voice, and the graphics are slightly blockier (notably around the tires, which turn realistically in the arcade version). Back then, this was the life of a gamer: You were watching for all of the details to see how closely the game matched the real version. The

Atari 8-bit Pole Position does exceedingly well otherwise, and the sensation of speed is palpable.

Figure 6.32: A popular third-person racing game, Pole Position offers just two stages (Qualify and Race), but delivers a fast frame rate and exciting gameplay.

The Atari 8-bit version also lets you configure some parameters; there are three courses in increasing levels of difficulty (Malibu Grand Prix, Namco Speedway, and Atari Grand Prix), and you can choose to run up to eight laps. The more you race, the more competing cars appear on the track, which makes absolutely no sense in real life. Primitive as it may seem now, Pole Position was an exciting game to play on its debut, and the home version was a compelling reason to pick up a 400, 800, or 5200.

Protector (Synapse Software, 1981)

A seriously slick Defender clone, Protector puts you in charge of saving 18 innocent victims from Fraxullan Slimehorde attacks. You must save the victims from the top of buildings and bring them one by one to the city of New Hope. When you finish bringing everyone there, a gate opens to the Verdann Fortress, to which you must evacuate all of the victims next. When you do that, a volcano erupts and eventually destroys New Hope. All the while, various alien ships, rocket bases, and stray meteoroids try to stop you. You're also working against a time limit, in case that wasn't already enough stress, and gravity slowly pulls down your ship as you play.

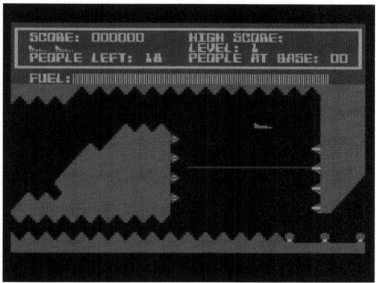

Figure 6.33: Synapse Software's Protector, a side-scrolling game that's more than just a shoot-'em-up.

To control the ship, you push the joystick in the direction you want to fly (right, left, up, or down). Pressing the fire button shoots your laser gun, and if you're carrying a passenger, it drops the person (hopefully to safety in the right place). Making things somewhat easier, you can fly straight through buildings, so picking up victims isn't as hard as it may have been otherwise. At the same time, you can't destroy the laser cannons, and most of the time you can't destroy the missiles (except when they turn red, which as an April 1983 review in *Electronic Fun* put it, "happens roughly every 50 years or so"). The game features six levels of difficulty. The manual helpfully offers the following tip: "Do not attack your computer when frustrated. It had nothing to do with designing this game." The sequel, Protector II, came out a year later; it's pretty similar, and saw somewhat wider distribution as Synapse Software grew larger.

Q*bert (Parker Brothers, 1983)

The M.C. Escher–inspired, isometric Q*bert is a popular arcade coin-op game, and it was practically a requirement that any serious home computing platform in the early 1980s had some version of it. You color all of the squares on a pyramid by hopping from one to next, while avoiding enemies like the snake Coily and the purple Ugg and Wrongway. Sam, a green creature, sometimes appear to turn the colors back on you while you're working. To avoid Coily, who kills you on contact, you can hop on one of the multicolored spinning discs on the side of the board and fly back to the top as Coily jumps off in vain trying to catch you, netting you 500 bonus points. On the tougher levels, you'll need to change the squares' color twice.

As with other ports of the time, the Atari 8-bit home conversion of this arcade classic is the best one, with colorful, proportionate (not stretched) graphics, smooth gameplay, and nearly all of the arcade version's elements. The trick with Q*bert is to hold the Atari joystick at a diagonal to match the board on-screen; otherwise the controls don't quite make sense. Sadly, even the Atari 8-bit version lacks the audible incoherent cursing, although you do get to see the cartoon bubble containing "@!#?@!" when you mess up. It's a fine game and holds up well today—particularly if, like me, you have mild OCD and like filling in all the squares the correct colors. Excuse me while I go play another round right now.

Qix (Atari, 1982)

Qix (pronounced "kicks") is a simple but addictive space game that pits you against the computer in trying to claim as much of the board as possible. You control the speed in which you draw Stix (lines) to create shapes; draw slow instead of fast, and you'll get more points from the completed shape. Plus, the larger pieces you draw and complete, the higher a score you receive. Unfortunately, each larger shape carries with it the risk of getting caught by the enemy Qix while you're drawing; if the Qix touches one of the Stix, you lose a life. So there's always a risk between going for big bonus points and drawing smaller shapes to build your empire more carefully. The object is to cover at least 75 percent of each board, at which point you move on to the next level.

None of the above conveys the actual pace of the game, which is certainly frenetic. Your reflexes must be top-notch. And to this day, there's something appealing about the *Tron*-esque, dawn-of-the-computer-age graphics, which echoes vector-based games like Tempest and Asteroids—even though the Qix coin-op isn't vector-based. There are two versions floating around: the original cartridge for Atari 8-bit computers, which is mediocre, and the 5200 conversion, which is superb and made its way over to the 8-bit computer lineup anyway (thanks to our old friend Glenn the 5200 Man).

Reviews in magazines and around the Web indicate this game had more of a cult following, and didn't have much staying power. "Qix was conceptually too mystifying for games," Tatio's own Keith Egging said in a June 1983 interview in *Electronic Games* magazine.[148] "It had a random mapping program that allowed for constant alteration. It was impossible to master and once the novelty wore off, the game faded." I still love it anyway.

Rainbow Walker (Synapse Software, 1983)

This exclusive, trippy, platform game developed by Steve Coleman is a kind of warped, but still imaginative, version of Q*bert. Rainbow Walker puts you, Cedrick, on top of a rainbow above the clouds. Unfortunately, someone did something terrible: They stole the colors of the rainbow! Your task is to color back in the rainbow's segments, which play music as you go, and complete full columns of the rainbow as the board wraps around. During the game, you have to avoid both holes in the rainbow you can fall through and various strange enemies out to get you and undo you work. For example, some of the creatures turn the rainbow segments back to gray, although once a column is completed, it's completed for good (at least until the next level begins).

Some of the creatures can fill in holes in the rainbow, and freeze squares let you stop all of the enemies for a few seconds. Sometimes, a shooting star flies across the top of the rainbow. If you touch it, it carries you off the side and drops you to your death. Each time you finish a rainbow, you get to play a quick bonus round. I call this

148. *Electronic Games*, June 1983, p. 84

game's graphics three-dimensional, but I'm using the term loosely—the perspective is 3D, even if the graphics are kind of a tricked-out 2D. But the effect certainly works. One other nice effect in the game is the gradual changeover from day to night; you see either the sun or the moon over the clouds. Overall, the game is original and impressively polished, and the sound design is excellent, as befits an Atari 8-bit game.

Figure 6.34: Synapse Software delivered a unique twist on the common platformer with Rainbow Walker, a colorful romp above the clouds.

Rally Speedway (Adventure International, 1983)

John Anderson's Rally Speedway is like a turbocharged version of the Intellivision's Auto Racing. The view is top-down, with your car at the center of the screen. The courses consist of straightaways, curves, and scenery such as houses, lakes, and clusters of trees. Each time you start a game, you can configure options such as top speed (40 to 100mph), slippery conditions (dry, wet, ice), a fun two-player mode, and memorably, the choice between Real Life or Only in a Computer mode—the latter of which lets you go through trees and buildings without a scratch. Your goal is to beat either the other player or your best lap times.

The game lets you set the joystick to one of two configurations. In the first, pressing right turns the car to the right regardless of how it's facing. You generally leave the stick alone as the car goes straight. In the second, you press the direction in which you want the car to travel (to go "up" the screen, you press up, for example). Pressing the button in either mode activates the brakes and lets you turn more sharply. In fact, of the racing games I played as a kid, Rally Speedway is the only one to accurately emulate oversteer, or the ability to swing your car's tail out as you slide around a corner using the brakes and accelerator (although the latter is automatic in this game).

The two-player mode puts both of you on the same screen, instead of using a split-screen view. If one player begins to lag behind, the game returns the offender to a side-by-side position and assesses a 5-second penalty. The game also comes with an enjoyable built-in track editor that increases the game's play value (similar to what Mr. Robot and His Robot Factory and Pinball Construction Set offered).

The best part: Whenever you crash, the car bursts into flames, and your character runs out of the car on fire and then rolls until he puts it out. Okay, someone burning to death may not sound like the best part. But come on, he's probably wearing one of those flame-retardant suits anyway.

Realm of Impossibility (Electronic Arts, 1984)

Zombies made a huge comeback in popular culture after the year 2000, but they were a popular foil back in the 1970s and 1980s as well. This was documented in the video game industry perhaps no more successfully than in Electronic Arts' Realm of Impossibility, a multilevel, fast-paced game. It puts you in the role of a human capturing crosses while dodging hordes of computer-controlled zombie beasties. Originally self-published by Mike Edwards under the title Zombies!, the EA version includes many more rooms (129 in all), and saw wider distribution at the time. More *28 Days Later* than *Dawn of the Dead*, the zombies in this game are fast—and quite scary.

In this game, you must travel through the "Thirteen Dungeons of Wistrik the Evil," to get either one of the seven missing crowns or a key (to unlock one of the locked dungeons). As you run through each dungeon, you can disperse crosses, which stick for a few seconds and block the denizens chasing you. In addition to zombies, the enemies include snakes, orbs, and spiders. You have a set number of hit points, which decrease as enemies run into you, or increase whenever you pick up special objects. Once you get the key or crown at the last screen, you must run all the way back to the entrance, upon which you hear a little audio motif, get a hit point bonus, and wave goodbye at the camera.

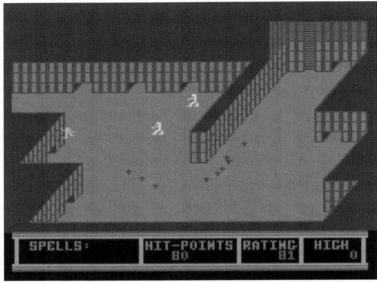

Figure 6.35: EA's Realm of Impossibility is an original and fun-to-play action adventure game.

There's also a two-player cooperative mode where you can both help each other, but you also must leave each room at the same time. If one person dies, the other can resurrect him or her. Realms of Impossibility contains four levels of difficulty, and you compete against yourself for the highest "rating" (or score) on each one.

Rescue on Fractalus! (Lucasfilm Games, 1984)

Rescue on Fractalus! was the second title, along with Ballblazer, that marked Lucasfilm Games's stunning debut. True to its name, the first-person space game employs computer-generated fractals to create a 3D landscape you fly over, using a compass-like tool and beacons to navigate the harsh, alien terrain. You must rescue other pilots in downed aircraft before the acidic atmosphere kills them, all while fighting off alien ships. The craziest part: Some of the rescued pilots turn out to be aliens disguised in helmets, and you must escape before they break through the glass of your ship and kill you.

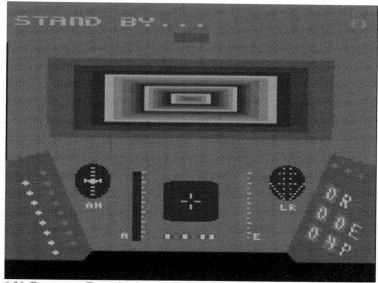

Figure 6.36: Rescue on Fractalus is a landmark game for the Atari 8-bit, thanks to its excellent graphics and sound design.

The fractal graphics were a revelation at the time, even despite the low-resolution look today. (An unfinished prototype version of the game, humorously called Behind Jaggi Lines, also made the rounds.) Project director David Fox said they purposely hid the score during gameplay so as not to break the illusion. Playing it today, you can even see the theatrical influence, from the opening Lucasfilm title screen and THX-like ramp-up sound, to the beautiful GTIA-shaded mothership during the loading sequence, to the main title screen theme, which sounded like something John Williams could have composed.

Even though the frame rate isn't perfect when flying over the actual landscape, it doesn't affect gameplay at all. For example, your laser cannon fires smoothly, and the controls are responsive in real time; only the rendering of the landscape itself sometimes stutters. The sensation of flying over the surface of an alien planet is there,

204 | Breakout: How Atari 8-Bit Computers Defined a Generation

quite an accomplishment for a machine of this vintage (to say nothing of the lack of 3D acceleration). This is one of the best games to grace the Atari 8-bit platform, and one of the clearest examples of how advanced it was for the time. Aside from a bump in screen resolution, this is exactly the kind of game you'd expect to play several years later on a 16-bit Amiga or Atari ST.

The Return of Heracles (Quality Software, 1983)

"Examine your options, and know thyself: May the gods favor you!" So goes the beginning of The Return of Heracles, a colorful and detailed turn-based adventure game based somewhat loosely on Greek mythology. It lets you play 20 (!) different characters, such as Great Ajax, Polydeuces, and Achilles; each one has RPG-like attributes, such as strength and dexterity, and the ability to use certain weapons or defensive techniques.

When you start the game, you're given 12 quests to complete, such as slaying the serpent of Ares or rescuing Helen from Troy. Most of these can be done in any order, though a few depend on completing other quests first. The Oracle of Delphi will provide you with clues, providing you contribute generously. In-game, you get several moves per turn. The interface is strange by today's standards; you get messages one at a time as computer-controlled opponents perform actions, and while you can speed up or slow down the messages, you can't just press the button when you're done reading them. The effect is to make you feel like you're only in control some of the time.

Otherwise, many traditional RPG elements are here, including the ability to buy weapons and choose your moves and attacks carefully. As *Computer Gaming World*'s December 1984 review pointed out, it's an enjoyable game, and challenging but not frustrating: "Unlike certain text adventures where you have to find the right words or you get nowhere, you will always be accomplishing something as long as you just move the characters... Error-handling is [also] superb. I couldn't make an error with this game, except in judgment."[149] Combined with comprehensive documentation and a detailed graphical presentation, The Return of Heracles is an excellent game, even despite the unusual interface.

---

149. *Computer Gaming World*, December 1984, p. 36

Robotron: 2084 (Atari, 1983)

In the year 2084, robots have taken over; you must save the last nuclear human family. The Robotrons stalk you endlessly, wave after wave, looking to kill the humans. (It quickly becomes apparent you must save the "last nuclear human family" over and over again.) You have to destroy all of the Grunt Robotrons before you can advance to the next wave. The only robot type you can't destroy is the green Hulk, which moves slower but is perhaps scarier as a result; your laser gun only slows them down.

You get large numbers of bonus points for saving the humans: 1,000 for the first, 2,000 for the second, and so on until you hit 5,000 for each, at least before the next wave begins. You get five lives, and a bonus life every 20,000 points you will come to seriously look forward to. Every fifth board is a Brain Wave, which can cause literal nightmares. Whenever a brain catches up to a human, it reprograms the human into a mutant prog, which moves fast and shoots cruise missiles at you. Later waves contain spheroids, which spawn embryos. The embryos grow into Enforcers, which shoot sparks in all directions. There are also dangerous electrodes, quarks, and tanks.

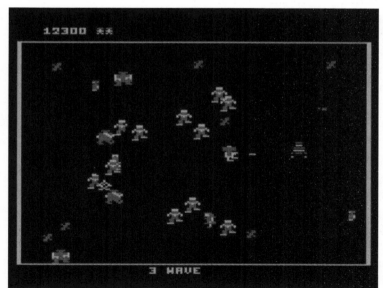

Figure 6.37: When played with two joysticks, the Atari 8-bit version of Robotron: 2084 really brought the arcade experience home.

This arcade game is one of my all-time favorites and still stands up today, even despite countless derivative versions (like Smash TV, which I also love). Nothing looks, sounds, and plays quite as intensely as the original. The 400/800 version played almost as well as the arcade, aside from some choppiness and the slight loss of color vibrancy that afflicted all Atari 8-bit titles.

Robotron: 2084 came with a plastic tray you could use as a dual joystick holder. This way you could move using the left stick and shoot your laser gun using the right stick independently of each other, just like the arcade version. The cartridge for the 5200 also allowed this, and came with a different joystick holder to fit the 5200's longer analog sticks.

Salmon Run (APX, 1982)

Salmon Run may not win any awards in the graphics department; even back in 1982, it was pretty simple-looking. But it's significant for a number of reasons. The legendary Bill Williams coded this soulful arcade game—his first—in machine language using Assembler Editor.[150] The game was distributed on APX. Your task is to swim upriver to find your mate. Gameplay is both smooth and fast; you moved side to side and sped upward as the river scrolled from top to bottom.

I lost many blissful hours speeding my salmon upstream while avoiding the large, scary-looking fishermen and even bears. You also must avoid seagulls and navigate around waterfalls. You can jump over the rapids by pressing the button. Holding down the button keeps you underwater and safely hidden from the various enemies. When you finally reach your mate, you'll hear a victory theme as the two gradually approach each other. Then the world's wettest kiss sound effect plays and hearts spray all over the screen. It's a glorious mess.

By the time Salmon Run came out, the world was already awash in space games and other shoot-'em-ups, so anything well executed like this that didn't involve killing things was a revelation. The sound design is particularly good, and I can still hear the splashing water effects as I write this. It's such a simple game, and yet addictive, inspir-

---

150. *Antic*, November 1983, p. 116

ing, and even a little sad at times. Salmon Run, even in its tiny ambition and simplicity, is an example of what happens when you nail the concept, graphics, sound, controls, and pacing all at once. Some of today's iPhone and Android games succeed precisely because of this level of arcade polish, and not because of the expected vastly improved graphics and sound.

The Seven Cities of Gold (Electronic Arts, 1984)

The Seven Cities of Gold puts you in the guise of a Christopher Columbus type—and the natives in America may not be especially welcoming. It's an open-world historical game where you balance exploration with diplomacy and trading. The game generates the world randomly each time. You start with four ships, 100 men, and some goods, and can buy more in town before setting sail for the New World. The ocean contains many perils; you have to monitor your speed and the depth of the water, and make sure you have enough food for your men to make the trip.

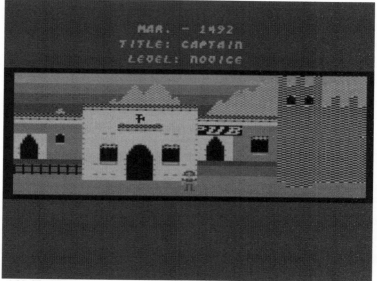

Figure 6.38: The Seven Cities of Gold is a compelling adventure in the New World that paved the way for Pirates!, Civilization, and other historical strategy games.

Once in America, you can explore and interact with the natives, and either peacefully trade with them, slaughter them, or convert them. Developer Dani Bunten said in a January 1985 interview with *Antic* that she didn't want to preach morality to the player, but instead wanted to give them an opportunity to get in touch with themselves about how they feel. "The peaceful approach really works best. I have not used a totally depraved approach and won. You've got to have some friends somewhere. If something goes wrong, you need a friendly mission where you can go back and not have to worry about an insurrection or something. A place you can return to and know that there will be food, for example. You need a series of these relatively safe places even if you are going on a conquest mission... If you continually abuse the natives you will eventually see a message from the king saying 'Don't treat the natives so badly. But keep the gold coming.' This double standard is straight out of history."

Bunten has also spoken about the difficulties of programming games in the early-to-mid 1980s: "Our biggest frustration with [The Seven Cities of Gold] was that it was developed in the days when you had to write a number of different versions since no platform was pre-eminent. There were Atari 800, C64, Apple, Mac and IBM PC versions of the game put out, but the only 'full' version was on the Atari. On the others we did the best we could with what we had."[151]

The Seven Cities of Gold is a true original. It inspired others down the line, perhaps most famously Sid Meier's games, including Pirates! and Civilization, and The Sims—which developer Will Wright dedicated to Bunten's memory after she passed away in 1998.

Shamus (Synapse Software, 1982)

Shamus is kind of derivative of Berzerk, but the gameplay is still quite different. You must traverse a 128-room, persistent-world maze in an effort to find the Shadow's Lair, collecting important items along the way. Various robots try to destroy you as you go, and just as in Berserk, the walls are electrified. There are four levels to complete, each one tougher than the last. Anyone who played Shamus probably still remembers the music, which is the theme song from *Alfred Hitch-*

---

151. www.atarimania.com/game-atari-400-800-xl-xe-seven-cities-of-gold-_s4599.html

cock Presents. (Video games had yet to garner the attention of the music and movie industries in 1982, so copyright was ignored with abandon.)

In the January 1983 issue of *Softline*, a review of Shamus said, "To know it is to love it, play it constantly, and not get enough of it. In an industry where attention span is everything, Shamus has the imagination and depth that demand repeat play." Shamus was highly successful; in an interview in the April 1983 issue of *Antic* magazine, Synapse Software cofounder Ihor Wolosenko said that after Shamus, the "ball really started rolling for the company."

The sequel, Shamus: Case II, came out a year later. It's a completely different game. This one is more of a side-view platformer, and even has some elements of Montezuma's Revenge and Breakout, with gravity pits, snakes, and ladders. It also has good game balance, and it's the rare "sequel" to deliver a new and exciting experience instead of just more of the same. Both Shamus and Shamus: Case II hold up well today, are worth playing, and remain significant examples of original Atari 8-bit games.

Sinistar (Atari prototype, 1984)

In Sinistar, you control a craft in open space; you have to create "Sinibombs" by shooting at asteroids and collecting the crystals they release. Meanwhile, enemy ships work on building the giant enemy Sinistar. It was downright scary to me as a kid whenever Sinistar himself was fully formed, thanks to then-new voice synthesis: "Beware, I live!" You then use the Sinibombs to destroy Sinistar.

Sinistar was one of my favorite arcade games. The Atari 8-bit conversion of the Williams classic is fantastic, and even contains the voice synthesis as well—quite a feat for the limited memory available. Unfortunately, the game was never released because of the Great Video Game Crash; management canceled it in 1984. And according to AtariProtos.com, the circumstances were even worse: "Apparently marketing decided the game wasn't going to make enough money and canceled the project... without telling the programmers! Jeff [Milhorn] and his team continued to work on the project for almost two months after it was canceled, due to lack of communication between [the] marketing and programming departments. Incidents like this were not uncommon, and just goes to show how badly out of touch the managers were at the time of Atari's collapse."

As has been a running theme here, copies of the completed Sinis- tar made their way out onto warez BBSes and were traded back and forth. Given the arcade game's popularity at that moment in time, enough people knew to look for it. I'll bet if it had come out, it would have been a big seller for Atari. The game showed up in vari- ous retro bundles for Sega, Sony, and Nintendo consoles throughout the 1990s and 2000s. But it's intriguing to see even now how close Atari got to the arcade version with this 8-bit computer conversion.

Space Invaders (Atari, 1980)

This one was a puzzler—and I don't mean the game genre. In Space Invaders, you control a laser cannon at the bottom of the screen. You must defend your planet against an ever-descending array of space aliens, shooting them one at a time along with the "bonus" saucer that occasionally flies across the top of the screen. As you eliminate the aliens, the remaining ones move faster and faster. If a single alien reaches the bottom of the screen, the game is over.

The Atari 8-bit version of Space Invaders is good, mind you, and features nice graphics and well-paced gameplay. But it looks *nothing* like the arcade game. Usually arcade ports for the home tried to re- semble the "real thing,", and this one looks different. It turns out, as detailed in *Atari Inc. Business Is Fun*, the developer behind the 8-bit version of Space Invaders, Rob Fulop, was given full rein to make his own version. Fulop believed trying to duplicate the arcade version was a missed opportunity for doing something creative.

"The reason Atari 800 was different from the original was very simple and somewhat embarrassing," Fulop wrote in an email to Ata- ri historian Steve Fulton. Fulop said he was 23 years old at the time, and with one "port" already under his belt (Night Driver for the VCS), he thought he was "far too cool" to do another straight port of an existing coin-op game.

"You have to remember that at Atari, programmers had nobody that ap- proved their plans, basically people like myself were given 100 percent liberty to create whatever we wanted. There was no approval process, no 'pitch meet- ings', no specs that needed sign off... In retrospect, such freedom is really

astonishing to me given what is now required to put something into production. But at that time, it was totally up to the programmer. Nobody told me to do Space Invaders, it was my choice. I decided to change the original, not because I thought the original was 'broken' in any way, but simply because I was looking to 'make my mark' whatever that meant."[152]

It was an interesting experiment, for sure. I would have preferred a true arcade conversion, as was the norm at the time; everyone wanted to play the game they knew from the arcade, not a new interpretation of it.

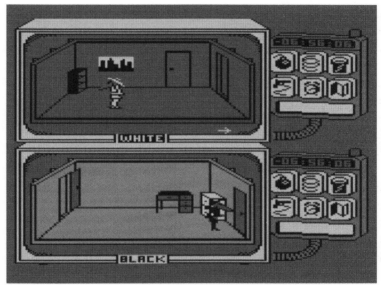

Figure 6.39: The famous *Mad* magazine duo comes to life in this split-screen caper, complete with cartoon graphics and ambitious sound design.

Spy vs. Spy (First Star Software, 1984)

Based on the *Mad* magazine cartoon strip of the same name, Spy vs. Spy is a clever, fun game where two spies—one dressed in white and one in black, complete with fedoras, just like in the strip—must compete against the clock to collect the key, the passport, the briefcase, some money, and the secret plans hidden in a series of rooms, and

152. www.gamasutra.com/view/feature/132160/atari_the_golden_years__a_.php_

then head to the airport to win. Of course, the other spy is trying to do the exact same thing, with the exact same items.

Each spy can set booby traps like buckets of water and bombs, which, when triggered, make the other spy drop whatever he's carrying and stop the corresponding player for a short while. Each spy can also make use of remedies for the traps (except for the bomb). For example, you can use scissors to cut a string attached to the trigger of a gun, thereby defusing the trap. Setting and diffusing traps each take time, naturally, so you want to make sure you're always making progress in getting the right items.

Each room is three-dimensional. You can walk toward the back and front walls, as well as to the left and right. The best thing about the game is the split-screen view; you can see what the other player is doing, which then clues you in on how you should proceed on your own. Whenever the two players enter the same room, it then shifts to just the half-screen view. At this point, you can beat each other over the head with clubs to get some of your frustration out.

The Atari 8-bit graphics and multichannel sound in this game are well done. The first sequel, The Island Caper, is also good, and lets you run around a horizontally scrolling island. The second sequel, Arctic Antics, adds a "body heat" component each player has to mind during gameplay.

Star League Baseball (Gamestar, 1983)

Not being a huge sports fan, I'll readily admit that I'm not the best judge of sports games in general. But I did play an awful lot of them as a kid, especially on the Intellivision, which had 16-direction disc controllers and was famous for its advanced (for the time) sports titles. Still, Star League Baseball is tremendous fun, and has a fast and addictive pace. Notably, it isn't overhead or in 3D from a batter's perspective. Instead, you watch and play the entire game from right field. Somehow it works, thanks to the accurate physics as much as the pacing. The game automatically activates the correct fielder to go after a hit; you don't have to waste time selecting one.

While the game isn't as realistic as the later (and better known) Hardball, Star League Baseball incorporates several levels of sophistication: In addition to tracking the usual runs, balls, and strikes, your pitcher can also get tired, relief pitchers throw knuckleballs, and the ball's shadow follows it on the field. You get a good sense of the depth of perspective from the unusual camera position. In-game, you can also steal bases. Getting hits is quite difficult; this game is no pushover to play. The sound design is well handled, too, from the roar of the crowd to the crack of the bat, and there's even an organist. The insistence on listening to the national anthem in the beginning of each game was a novelty at the time, but you can't interrupt it; fortunately, it's not long. While computer baseball games may seem too common to matter much, Star League Baseball is an excellent and original example.

Star Raiders (Atari, 1979)

Star Raiders has the distinction of being the first 3D space combat simulator ever made. Obviously derived from the original *Star Trek*, it puts you in command of a ship clearing out enemy space fighters from the sectors surrounding your bases. Harder difficulty levels make it tougher to warp between sectors accurately, and introduce shield damage and other variables to make the game more realistic.

This seminal 800 title fit into just 8KB of memory—8,192 bytes!—and became the first true killer app for the platform. Doug Neubauer, who worked on the POKEY chip during the Atari computer's development phase, also began work on a game to properly demo the system. Star Raiders was released either with or shortly after the 400 and 800—Atarimania's History of Atari section has the launch pegged in the November-to-December 1979 time frame, the same as the computers themselves. The game quickly became a system seller.[153]

"Star Raiders was to be a 3-D version of the Star Trek game played on the mainframe computers of that time," Neubauer said. "The Star Trek game was all text and not played in real time, but it had the idea of ship damage and sector scanners and charts."[154]

It's also not what Atari wanted. Under the direction of Ray Kassar, the company wanted its home computers to be taken seriously, and not just as game machines, which is what the Atari brand had meant up until this point. It's why the original lineup of software was

---

153. Atari.com - Game Titles history page.
154. www.atarihq.com/othersec/library/neubauer.html

stocked mostly with business and educational titles. The success of Star Raiders killed the idea.

"The employees in the company went bonkers over the game, which was the first true-to-life, three-dimensional video game," wrote Michael S. Tomczyk in *The Home Computer Wars*. "The visual effects were dazzling, especially when the stars whizzed by when you warped, or when the four kinds of enemy ships came zooming out of nowhere either behind or in front of you."

I'm assuming most of you reading this book have played this game, but if not, you have to see it to believe it. Sadly, as with many things Atari in those days, Neubauer didn't make a penny off of the game, as Atari owned the full rights to the software.[155] "It's pretty amazing, the way the game caught on," Neubauer said. "I think it was the first game to combine action with a strategy screen, and luckily, the concept worked out pretty well."[156]

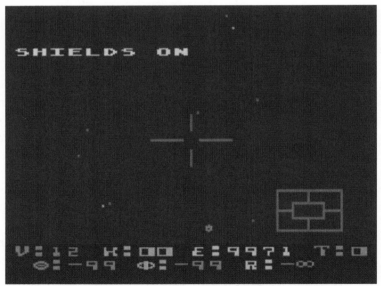

Figure 6.40: The killer app for the Atari 400 and 800, Star Raiders still holds up today despite being packed into an 8KB cartridge.

Star Raiders both loomed over and influenced all of the early game developers on the Atari platform. "Anybody who has seen Ata-

155. Atari.com - Game Titles history page.
156. www.atarihq.com/othersec/library/neubauer.html

ri's Star Raiders knows the Atari Personal Computer System has vastly greater graphics capabilities than any other personal computer," Crawford wrote in *Compute's First Book of Atari* in 1981. "Owners of these computers might wonder if they can get their machines to do the fabulous things that Star Raiders does. The good news is that you can indeed write programs with graphics and animation every bit as good as Star Raiders."

Star Wars: The Arcade Game (Parker Brothers, 1983)

Right after discussing Star Raiders, let's continue with a cautionary tale. By the time *Return of the Jedi* rolled into theaters in 1983, there was still nothing like the *Star Wars* movie trilogy—and certainly nothing like Star Wars: The Arcade Game, which rendered the first film's battle sequences in colorful, laser-like vector graphics, complete with snippets of digitized dialog from actors Mark Hamill and Alec Guinness. This game, which appeared in both stand-up versions and custom sit-down cabinets, delivered the three-dimensional flight and space combat experience like nothing else before.

The rushed Atari 8-bit port's reviews were mixed, and I agreed at the time. It isn't just the obvious problem of replicating vector graphics with limited screen resolution. It's more that the game just isn't challenging or fun with a regular Atari joystick, as opposed to the arcade machine's dual-grip flight stick. There's little sense of movement; too many of the on-screen elements are fixed in place, the Death Star doesn't appear to get closer as you approach it, and flying through the trench doesn't deliver the proper 3D sensation. None of the digitized voices of each actor from the movie made it over to the Atari 8-bit, either.

It's strange to compare this game, which isn't much fun on an Atari computer, with Star Raiders, which delivers a phenomenal sense of movement and a real, addictive challenge from the same hardware. Remember Star Raiders came out several years earlier, and required only two-thirds of the memory of the 12KB Star Wars: The Arcade Game cartridge. It's an unfortunate but important early example of two things: Movie tie-ins don't necessarily make for good games, especially if you're working against a marketing deadline; and even programmers with plenty of hardware resources can create a substandard game if they don't take advantage of them (or, as is usually the case, aren't given enough time to do so properly).

Stealth (Brøderbund, 1984)

This game had beautiful graphics and sound effects for the time. It's a three-dimensional shooter; you fly past enemy lines and destroy a dark tower, which contains the Council of Nine, "cruel overlords of a conquered world." While flying your stealth starfighter low to the ground, you must avoid negative energy fields and active volcanoes while destroying robotic tanks, scout planes, and fighter planes. Radar towers track your approach, and on later levels, they can shoot at you. Positive energy fields give you more energy when you pass through them, though if you're like me, sometimes you'll shoot them by accident before you reach them, thinking they're the other kind.

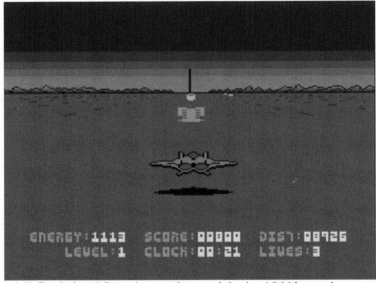

Figure 6.41: Brøderbund flexes its muscles—and the Atari 8-bit's—and comes up with an amazing third-person shooter that doesn't reek of being programmed on the Apple II first.

The controls are simple; you push forward to accelerate and back to slow down. Pushing left or right on the stick will bank the fighter in the appropriate direction. The game features five levels, distinguished primarily by their color scheme and the number of enemies you face. On the first level, you'll need one shot to destroy the tower, on the second level you'll need two, and so on. You get a total of three lives before losing the game. As you approach, a distance counter counts backward from 10,000; energy also trickles away just from flying, so you need those positive energy fields to stay alive as the tower gets closer and closer.

Antic's February 1985 review of Stealth was dripping with sarcasm about how impressive the graphics and sound were: "Could it be this game was not originally designed for the squeaking Apple?" The multi-lined graded sky, distant tower, and fast landscape movement lend a serious, frenetic pace to the proceedings. Looking back on it now, something about the design and colors evokes what was to come with F-Zero on the Super Nintendo, although that was a faster and more advanced racing game instead of a shooter. A prototype version of Stealth called Landscape also made the warez rounds, ahead of the game's official release.

Super Breakout (Atari, 1979)

One of the most famous early video games was Breakout, created by Steve Wozniak and Steve Jobs for Atari in the mid 1970s. Pong, and variations on its theme, helped put the company on the map, so a version of Breakout was a natural early release for its 8-bit computer platform. The VCS console version of Breakout was an early breakout hit (sorry). For its computer, Atari decided to go with Super Breakout, which was a 6502-based coin-op game and therefore an obvious choice.

The concept is deceptively simple: Use a paddle controller to move a bar, which bounces a ball up at rows of bricks above. Once you break a hole clean through the wall, the ball hits the ceiling, bounces all over the bricks on the top, and takes out many of them at once before returning to the bottom of the screen. The game features four variations: Breakout, Progressive, Double, and Cavity, which periodically releases trapped balls as you break through the lines of bricks. The game requires Atari Paddle Controllers. Unlike with the VCS version, you can see a little space between each brick that functions as an outline.

While games like Clowns and Balloons introduced variations on the Breakout concept, it wasn't until Taito's Arkanoid coin-op in

1986—along with home conversions primarily for 16-bit systems, although the Commodore 64 and NES also saw ports—that the bar truly moved forward for games like this. In the meantime, Super Breakout still plays well today, although it barely takes advantage of the Atari 8-bit platform. Given that we're still seeing clones left and right, even on modern iOS and Android devices, it's a well-proven concept and deserves its place in Atari computer history.

Super Pac-Man (Atari Prototype, 1984)

Super Pac-Man delivers a totally different experience than its predecessors. In this game, you gobble up giant fruit—what used to be the sole prize on each regular board in Pac-Man—one after the other. The mazes contain gates you can unlock by gobbling up keys. New "Super" power pellets turn you into Super Pac-Man, meaning you can go faster and eat the gates in addition to the ghosts as with regular power pellets. The harder levels of the game put the keys farther away from the doors they unlocked.

As with Jr. Pac-Man, Super Pac-Man was another finished, unreleased prototype (complete with intermissions!). Tramiel canned it along with many other games when he took over in 1984. Interestingly, programmer Landon Dyer at Atari coded a software switch. It detected which system it was being played on (either an 8-bit computer or the 5200); this way Atari could have used the same exact code in both types of cartridges.[157]

True story: Back when I was running my Atari BBS, one of the regular callers was a guy named Alfred Krumb, who said that he was 74, retired, and had bought several extra Atari 800XLs so he could put them around the house and play Super Pac-Man wherever he wanted. It was his favorite game. He even hired me once to help him create a custom version of his FoReM XL BBS, and then sent me $20 as payment (which I hadn't asked for, since I was 12 and didn't know from such things yet). I always wondered what happened to him; this was back in the mid 1980s, so chances are he has since passed on to a better place. But whenever I think of Super Pac-Man, I think of Mr. Krumb.

---

157. www.atariprotos.com/5200/software/superpac/superpac.htm

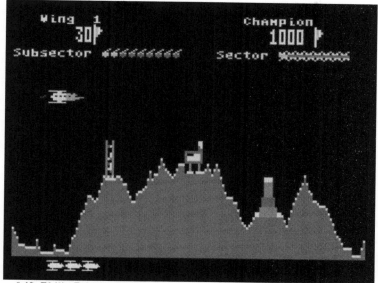

Figure 6.42: Philip Price's side-scroller for Datamost was fun to play and a good warmup for writing Alternate Reality: The City.

The Tail of Beta Lyrae (Datamost, 1983)

Scramble was a popular enough arcade game in 1981 to inspire many other side-scrolling space shooters. Datamost's The Tail of Beta Lyrae follows in this vein—although it has some elements of randomness to the playfield, unlike later titles like Gradius for the Nintendo, which keep all of the enemies in the same place and order each time. The game puts you in control of a spaceship; you must use it to destroy alien surface installations and force them to retreat from mining settlements. The Tail of Beta Lyrae is notable not so much for its gameplay—which is good, if derivative—but because the famed Philip Price developed it for the Atari, honing his skills here before going on to create his magnum opus, Alternate Reality: The City.

"Since I only had 32K of memory and no floppy drive, the first game I wrote had to be an action game," Price said in *Halcyon Days*. "I enjoyed side-scrolling arcade games the most, so I had decided to try creating one. Since I enjoy playing as well as writing, I used an infinite scrolling field and a probability engine to generate terrain and objects. I wanted the game to last; I hated playing a game where all I had to do was remember where all of the items were. I liked the future to be unpredictable, but with a degree of order. I also enjoyed surprises, so I made the game change after you had owned it for a while."[158]

Gary Gilbertson also composed the excellent music. "Even today most game companies I have visited vastly under estimate the value of music and sound," Price continued. "Beta Lyrae had only one song, but it didn't sound anything like what was out there, thanks to the combined strength of a great musician and a language that allowed him to express music in ways much more flexible than were currently available. Almost all games out at that time used classical music and transcribed the music literally. They also used pure tones for the notes. I had added forms of vibrato, time and frequency shifts, random jumps, and greater frequency accuracy. Gary used these to enhance the effect of the music. He also used the increased resolution of the timing to express emotional context of his songs. Later, I added synchronization of video to audio; this was used in the Alternate Reality intro."[159]

Ultima III: Exodus (Origin Systems, 1983)

One of the best role-playing games to grace the Atari 8-bit platform, Ultima III: Exodus brought a four-character party and a moving four-voice musical score by Kenneth Arnold to enterprising RPGers everywhere. Your quest is to rid the world of Sosaria of the evil Exodus, a cyborg contraption and the offspring of your arch nemeses from the first two Ultima adventures. Along the way, you explore the land, battle monsters, descend into dungeons, and talk to people in towns for one-line hints and tips. The game contains many kinds of weapons, armor, and spell types, with 11 character classes and five races to choose from.

The Atari 8-bit conversion uses artifacting; if your television or monitor isn't set up properly, you'll see the game in black and white. While Ultima III isn't quite as well remembered as Ultima IV: Quest of the Avatar, it was considered one of the best role-playing games of its time. It's a hard game as well, and if all four characters die, you're done for and have to start from scratch. There's even ship-to-ship combat, which can wipe out your party quite quickly, and you

---

158. www.dadgum.com/halcyon/BOOK/PRICE.HTM
159. Ibid

need to navigate a ship through various winds to get to the mystical land of Ambrosia. Moongates let you teleport from location to location (and sometimes secret places), but are hard to find, and it's tough at first to figure out how they work.

On a personal note, this was absolutely one of my favorite games, and I especially enjoyed reading the accompanying two manuals and cloth map. I credit this game's audio as one of the main reasons I got into creating sound effects and music for video games later in life. I loved the music from this game so much that, when I was 11, I taught myself to play a few of the songs on the piano; they were deceptively simple to play. Ultima III didn't have music on most of the platforms on which it was available, which made the Atari 8-bit version even more significant.

Figure 6.43: The RPG that raised the bar for all to follow, Ultima IV: Quest for the Avatar was well worth the wait for the Atari 8-bit version.

Ultima IV: Quest of the Avatar (Origin Systems, 1985)

If Ultima III: Exodus was an important milestone in modern computer role-playing games, Ultima IV: Quest of the Avatar was a soaring achievement. As the Avatar, in a time of peace, you must conquer any remaining evil in the land of Britannia, a world 16 times larger than Sosaria in Ultima III. Your success in the game depends on how well you stick to eight virtues, including compassion, honor, and justice, rather than vanquishing an evil being at the end. Ultima IV introduced morality as a gameplay mechanic for the first time in RPGs.

The game was the first in what was eventually called the "Age of Enlightenment" trilogy, although only Ultima IV made it to the Atari 8-bit platform. The game takes hundreds of hours to complete. As you play, you can eventually build up a party of eight characters, only one of which is your own creation; the rest join the adventure from various cities across the land. The game's conversation system, which spans hundreds of non-player characters, and its sophisticated component-based spell system sets Ultima IV apart from contemporary RPGs.

The Atari 8-bit port of Ultima IV looks and plays well. It's a difficult game to get all the way through, and you need to take plenty of notes as you play. Knowing what I know now, though, the Atari version lacks the excellent music found in a few other ports. Even I noticed at the time it was strange to play this game in relative silence after experiencing Ultima III's stunning four-voice soundtrack. Like Ultima III, Ultima IV uses artifacting, which means you need a special display hookup to see color. This is an excellent game and a defining role-playing experience of the mid 1980s, even if the Atari 8-bit version isn't the best port.

Universe (Omnitrend, 1984)

A strategy game clearly ahead of its time, the space trading and fighting game Universe came on a then-astounding four floppy disks. In 1984, it cost a whopping $89.95, and came in a metal box with a three-ring-binder manual that ran over 75 pages, complete with quick index cards. Universe is set far in the future; humanity figured out centuries ago how to settle planets around other stars in the Local Group after discovering an alien-made hyperspace booster. Since then, Earth has been sending supplies out to the colonies, but the supplies have mysteriously stopped arriving. Your goal is to attempt to contact the lost planet Earth by searching for a second hyperspace booster.

The game begins by giving you credits so you can put together a ship. You must employ a mix of mining, trading, and piracy to stay alive. Mining tends to cost the most at the outset, while trading and transporting passengers tends to be easier. By doing any of these, you can make money and then upgrade your ship to explore farther into the Local Group.

William G Leslie developed the game on an 800; it was later ported to the IBM PC and Apple II. Reviews were mixed, with the game coming in for some criticism for all the disk swapping and overall slow performance. *Computer Gaming World* took the unusual step of running dual (unsolicited!) reviews in its June 1984 issue. Both writers enjoyed the game, with one emphasizing that while gameplay was comparatively simple, it was difficult to make the right decisions.

No VCS or Intellivision game console would give you a game like Universe. It took the average player several months to complete, according to reviews at the time. The game even came with two free months of access to a dedicated Universe BBS, which you could dial in to get tips and other assistance for the game.

Vanguard (Atari 5200, 1983)

Vanguard was one of my favorite early arcade games. It's similar to Scramble, except you can shoot in multiple directions simultaneously. The game also contains multiple zones, which play differently and even change between horizontal, diagonal, and vertical scrolling. While you're playing, you're constantly running out of fuel, although you replenish it by destroying enemies. Periodically, you'll come across an Energy module; fly through it and you'll start flashing different colors and become invulnerable for a time, and even able to destroy enemies with your ship itself (although you can't shoot your lasers while in this mode).

This 8-bit 5200 conversion plays almost exactly like the original, aside from how you only have one joystick with one button on it, instead of four shooting buttons (one for each direction) as with the arcade version. There are two tunnels, each of which contains multiple zones: Mountain, Rainbow, Styx, Rainbow 2, Stripe, Rainbow 3, Bleak, and the City of Mystery, with an end boss for each guarded by force fields. Nonetheless, it's a hard game and satisfying to complete. An early ad for the coin-op version calls it "Centuri's First Talking Game," though the voices aren't included in the home versions. The game does include the proper Jerry Goldsmith rip-off of the theme song to *Star Trek: The Motion Picture*, which later became the music for my favorite TV series, *Star Trek: The Next Generation*. Maybe this is why I liked playing Vanguard so much.

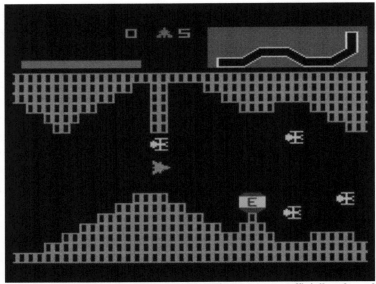

Figure 6.44: This fantastic port of Vanguard scroller was never officially released on Atari computers, but a 5200 console version made the rounds.

Unfortunately, the game never made it to retail shelves for the Atari computer specifically; of the 69 titles produced for the 5200, Vanguard was one of the few without any version (inferior or otherwise) available for the 400/800. Pirated versions of the 5200 cartridge were widely circulated on Atari computer BBSes anyway. I clearly didn't have a copy.

Whistler's Brother (Brøderbund, 1984)

This arcade-style platformer pits you against runaway boulders, poison arrows, and other obstacles as you search a ship and underground caverns to find priceless artifacts. The multiscreen boards seemed enormous at the time, and are still fun to explore. There are 13 levels in all, with names like "The Docks," "The Sailing Ship," "The Strange Tomb," and "The Lava Cave"; each one contains a portion of your brother's document. Once you complete the book, you start over, and can replay the game up to 16 times; it gets harder as you go.

The game also has a hilarious twist: Said absentminded archaeologist brother, a chap by the name of Fenton Q. Fogbank, is also following you around the entire time with his head buried in a map. So you have to keep whistling to him (by pressing the joystick button) whenever he goes off in the wrong direction; when you whistle, he then runs in the opposite direction and tries to find you, still never looking up from the map. If your brother wanders too far away, he'll turn white with fear, and the music will change to remind you to get closer to him again. The button also activates whirling, which you can do once you collect the two tools on the current screen. When activated, whirling paves a path in front of you and makes you temporarily invulnerable.

The graphics are a little basic even by 1984 standards, but the game is enjoyable nonetheless. The controls offer an extra layer: Pushing diagonally speeds up your character in the direction he's already heading. To this day, I keep wishing I could make a Whistler's Brother reference whenever someone doesn't seem to be paying attention to what they're doing. It's a shame few people would get the joke. (I know you would, dear reader.)

Yoomp! (No publisher, 2007)

If anything indicates a vintage computer platform has enthusiasts, it's the existence of a homebrew community that continues to develop new software for it long after it's officially died. While I don't have room to go into every significant release since the Atari 8-bit line went out of production in 1992, I certainly have room for one of the best-known games: Yoomp!, a futuristic action game with textured graphics, anti-aliasing, 21 levels, and an overall look and sound straight out of the famed European PC demo scene.

In the game, inspired by the relatively unknown D. Johannsen's 1986 title Jump!,[160] you control a ball that is continuously moving through a three-dimensional textured tube. As you go, you'll find holes in the floor you have to navigate around, and you'll encounter teleporters, ramps, additional lives, and even earthquakes. You get

---

[160] www.atarimania.com/game-atari-400-800-xl-xe-jump_2699.html

three special jumps you can use. The developers claim a perfect run-through of the game takes more than 20 minutes, and it's tough, so it will take many hours of play to master. Yoomp! even supports stereo sound, if you have a modded XL or XE system with dual POKEY support, and there are optimized versions for both NTSC and PAL machines. You can tell the developers put extra care into the entire presentation, from the load, title, and finish screens to the different music themes each game you play a round.

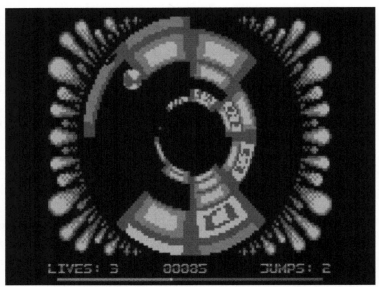

Figure 6.45: A "new" Atari 8-bit game developed in Eastern Europe that really shows off what a 1979 computer could do when fully maxed out.

The game runs on any 64KB Atari XL or XE, and actually takes up over 80KB; the developers used compression to squeeze everything in. The game runs in Graphics 7 with 128-by-96-pixel resolution. Unlike with any Atari game before it to my knowledge, you can balance and smoothly adjust the volume levels of sound effects and music in-game. Honestly, it's terrific to see people still developing new software for the Atari 8-bit. You can learn more about this excellent game at yoomp.atari.pl.

Zorro (Datasoft, 1985)

A fun side-scrolling adventure game with a Spanish-infused style all its own, Zorro puts you in control of the famous outlaw, complete with hat, eye mask, and rapier. The game takes place over 20 boards, and you go from one to the next, getting into duels with guards and looking for the missing Mission Bells. Then you get to the underground catacombs, where you search for and release innocent prisoners and ultimately find the kidnapped "senorita."

The controls are simple: You can climb up or down in addition to moving right or left, and in sword fights you defeat guards by pressing the joystick button when both swords are down. You can also push a guard off a ledge. Some of the items in the game are part of puzzles; you have to get keys to unlock doors, or figure out where a particular item is needed.

Datasoft's earlier Bruce Lee is still a better game, but Zorro—which clearly takes inspiration from its predecessor, especially graphics-wise—provides a good distraction, if at a more relaxed pace. Looking back now, Zorro didn't hold up quite as well graphics-wise as the other three games, even though it was one of the later titles. With Zorro, you also must travel through screens more than once in order to complete the game; it's a more nonlinear quest than Bruce Lee. In retrospect, Datamost clearly made good use of movie licenses over its lifespan, spawning Bruce Lee, Zorro, The Goonies, and Conan all within a two-year period. All of the games ended up being good, which is more than you can say for countless movie-licensed titles since!

Zybex (Zeppelin Games, 1988)

Zybex is a horizontally scrolling shooter; it didn't see wide distribution in the U.S., but it's gone on to become a cult favorite for its excellent graphics, music, and gameplay. It's one of the most popular downloads on Atarimania.com, and is frequently cited as one of the best games for the 8-bit Atari platform. Even though it's listed as coming from a different developer, three of the same people who worked on Draconus worked on Zybex—and you can tell by the style of the graphics and audio. (Draconus is listed as being developed by Cognito, but it's Zeppelin Games.)

I didn't have Zybex when I was younger, but I've played it recently and find it on par with some of the better shooters for the NES and Sega Master System. Not bad at all for a platform predating those game consoles by six years. I'm thinking of Gradius and R-Type in particular, given the graphics style and the ability to build up your weapons. Destroy a squadron of aliens and they'll leave behind bonus objects, similar to how Gradius works for power-ups. But when you come back to the screen after losing a life, your temporarily invincibility doesn't let you destroy enemies the way it does in Gradius. Zybex's auto-firing makes for a nice ability to spray enemies with multiple shots with little effort; the fire button changes the weapon you're using, rather than shooting it.

While the Atari platform didn't lack for Defender and Scramble clones throughout the early and mid 1980s, arcade games like Gradius and R-Type advanced the form, and Zybex is probably the closest you can get on an Atari 8-bit computer. It's certainly worth playing today, and it makes you wonder what Atari could have pulled off with the XE Game System had it taken the console (or the ST, or anything) more seriously by this point in its history.

7 | Emulation

The Atari 8-bit may have officially disappeared in the early 1990s, but that wasn't the end by a long shot. Nothing has done more for preserving computer history than emulators, which let you run programs for computers and game consoles that are no longer readily available. And for more than 20 years, it's been possible to emulate the 8-bit Atari platform on both the PC and the Mac. Quality and accuracy became pretty good early on, as even PCs in the mid-to-late 1990s had enough power to emulate Atari 8-bit hardware in software. Whether emulation is sacrilege compared with using the actual hardware and software is up to you. I'm as pro-Atari–8-bit as they come, so I think there's room for all kinds of enthusiasts. And there's a good chance I wouldn't have written this book if easy-to-use emulators hadn't rekindled my passion for the actual computer line in the first place.

One of the more interesting questions to grapple with is the importance of individual ports of particular games. For example, back in the early 1980s, most programmers strove to make home conversions as similar as possible to the arcade versions (with the notable Atari exception of Space Invaders, as discussed earlier). If you had an 800 and played Asteroids on it a lot, you may still want to do this today for nostalgia purposes, even though it's not a top-notch port. But for the most part, when it comes to a game like Asteroids, or even Joust (a better, but still not perfect translation), I'll probably play it in MAME before firing up the 800 version.

Deciding which version of a computer game to play is a little trickier. Some of them are easy—a game like Alternate Reality: The City was designed on the Atari 800. Playing the native version is a must, although even in this case, the Atari ST version added support for guilds and has added depth even though it wasn't as good otherwise. The same goes for something like M.U.L.E., with its four-player capability; it's Atari all the way. But then you run into another problem: A few games were (gasp!) better on the Commodore 64 than they were on the Atari—or at least prettier, if often slower. For example, Archon's characters have a nice black outline around them on the C64, whereas the Atari version looks simpler and a bit less colorful. On the other hand, the Atari is a faster machine.

In all of these cases, choosing a version of a game to play is obviously up to you. I grew up playing Ultima III on the 800, with its stellar soundtrack, and couldn't imagine playing it on another machine without the score. (Even the Atari ST version, while more colorful, had the soundtrack oddly kicked up an octave, which sounded strange in comparison. And the Atari ST had just three voices to work with instead of four, which never made any sense.)

For Ultima IV, it's a different question entirely. It's tough to play it on the 800 knowing the ST version had better color and included the soundtrack, whereas it was missing entirely in the 8-bit Atari version. For this one, I'd turn to the ST to play it now—or play the PC version I got off of Good Old Games and mod it for 256-color VGA and the soundtrack. (Go do this, by the way—Ultima IV is public domain, so you can download it from gog.com for free!) Or maybe you just want to play the game in the version you remember, regardless of whether it was the "best" version.

For proper emulation, you'll also need some type of controller. You can use the keyboard, but you don't need me to tell you it's just not the same. The easiest solution is to pick up a generic USB gamepad and just ignore any extra buttons aside from the first one. This works fine, especially if you're used to gamepads from console gaming.

If you're looking for an authentic Atari joystick-style experience, your options are more limited. Over the years, I've had perfect results with a genuine Atari CX-40 controller connected to an old (and unfortunately discontinued) Stelladaptor, which converts the original 9-pin connector to USB. If you can find a Stelladaptor on eBay or in an online store somewhere, grab it, used or new. Otherwise, there's not much else out there without using an actual Atari computer. I would avoid the Retro-Bit USB joystick floating around on Amazon for $10 or so. I own two of them, and neither works right; most of the customer reviews seem to say the same thing. Some of the USB Atari-style joysticks available are fully contained emulators you plug into a TV set to play VCS games. You don't want one of those either, for obvious reasons.

Image files

And now for the thorniest of problems when discussing emulators: ROMs, and the legality of getting them. It's still a gray area, so I won't provide direct links in this book. One of the packages below includes many of the most popular games, I'll describe some of the best web hosts with collections of program files, and a simple Google search will help you find exactly what you need if it's not in the aforementioned places.

But what do all the file extensions mean? It's a bit of a mess, and the various explainers out there tend to discuss the file formats in specific contexts (such as with Atari DOS 2.0, or with an SIO2SD interface). Here are the different kinds of files you may encounter, and what each one represents, roughly from most to least common:

ROM: This is a cartridge dump. Usually 8KB or 16KB, it should run as an Atari 8-bit cartridge in an emulator.

COM: This is a straight-up Atari executable image, which works on Atari computers directly. Plugging it into an emulator will get you nowhere, unless in the emulator you load DOS, load a virtual "disk" with COM files, and then load those individually.

SYS: This is an Atari system file; examples include DOS.SYS and DUP.SYS (for Atari DOS 2.0S), and AUTORUN.SYS (for a bootable Atari disk).

BAS: This is a BASIC program that must be loaded from within Atari BASIC with a RUN command (for example, LOAD "D:MYFILE.BAS" and RUN)

ATR: This is a one-sided disk dump (88KB) that works with nearly all current emulators, as well as APE and SIO2PC-type hardware interfaces. A game that requires both sides will have two ATR files;

you'll be able to insert them in an emulator in two different drives so as to avoid virtual "disk flipping." You'll most likely need files in this format, especially if you want to run some of the larger Atari 8-bit games that only came on disk.

CAS: This is a dump of a program recorded on a cassette. It will work in an emulator simulating a 410 Program Recorder cassette drive or equivalent.

XEX: This is an executable file, and would have been called EXE; the XEX convention is used so as to distinguish Atari 8-bit executable files from MS-DOS files. You'll need these if you go with a modern-day upgrade like an SIO2SD interface (more on this in the Mods chapter).

ATX: These are VAPI-format disk images. VAPI is an Atari 8-bit software preservation project for copy-protected Atari disks. You can make new VAPI images using a 1050 drive with a Happy, Speedy, or Duplicator enhancement installed.[161]

PRO: Atarimax APE disk images; these files only work with APE.

XFD: Atarimax lists this as similar to the ATR format, but without ID and format headers, making it "an unmarked blob of data," which is "compatible only with the [now-defunct] PC-Xformer emulator."[162] You probably don't need this one anymore, unless you have a setup using it now and want to continue using it.

Altirra

Virtualdub.org's Altirra is arguably the best-known Atari 800 emulator today. Well, it's more than that—it's an Atari 400/800, 1200XL, 600/800XL, 130XE, XEGS, and 5200 emulator. All it requires is a PC running Windows XP SP2 or later. This is an incredibly accurate emulator, with tons of configuration options. You can choose exactly the OS, RAM, and ROM configuration you want to emulate, such as Atari OS/A (48KB), and it "gives" you four disk drives, a cartridge slot, and a cassette deck with which to load ROMs. Altirra also has enhancements, such as scan lines to properly emulate the appearance of a cathode ray tube television, a smoothing effect to increase perceived resolution, and a 16-bit stereo sound algorithm.

---

161. vapi.fxatari.com/vapi-faq.html
162. www.atarimax.com/ape/docs/DiskImageFAQ/

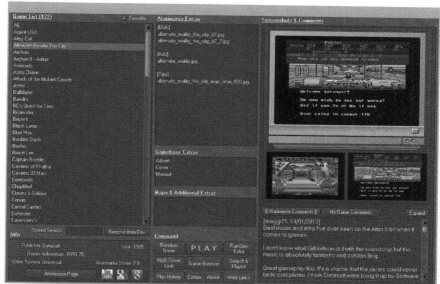

Figure 7.1: One of the easiest ways to get started playing lots of Atari 800 games is to grab a copy of Atari Best Game Pack from the AtariAge forums. Works fine on my Windows 10 PC.

Atari Best Game Pack

A few years ago, AtariAge forum members Starwindz, Paul "Mclane" Irvine, and Greyfox put together a downloadable package including more than 600 of the best 8-bit Atari games, screenshots, advertisements, manuals, and cover art sourced from Atarimania.com and Atariage.com, all with a slick front end. Simply enough, it's called the Atari Best Game Pack, and it's based on both Altirra and Atari800Win Plus; you can choose one or the other. To grab a copy, head over to atariage.com/forums/topic/226801-atari-800-best-game-pack-releases/ and click the Download link; it's a simple install.

The Atari Best Game Pack has a high-score spreadsheet from the community, and lets you favorite a group of games so you don't have to sort through the massive list each time you want to play something. The Best Game Pack also runs under Wine, so you can play with it on a Mac or a Linux machine. Not all Atari 8-bit games you may want to play are included, and there's no way to add new ones yourself I could find. I can't do without Gateway to Apshai or the

5200 versions of Centipede and Pac-Man, and most Infocom games are missing. You'll have to send requests to the developers and wait for the next version to see if it has been added. But this is a minor quibble, as practically every game of importance is included. Like most things Atari 8-bit–related these days, Best Game Pack is clearly a labor of love, and the developers don't always have the time to keep it fully up to date.

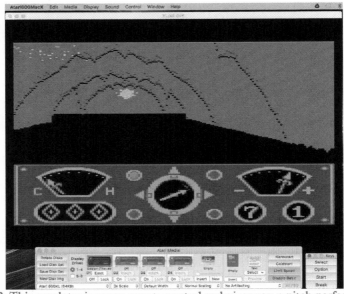

Figure 7.2: This emulator is super-easy to control and gives you a pitch-perfect Atari 8-bit experience on today's Mac; it even works fine (in my experience) on macOS Sierra, which was relatively new at the time of this writing.

Atari800MacX

You may have heard of Atari800Win Plus; it's an older Atari 800 emulator for PCs that has since found its way over to GitHub and is no longer being developed. But if you're running Max OS X, you'll want to head straight to Atari800MacX, the OS X version of the same emulator. The latest update—over four years old at the time of this writing—still works even on OS X 10.11 El Capitan machines (though I haven't tested it on Sierra). The latest version also supports virtual hard drives, copy and paste, and a graphical debugger.

The main window is quite attractive and easy to understand. Starting from the left, there's a series of buttons to control loading and saving disks, a trigger to display the first four or next four virtual floppy drives, and icons of actual Atari 810s representing D1, D2, and so on with buttons to turn them on, insert disks, and lock the disks. After this are cassette and cartridge inserts, a printer emulation button with Preview, and finally, buttons to Warm or Cold boot, limit the speed of emulation, and disable built-in BASIC. Below are several drop-downs for choosing the exact machine to emulate (such as an 800 or 800XL), a multiplier for zoom magnification and some other display options, and a toggle for artifacting for games like Ultima III to display in color.

Here's how to install Atari800MacX:

- Head over to www.atarimac.com/atari800macx.php and click the Downloads tab.
- Download the current version of Atari800MacX.
- Double-click the installer, first to unpack the .gz archive, and then to mount the .dmg file.
- Drag the folder to your Mac's hard drive.

If you try and run it now, it will pop up a familiar-looking Atari 800 window, but it will say, "Sorry, this program needs a real Atari OS. Visit the Web pages to find out more." To get it up and running, you'll need separate ROM images. Here are the files you want to look for:

- ATARIOSB.ROM (Atari 800)
- ATARIXL.ROM (Atari 800XL)
- 5200.ROM (Atari 5200)

You'll also want the following:

- DOS_20S.ATR (Atari DOS 2.0S)
- ATARIBAS.ROM (Atari BASIC)

When you find the OS ROMs, drop them into the OSRoms subfolder. Then, the next time you start Atari800MacX, you should see

"ATARI COMPUTER - MEMO PAD." This is how you know you're in business.

Next up, you'll want to find some actual programs to run. Look for files with the extensions ROM (cartridges), ATR (disks), or CAS (cassettes). Or just Google "Atari 800 ROMs" and see what comes up. If you find disks, put them in the Disks folder. Then, while in the emulator, click the Atari 810 D1 drive on, click Insert, and choose the ATR file you want to load. You'll see the grayscale drive icon "color in." The Eject button also lights up, but don't press it yet. Instead, click Coldstart on the right side of the menu bar. If all goes well, voilá: You should see it light up and play the game. Notice how the load time is immediate; you won't hear any of those repeated "beep" the Atari computer made as it chugged through each sector of the program. Emulators do have their benefits.

I usually increase the display to 3x scale and turn on scan lines, although the scan lines dim the display a bit; personally, I just prefer the authentic CRT look. Some games have both cartridge and disk versions. The cartridge versions are usually 8KB or 16KB, whereas the disk versions may take up more memory. And sometimes, the disk versions offer additional features or game levels compared with the cartridge versions, although it's rare.

For controllers, I use a Stelladaptor USB device connected to an original Atari Joystick. To enable this, I had to tell Atari800MacX I was using a gamepad for Joystick 1 (Preferences > Controllers). You can also set it to let you use the keyboard, though it doesn't default to the typical emulator-style Arrow and Ctrl key controls. Instead, the "left" joystick is set to use the left side of the keyboard; open the same Controllers tab, click Left Joystick, and you'll be able to look at and adjust the keys as needed.

Atari800MacX also has some extra useful features. You can display the frame rate, or even the current disk "sector." You can pretend-connect an XEP80 for an 80-column terminal. You can simulate RAM expansion modules, like the old Mosaic 64KB upgrade. All-in-all, it's a solid solution for playing Atari 8-bit computer games on Macs.

Atari800

Atari800, the original Atari 8-bit emulator, was developed in C by David Firth in 1995 and released under the GPL. Development work stopped two years later, but then some other programmers picked up the slack. It's known to work on everything from MS-DOS to BeOS, OS/2, and AmigaOS, and supports up to eight disk drives, 42 cartridge types, and stereo POKEY emulation. The most recent release, version 3.0.0, was in 2013. You can find more info at atari800.sourceforge.net. Atari800 is what you'll want if you're trying to get 8-bit emulation up and running on a Linux machine, a Raspberry Pi, a phone, or another configuration not straight-up Windows or OS X.

Phones and Tablets

Some enterprising fans have worked hard to develop versions of emulators for various phones and tablets. Your options here are more limited, though. First, your device has to be running Android; there's no way to boot into an Atari 800 emulator on an iPhone or iPad, at least without jailbreaking (an increasingly unreliable and even risky proposition). Even if you are running Android, there's only one truly operational emulator, Colleen. And even then, you may not find the on-screen touch controls to your satisfaction.

If you want to give it a shot anyway, you can find Colleen on Google Play. Essentially, it's a port of the venerable Atari800 open-source emulator mentioned above. Colleen emulates a joystick with on-screen multitouch, a hardware keyboard, or an external Bluetooth peripheral. You can load or save game states, and it supports sound. The current version, 3.0, works on any version of Android 1.6 or higher. It's definitely a thrill to pull a device out of your pocket and fire up an Atari 800 game, even if its ultimate use for long periods of time is questionable. Droid800 is an older Android-compatible front end for Atari800. Unfortunately, development work stopped in 2011, but the code is out there if you want to look at it.

My vote: Stick with a PC or Mac, plug in a proper joystick, and do this the right way. If a $35 Raspberry Pi can do it, any 10-year-old computer you have sitting around should be able to handle it as well. Or you can pick up an inexpensive netbook or current budget-level equivalent, or build a $200 PC; you certainly don't need a lot of CPU or GPU firepower for this task.

8 | Collecting

It's certainly tempting: You may want to pick up some old Atari hardware so you can check out your old favorite games and reexperience the magic. Or maybe you've kept your original equipment in a closet or in the garage, and you're now thinking of breaking it out and setting it all up again. Maybe now's the time to get the expensive peripheral you couldn't afford back when it was the latest and greatest. Or maybe you just want to build or flesh out a collection of Atari 8-bit gear, since now you have the room and (presumably) a little bit of disposable income you can use for the purpose.

There's another possibility: Like me, you regret getting rid of your old Atari gear. When I first upgraded to an ST, I still had my two 800s: one was alive running the BBS, and the other I used to play games. As the 1980s wore on, I took down the BBS, entered high school, and primarily used the ST for schoolwork, games, and getting online. But I kept one Atari 800 set up with two disk drives and lots of my favorite games nearby; and by this point, I had learned to make backup copies of just about everything, so I had a separate disk case just for those. I kept this setup throughout college and my first few jobs, even though I had PCs and Macs by that point.

I only stopped owning Atari hardware in my mid 20s, right around the year 2000, when I had already moved several times and my dad found himself constantly having to shuffle around old computer stuff in the basement apartment of our house in Brooklyn to make room for other things. I eventually let go of everything and we gave it all away, because when you're living in New York City apartments, every square inch of storage space counts. Now I live in a house and there's some room—and I certainly could have used some of the equipment again while writing this book. Hopefully you still have your old gear—but even if you don't, it's quite easy to remedy the situation.

For the above reasons and others, there's a thriving collector's market out there for vintage Atari computer gear. With some diligent shopping and a little cash, you can make some of it yours. Make no mistake: The majority of people would be served just fine by checking out an emulator and playing some of their favorite games this way, as well as poring through some of the old literature out there. But if you're a tinkerer and you miss your old computer, or if you want to get your hands on some plastic and metal and see what the fuss was about in person, read on.

Choosing Atari Hardware Today

Before we get started, make sure you keep in mind what you're getting yourself into. Most Atari 8-bit computers are 30 years old or more, and not all of them work as well as they used to. Plus, some of them didn't work all that well to begin with! Atari switched up its production methods and some internal parts throughout. As a result, methods of fixing one particular problem on one machine may not work on another machine, and some batches of a particular machine or peripheral were known to fail in specific ways others didn't. I know one of my Atari 800s developed a stiff, hard-to-type-on keyboard in just a couple of years, and as I mentioned earlier, my Indus GT drives had occasional trouble reading floppy disks my dad's Rana Systems 1000 drive read without issue—and this was back in the 1980s, when it was all new. I also had some hardware that worked perfectly the entire time I had it. It was a crapshoot.

These days, you'll have to factor in not just a piece of equipment's apparent condition and Atari's original manufacturing methods for the particular unit, but its age and the way it was used or stored all this time. If you're thinking about acquiring some "new" vintage gear, more power to you! Nonetheless, I recommend you either have some experience with repairing electronics—or have the desire to learn—and the space and money to pick up some tools (multimeter, soldering iron, defogger pen, a basic screwdriver kit, and so on).

Consider using and maintaining Atari 8-bit gear less like using a PC and more like caring for a classic car or antique furniture. While you may certainly get lucky and find someone trustworthy selling gear in tip-top shape, it's not the kind of thing you should expect to just order off the Internet and plug and play—or expect to keep working perfectly for the next 10 years.

Figure 8.1: Cleaning up and organizing some gear I received in an eBay haul.

Still with me? Excellent. This brings us to the wonders of eBay, along with some old-school, dedicated shops that have kept their doors open for longtime Atari fans. The good news is that collecting Atari 8-bit systems is still a reasonably priced hobby. It's true that the earliest Atari computers, the original 400 and 800, are becoming rarer by the day. They're still out there, but I'm seeing prices exceeding $100 to $200 for each model, whereas in the early 2000s you could buy one for $30 or $40. And even newer XL and XE machines are going up in price a bit.

Many fans who were there from the beginning, or who just want to experience the first Atari computer, head straight for the 400 or 800. Just be alert: There's a small chance you could end up with one with 16KB of RAM instead of 48KB, or with the CTIA chip instead of the GTIA chip. Or, if you buy a 400, you could get one with just 8KB of RAM instead of 16KB. None of these things are the end of the world. Depending on your viewpoint, an unusual configuration just adds to the rarity and collectability of the gear.

If you're not dead set on an original 400 or 800, you'll be able to capture more of the Atari 8-bit experience with one of the newer computers, which have more memory and run more software, and work with more of today's modifications to enable the use of flash storage or other upgrades. The 600XL and 800XL are a couple of years newer, for starters, and they sold at lower prices than the 400 and 800 did, so more people pulled the trigger at the time. If you're deciding between the two, the 800XL is the easy choice. While going for a 600XL and adding a monitor port and 64KB memory would be a fun project, and you'll get a smaller machine as a result, it's more work and won't run a wide variety of programs until you upgrade the memory. The 800XL has it all done for you, and is the simpler and more economical route overall to take. The XL line is known to have slightly worse video quality than the 800 or the XE; it's just a bit less vibrant, though you could turn up the color knob a bit on your monitor to compensate, and there are S-Video upgrades floating around (more on this in the Mods chapter). The cartridge slot is on top and doesn't have a power-enabled door, both of which make it easier to use.

Although the 1200XL was troubled in its short production run, a select group of Atari enthusiasts consider it the best machine the company produced. It's attractive and had interesting luxuries like a colorful startup screen and that fantastic-feeling keyboard. Plus, a 1200XL can be a bit of a project, as you can fix most of its issues with upgrades, and then get an absolutely stellar machine you could use every day. These are hard to find, and they were only sold as NTSC models in the U.S., so keep this in mind when looking.

Depending on the machine you get, the XE line could be the best choice of all for compatibility reasons, especially with later software—and the easiest to find relatively unmolested. An XE model, with its composite video output, will deliver the best stock video quality—seriously, I hadn't realized the difference in vibrancy from an 800XL until I bought one and hooked it up recently. If you can find a clean 65XE and don't need the extra memory, it could be the way to go. The 130XE version includes the composite output and also has

128KB of RAM (although upgrades exist for the 800XL to bring it to 320KB). The only problem with the XE is the location of the cartridge slot, which is inconvenient compared with the top-mounted slot on the XL machines. Style-wise, it's clearly more modern than the 1970s-retro 400/800 and brown-and-beige XL, both of which may look dated to you in comparison.

Most enthusiasts today don't bother with external peripherals (except as collector's items). For example, it's easier to run software over flash-based storage, using one of the mods outlined later in this book. You probably don't need a floppy drive if you're going to use flash storage, or if you're only going to play games on cartridge. Floppy drives weren't the most reliable to begin with, and now you're adding an additional couple of decades on top. If you have some old software you want to run, or if you absolutely want to use floppy disks again now, then it's certainly worth getting a drive or two. Just keep in mind that if you're hell-bent on running specific disks you still have around or are thinking of purchasing on eBay, you may need to put some work into getting what you want up and running.

Do you need an Atari-compatible printer? You might if you still plan on programming or writing on the computer. If you just want to play games, though, you don't need one. Many bundles I've been seeing come with a printer anyway, and it's doubtful anyone selling an entire haul as a single unit is going to want to part it out; otherwise, they would have already done so in separate ads or listings.

The Hunt

Let's say you've decided to buy some Atari gear. Where are the best places to look? In addition to eBay, garage sales and thrift shops are still known to conceal the occasional machine or accessory. If you find yourself at one, and see any Atari 8-bit computer gear at all, my advice would be to pick it up, as long as it's a pennies-on-the-dollar purchase. Run from anyone who claims a particular machine is "vintage" or "rare" and "priced accordingly." Atari computers are still relatively common compared with, say, an Apple I, and you won't know if it's working. (Unless, of course, it's an ultra-rare 1400XL or 1450XLD prototype, in which case you should buy it at whatever the sticker price says and then sell it on eBay for $5,000!)

All other things being equal, for a few hundred dollars you should be able to put together a nice Atari 8-bit system with a disk drive and whatever other peripherals you need. These machines are so old that not everyone posting them knows exactly what they are. When I came across a number of bundles with vague descriptions, I had to look quite closely at the pictures to see just what was included.

More troubling is how many people believe it's okay to say "not tested." There's not much you can do here other than pull the trigger and hope for the best—or keep looking until you find one that is fully tested. Otherwise, you may get one in and find out that part of the keyboard doesn't work correctly, or the sound isn't working, or the cartridge door isn't making contact and the machine won't power up. If worse comes to worst, you could resell it and list the problem; another Atari enthusiast comfortable with electronic repairs may well pick it up, given the entire lineup's increasing rarity. Some people listing don't bother to plug them in and test them. They say things like, "Was working fine a few years ago; untested." I'll give some the benefit of the doubt. Maybe they're listing it for a relative, because it's been sitting in the closet or garage, and they themselves don't know how to hook it all up. But some of it reeks of laziness, unfortunately.

If you have the extra bucks and storage room in your home, you may want to order a couple of extra systems or peripherals just to keep the best ones for yourself, and then turn the others around (or repair them first, if they're not working). You'll also find people listing specific parts, like a motherboard from an 800XL. If you're electronically inclined, you could put together a working system from parts.

If you're planning on selling some gear, there are eBay selling tips all over the Internet, so I'm not going to waste much space here: Be clear, be specific, take lots of pictures (six to 10 if possible), and make sure the pictures are in focus and well lit (not with a flash). When the auction sells and you get paid, pack carefully and ship promptly. As far as listing type is concerned, I've found over my 16 years on eBay that risking it—going for an auction, setting the starting price low, and leaving no reserve—gets the most viewer interest and the best prices in the end. Just don't make any spelling errors in the title and make sure you get all the keywords in there.

As long as you remember that real Atari 8-bit enthusiasts are human beings and in this for a good time and not to rip you off, and you keep a wary eye out for the occasional clueless person, you'll be fine. Do the obvious and everyone will thank you.

If you'd rather skip the hassle of searching for used gear altogether—although it's a huge part of the fun for many of us—there are also some well-respected and long-running outlets selling new "old" stock Atari products. The two big ones are Best Electronics and B&C ComputerVisions, both of which have been around for more than 30 years. Best Electronics' website is all text, in various colors, with a smattering of blurry product photos, and the business still proudly displays its Atari Authorized Sales & Service logo on the screen. B&C ComputerVisions has also been operating for decades—*Antic* magazine contained ads for it in 1984! It's still around and is still updating its pricing lists for old Atari 8-bit and ST computers and peripherals. This is another good source for equipment if you'd rather not deal with the vagaries of eBay. Back in 1997, I purchased a Lynx system and a number of games from B&C, and it was all delivered as promised. The company's website still reeks of the original dot-com era, and the ordering process is convoluted by today's standards. But in the world of hobbyist electronics, it's nothing compared with finding the long-since-discontinued objects of your dreams in good condition.

The Purchase

As I wrote this book, I decided to replace some of the gear I had eons ago. Of course, I had to go a bit further than just repurchasing what I had before. My original collection consisted of two Atari 800s, an Atari 850 interface, three Indus GT disk drives, a Hayes Smartmodem 1200, two Commodore 1702 color monitors, and an Epson FX-85 printer. I also had a 5200 SuperSystem with the trackball and dual-joystick tray holder. I didn't see a need to replace the 5200, since I have an X-Arcade Tankstick with the trackball and two arcade joysticks, and I can use it to get the authentic Robotron: 2084 and Missile Command experiences whenever I wanted.

I decided to buy one model from each of the three main product lines. For the 800, I'd pick up an Atari 810 Disk Drive and 410 Program Recorder. For the XL, I'd buy a 1050 disk drive. And for the XE, I'd probably get an XF551. I also wanted an SIO2SD interface with an SD card for use with the XL and XE, and I decided to get another Commodore 1702 monitor, since I loved (and still miss) the two I had 30 years ago.

Figure 8.2: An Atari 800XL system in my office doing something important.

Securing the monitor immediately proved to be a problem. It turns out the 1702 is quite popular, and there just aren't many on the market; the people who have them know they're good and are holding onto them. I found several in poor condition, and I lost the auctions on a couple that appeared to be in good condition. In the end, I managed to snag one on a relist, and it showed up virtually unmarked and in perfect working order. You don't have to buy this particular monitor, of course—even an old TV set will work, and there are other monitors compatible with the Atari line available as well.

Next up, I searched for an Atari 800XL. It seemed like the best compromise for what I wanted: It would work with the SIO2SD SD card interface, it had a nice keyboard if I found the right one, and it would work with some of the other mods out there (I'll go into this in more detail in the next chapter). I found a number of systems on eBay, and several were surprisingly still listed as new in the box, or at least "new in a box," meaning the box had been opened, but the computer was supposedly never used.

I zeroed in on an "untested" model still in the wrapping, with all original packaging and documentation and even a 1985 receipt from Kmart. This particular 800XL had a slightly wider "800XL" font on the front label, instead of the taller and thinner 800XL letters on most of them, and I remembered my dad's 800XL like this had the best keyboard I had ever used. So I took a chance and sprung for it, and probably paid a bit too much: $174. It turned out to indeed have a fantastic keyboard, and it arrived in perfect working condition. And it worked for a whole month. (I'll get to this in a moment.)

I had a bit less luck looking for an original 800. I ended up buying two of them, one of which was promised in "excellent working order" but lacked everything, even the power supply. The other was a little yellowed-looking, but came in a lot with an 810, a 410, some manuals, two joysticks, and some other diskettes holding what looked like personal data I didn't want to touch. This lot ended up costing $107 plus shipping, and the working Atari was $61. Unfortunately, I bought myself some problems here; the 800's keyboard was only half functional, and the 810 booted and powered up (as promised) but the 800 wouldn't recognize it. On the plus side, both Atari 800s had the GTIA chip, and both of them were maxed out at 48KB.

I saw some 130XEs go by, but they were priced on the high side ($150 and up). On a whim, I searched for a 65XE and found one in mint condition in its original box for $97 with shipping from Canada; I snapped it up immediately. I also picked up a second 800XL system at the time, one with the thinner 800XL font and different keyboard lettering. This one wasn't in as nice a condition as the 1984 Olympics model, but more importantly, it worked properly. I found a clean 1050 and never did bother with the XF551, but as I accumulate more software on disk again, it may become more tempting.

Right from the start, I relearned what everyone knows: Pricing is whatever the market will bear. As a result, and since eBay has moved more toward a buy-at-this-price model, there are comparatively fewer auctions going at any one time. That may leave you with a quandary: Say, for example, you want a copy of Star Raiders with the box and manual. The only one you can find now is listed at $19, but you're sure you saw one go by last month that sold for $12 in similar condition. Does that mean this new one isn't worth $19? Probably; you could keep waiting, especially if you've seen lots of copies recently, as is normally the case with the quite-common Star Raiders cartridge.

On the other hand, a new-in-the-box Atari Trak-Ball appeared listed at $49.95. That seemed high, but 43 people were already watching it within a few days because it just doesn't come by often.

Figure 8.3: Later Atari 800s had just the RAM and ROM boards maxed out from the beginning, and without cartridge enclosures. The black plastic clips used to open and close the lid were also deleted. Instead, two screws (removed here) and a plastic bar kept the boards in place.

For me, the nostalgia factor is the most important. There's no need for me to buy a rare, boxed copy of a game I haven't played just to have it, because it's all about reexperiencing what I loved so much in my childhood—or even better, being able to buy now what I couldn't afford then. You may have wanted a hard drive for your 800 in the 1980s, but since $8 SD cards can hold hundreds or thousands of programs, you can finally have the seemingly limitless computing or gaming you always wanted. Or you may be more of a collector and want a specific set of original products in the best condition possible, in which case, more power to you! Just keep in mind what your goals are, and with some patience and planning, you're sure to find bliss.

At the same time, there's no reason to pay extra for something. Just be patient and watch the listings over a period of a few days or weeks, and you'll eventually score. For example, I came across a copy of Boulder Dash new in the box for $300! I think it was a bit much, but where there's a seller, there could be a buyer just waiting for this moment. I also found some outright rip-offs, including $290 for a new-in-box 410 Cassette Recorder and $150 for an untested, basically destroyed 800 with missing keys, heavy discoloration, and a giant crack in the top of the enclosure. At the risk of stating the obvious, don't assume that if something is listed at a high price, it's worth it. There's a cottage industry of people who buy a bundle of gear for $50 or get hand-me-downs from someone, and then break it all apart into individual pieces and list each one to see what they can get.

Figure 8.4: I recently moved my office upstairs so our toddler could have a playroom on the first floor. This was part of the move.

Repairing Atari Equipment

Reliability is a concern with any electronics equipment more than 30 years old. Atari 8-bit computer gear has proven surprisingly durable, especially given the somewhat haphazard way it was manufactured at various points in its history. Original 400 and 800 systems and cartridges should generally be fine unless listed otherwise. Disk drives and floppy disks, however, are another thing entirely. Remember what I said about making occasional backup copies, and how some software developers printed out their exchange policies in the manuals? There was a reason.

With all this in mind, if you have working Atari equipment, you'll want to maintain it, which is easier than it sounds. The Atari 8-bit FAQ advises using an Atari computer as much as possible to keep it in working condition. For example, to keep the keys working, use the keyboard more often, and if your machine develops a nonfunctioning key, pressing it lots of times may restore its functionality. This does work, so don't hesitate to give it a try if your computer has similar problems.

While I was writing this book, my Atari 800XL developed the opposite problem: a stuck Slash ("/") key. No matter what I did, or what was or wasn't hooked up to the computer, whenever I powered it on, it played the raspberry-like startup sound, and then proceeded to paint slashes across the screen with a rapid-fire keyboard click. I could hit the Break key, and it would skip to the next line, but it would keep printing the slash mark. I'm still working on this problem as this book goes to press. In addition, my 810 disk drive powers up but none of my computers can see it, and maybe half the keys have stopped working on one of my two 800s.

There's a lot of information out there about joystick repair, at least if you're using Atari joysticks (don't forget there are plenty of third-party products, most notably from Wico). Best Electronics has a stock of improved, upgraded circuit boards for the internals of a stock Atari joystick. Get them on the horn if you have some older sticks around that aren't working quite right. One of mine didn't move "up" reliably and also squeaked a lot; I pulled it apart to find the clear tape over the circuit board was no longer attached, and therefore pulling the "up" button from the surface of the board. Moreover, two of the internal black plastic posts were broken off entirely and squishing around inside against the white plastic part of the stick. I superglued the posts back in place, taped down the button with clear plastic tape, and screwed the unit back together. It's still not quite perfect, but it works reliably again and doesn't sound like a creaky window shutter anymore.

Many enthusiasts using Atari computers today have moved on to SIO2SD, SIO2PC, and other more reliable (and much faster) methods of data transfer. But if you do chance it with older media, you probably won't be surprised to find that floppy disks aren't known for their extended lifespans. Not everyone was diligent about putting disks back into their proper paper sleeves when not in use. And once a family upgraded to a different computer, Atari gear often ended up in the back of a closet, in a dusty attic, or (heaven forbid) in a damp basement. While the gear may still work, the floppy disks may be toast after several decades, even if they *were* stored properly. Still, you may have or come upon some older floppy disks you want to read—give it a shot. But before you give up, the Atari 8-bit FAQ has some solid advice from enthusiast Lee Hart:

Most disks stored in plastic boxes or ziplock baggies survived. Most disks stored in cardboard boxes or just their sleeves did NOT survive. Some brands lasted better than others, but I haven't collated the information so as to make any kind of definitive statements. If a disk cannot be read, CLEAN THE DISK DRIVE HEAD before attempting to read another disk! Otherwise, crap from the bad disk will remain on the head, and will scar and destroy any SUBSEQUENT disk you put in the drive! (the voice of painful experience)... For lack of a better plan, for each of my surviving disks I am: a) reformatting another blank disk; b) copying the data from an old disk onto the blank disk. Then I have a more recently-produced backup disk in case the original disk later fails.

9 | Mods

When I began researching this book, I was stunned to find so much activity still going on in the 8-bit Atari forums. There were tons of mods and upgrades available during the Atari 8-bit's time in the 1980s, such as the Happy enhancement and Doubler I discussed earlier. But this is nothing compared with the mods that began appearing in the 1990s and 2000s, after Atari discontinued the 8-bit line. You can upgrade an 8-bit Atari computer to do far more than it was capable of in the 1980s. That's the subject of this chapter.

I'm no stranger to upgrading old Atari hardware. In 2005, my friend Sascha Segan and I built a semiportable Atari 8-bit computer, and wrote about it for *ExtremeTech* (which back then was both in print and online). To build the hardware, we bought a 130XE off of eBay, an analog-interface 13-inch Gateway LCD TV, and one of those metal suitcases you see in spy movies, complete with foam padding inside. We ordered a custom third-party CompactFlash card interface from Poland. We soldered it into the 130XE (using 44 separate connections!), and then inserted a 256MB CF card as a kind of internal "hard" drive to store hundreds of games, using a special cable to transfer them over from a PC. That was a fun project, but since then, several modders have built machines that totally put our creation to shame—most notably Ben Heckendorn, who has built a series of truly impressive, portable Atari 8-bit computers I'll go into later on in this chapter.

More relevant to our purposes, I'll also go into how to set up something similar to what we did in 2005 in a much simpler way. If you're looking to mod your Atari computer, there are several key shops to check out for parts. Lotharek's Lair (www.lotharek.pl) is a popular one, and includes a wide array of SD card interfaces, sound and video upgrades, and more. 8-Bit Classics (www.8bitclassics.com) offers an array of hardware upgrades, including MyIDE II, Happy 1050, APE Warp+ OS 32-in 1, and SIO2PC, and you can get spare 5-pin DIN monitor cables and other accessories there as well. Finally, Atarimax (www.atarimax.com) sells popular multi-carts to let you store hundreds or even thousands of Atari programs in a single place, and also sells versions of the SIO2PC interface.

Combining modern-day tech with an Atari 8-bit computer makes more sense than ever. As I mentioned earlier, all this time passing hasn't been kind to 5.25-inch floppy disks. The data may have long since disintegrated or become corrupt, although some may still survive. Besides, if you're anything like me, you won't have the patience (or at least the time) I did as a kid to watch and wait for 300-odd sectors to load into RAM before you can play a game. Let's take a look at some of the most common mods and upgrades available for the Atari 8-bit line—starting with a newer and easier-to-use SD card interface than the one Sascha and I soldered into the 130XE.

SIO2SD

One of the most popular Atari 8-bit mods, and my personal favorite, is called SIO2SD. It's either an internal or external box, depending on what you order. Adding this interface means you can load lots of Atari file images to an SD card (up to 32GB in size), which you can then insert into the SIO2SD interface. The computer sees the SIO2SD as a drive to load from, as if you were loading from an actual floppy disk or cartridge image. To choose a particular file—a virtual cartridge or disk—you scroll to it via the two-line LCD on the device itself, and you can load new software onto the SD card from your computer if you get tired of the selection there.

Setting up SIO2SD is simpler than it looks. All you have to do is quick-format an SD card on a PC or Mac, create a folder called ATARI, and then copy your program files to it. The program files must be in either ATR or XEX format; the latter isn't always easy to find on ROM sites, but you can do so with a quick Google search. Once you set up an SD card, plug it into the interface, plug the interface into your XL or XE computer, and power it up while holding down Option (to disable BASIC). You'll quickly see a prompt at the top of the screen. From there, on the second line of the display, you can scroll between your program files using the K2 button (hold Shift while pressing K2 to scroll the other way). When you see one you like, press Enter on the SIO2SD, and you'll see the name of the file copied to the top line. This means it's ready to go; hold down Option and press System Reset, and the file will start loading at seemingly warp speed (at least compared with a stock 810 drive).

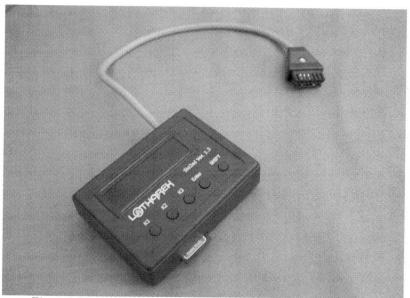

Figure 9.1: Lotharek's SIO2SD device with an SD card installed.

SIO2SD also supports multiple drives, labeled D1, D2, and so on. So you can switch between these virtual drives by pressing the K1 key, and then load multiple disks for a particular game into each one. Lotharek advises on his website that you probably don't want more than 100 or so files in a single folder, and you should use subfolders. This is because you'll just spend forever scrolling between them one by one on the display, not because of any inherent reliability limitations I could find. All told, an Atari XL or XE machine, a monitor, and the SIO2SD interface provide a clean setup that doesn't take up much space on your desk and allows for the authentic Atari experience without the need of an emulator. You can buy an SIO2SD prebuilt from Lotharek's website.

The only downside of this method is having to manually search for files using the small display and hardware buttons on the SIO2SD. You may prefer to use your computer directly for this purpose, using SIO2PC, or you may prefer a cartridge from Atarimax, which lets you load hundreds of programs you can then choose from using an on-screen menu on the Atari itself. The way I look at it, SIO2SD is still easier than keeping around several suitcases full of floppy disks, all of which are slower to load and developed bad sectors even back in the 1980s, much less now!

Storage, Memory, and OS

Let's step through some of the best of the other mods available. While there are pure memory upgrades out there, those were already available back in the 1980s when the Atari 8-bit was current. These later, post-production enthusiast mods tend to add additional capabilities on top of the memory upgrades. I haven't used every single one of these personally, but lots of people speak favorably about each of these, so I wanted to round them up here; maybe you'll find you prefer a different setup than the ones I've discussed.

The Incognito "personality board," as it's called, adds a variety of upgrades to the original Atari 800. First and foremost is XL compatibility; it lets you play newer games and run XL/XE-compatible software. It also adds 1MB of RAM, a real-time clock, a battery-backed RAM disk, SpartaDOS X, Compact Flash–based internal storage, a CF external slot you can use to sideload software, a PBI port, and a choice of Atari OSes to boot from, all switchable from an on-screen menu. The board was introduced in 2012 by Jonathan Halliday, and in 2015 he rewrote the main BIOS, PBI BIOS, and XEX loader to include new high-speed SIO code, a system information page, BIOS hotkeys, and support for multiple FAT partitions.

Another option for sideloading SD cards is the SDrive, an external box to connect to the XL or XE's SIO port and simulate a floppy drive, including read/write capability, for SD cards. A newer NUXX version adds faster read and write speeds, a sleeker enclosure, and an internal SIO connector. It supports up to four virtual drives, and cards up to 2GB. You can find schematics and parts lists around the

Web if you want to make your own SDrive or SDrive NUXX. Most users would be best served ordering a prebuilt SIO2SD at this point, since they're available.

In lieu of a separate SD-card-based drive, another option is to use a so-called SIO2PC cable, such as one from Atarimax, which it sells as the Universal SIO2PC/ProSystem interface. The idea here is to put your PC or Mac into duty as a storage device for games you then run on an actual Atari computer directly, with the cable serving as a conduit. This means you can easily add or subtract software, since you can control it from the computer, as well as navigate more easily than using the small two-line LCD on the SIO2SD.

The Atari Peripheral Emulator (APE), by Steven Tucker, lets you use your PC as a peripheral for your Atari computer. In other words, instead of hooking up an Atari disk drive, you hook up your PC to your Atari, using a variety of methods, and APE will communicate with the SIO bus to fake it so the Atari thinks it's a regular SIO-compatible product. It's similar to SIO2PC, but works at a faster speed, works with PC modems, and lets you print to PC printers. Originally, APE used a PC's serial port, but now there are better versions that are compatible with USB. Then, on the PC side, you load up free software that lets you set up the disk images and data you want to run on the Atari.

Atarimax sells a series of X-in-1 cartridges that expand the capabilities of your Atari computer. The one I'll focus on here is APE Warp+ 32-in-1, a $49.99 switchless OS upgrade module. There are versions available for the XL/XE and for the 1200XL. The cartridge gives you a slew of official Atari versions from the 400/800, XL, and XE, all the way to the XEGS, and some custom OSes like Warp+ OS (its namesake), four versions of MyIDE, and Omnimon R-Basic. Buy this upgrade and your machine will be compatible with anything, or so goes the theory.

If you're not familiar with Arduino, it's an open-source microcontroller platform that lets you build interfaces for real-world devices. You can buy Arduinos in kits or preassembled, and you can also design your own devices, since the hardware specs are available for anyone to use for free. SIO2Arduino is an Atari 8-bit-specific project emulating a 1050 disk drive; you plug it into the cartridge slot, and then pop in a microSD card full of disk images you can run directly on the computer. SIO2Arduino is open source as well, so you can make your own or buy a prebuilt one. It works with several existing Arduino kits and SD card readers, and you can even wire in an LCD and physical buttons to select disk images instead of using on-screen software, so a custom combination is possible.

Figure 9.2: Atarimax sells a series of X-in-1 cartridges and programming utilities from its website, Atarimax.com.

SIDE2 is another cartridge-type interface. It includes SpartaDOS X, a switchable loader, an extra 256KB for applications to use, and a real-time clock. SIDE2 works with Compact Flash cards, which are a little harder to find these days, but the effort is worth it: With SIDE2, you can use SpartaDOS X's hard drive capability. SIDE2 is available from Lotharek's website.

IDE Plus 2.0 is a PC IDE-style interface that brings mass storage capability to an Atari computer via a PBI adapter. Like SIDE2, IDE Plus 2.0 includes a real-time clock, built-in SpartaDOS X, and you connect a 2.5-inch IDE hard drive to it as well as a CF/SD card adapter. Various switches on the board enable or disable write protect and signal which partition the drive should show up as. This could be a good option if you have an older PC laptop hard drive lying around, and want to use it as storage for your Atari XL or XE.

In 2013, AtariAge members BigBen German and santosp unveiled a 4MB version of Megacart, a formerly 512KB flash cartridge that lets you back up and restore files, boot from disk images, and store tons of programs. The cartridge comes without an enclosure; it's a board that acts as a 16KB cartridge, but uses bank switching from 0 to 254 (255 isn't writeable) to achieve the 4MB. There's also an accompanying program suite written in Java that lets you build a catalog to transfer to the cartridge, which the authors say takes about 17 minutes to flash. As with many of these prebuilt mods, it's best to inquire about how many are still available, or see if anyone is selling used ones on the forums or on eBay, because none of this stuff is mass-produced in any way.

Turbo Freezer is a useful tool for developers looking to debug code, as well as anyone trying to snapshot their progress in a difficult game. Essentially, it lets you "freeze" the machine in progress so you can debug the software you're writing. A newer version introduced in 2011 comes with 1MB flash storage and 1MB battery-backed RAM, has exchangeable adapter boards for both XL and XE computers, and the ability to save and load snapshots to various locations, and it even supports stereo POKEY-equipped computers. A red button on the board triggers the freeze.

The Ultimate 1MB Revised 2K14 upgrade may well be aptly named. Designed by Sebastian Bartkowicz (Candle), it's a simple electronic upgrade to the XL and XE that gives you SpartaDOS X with 320K, a real-time clock, 4 OS ROM slots, hardware write protect, and further RAM expansion up to just over 1MB. A recent update to the BIOS also adds Turbo Freezing capability, new Settings menus, and customizable shortcut keys. You can buy this board from Lotharek's website.

Not many people hooked up hard drives to Atari 8-bit computers in the 1980s; most people needing a lot of fast data storage either moved to the Atari ST, or left Atari completely and ran a PC or early Macintosh. But today's AtariAge forums show many people have interest in hooking up SCSI drives to an 8-bit Atari, and one of the easiest ways was to land an Adaptec 4000 or 4070 controller board. An easier and better option: Atarimax sells MyIDE II, a cartridge that gives your Atari a basic Compact Flash interface with a FAT32 loader and built-in BIOS and MyDOS. As with some of the other flash storage devices I've noted above, MyIDE II is a neat way to add lots of storage capability to an Atari 8-bit, and lets you select between them with on-screen software. MyIDE II also lets you control power via software, and it supports boot ROMs directly from the card. And since Atarimax custom-builds these cartridges, you can order one in clear, red, blue, or green for $69.95 each.

Finally, there's QMEG 4.0. According to Thomas Havemeister, a USENET poster in 1997, the OS delivers a disk speed boost, two simultaneous RAM disks, a disk copier, a freezer for poking memory while playing games, and a bunch of other functions. There's not much out there about this now-ancient Atari OS upgrade aside from a quick mention in an 8-bit Atari Hardware Upgrade FAQ and a couple of other Usenet posts dating to 1997. A few AtariAge forum owners still list it in their .signatures, with one saying a machine running QMEG 4.0 remains his "daily driver."

Video and Networking

Many Atari fans would prefer a sharper picture from their computers, and it turns out there are several ways to achieve this. The 800XL has built-in S-Video provisions out of the box, even though they're not hooked up; you can buy a 5-pin DIN plug and install it for both video and RCA audio. There's some back-and-forth about the best way to do this, and whether you need an extra resistor. I would search AtariAge forums for S-Video to get the lowdown on what's been done already and the best way you want to approach it. There's no prepackaged upgrade I've seen, though.

Tomasz Piorek and Candle began the VBXE project in 2005; the current version delivers RGB output using an LCD TV or CRT, up to 1,024 colors on screen instead of 256, and graphics resolution up to 640 by 480i (640 by 240p) in 16 colors, and 320 by 240p and 160 by 240p in 1,024 colors. You also get an 80-column display mode for text; a blitter chip with zoom, transparency, and collision detection; and full GTIA backward compatibility. You'll need a 65XE, 130XE, or an XEGS to use this board, which you can currently buy from Lotharek's website.

At some point, you may decide a small CRT monitor isn't enough, and you'd like to blast your Atari 8-bit's display across your giant living room HDTV. A few lucky people got to experience Star Raiders on a giant projection screen TV in 1980, but you can do better now, and with a far superior, more reliable, and more vibrant TV—one you most likely paid far less for, too, as projection-screen TVs often ran into the thousands (in 1980 dollars!). It turns out you can do this with today's flat-panel TVs, though you may need to build a cable or modify some hardware for an 800 or 800XL. XE machines have composite and S-Video built in, which makes the conversion easier.

A while back, a small group started an Atari 8-bit Ethernet project to add wired networking to the lineup. The idea was to come up with a small IP65-based client that would still leave enough memory for running telnet, text-based Web browsing (like Lynx), FTP, or even some Internet-based gaming. In 2013, a short run of so-called Dragon carts was made and put up for sale, but they are unfortunately out of production as of 2015. Wired networking is past its prime, but if you're interested, you can find plenty of information about this open-source project at atari8ethernet.com.

Sound and Music

The POKEY chip is a fantastic four-voice synthesizer, so why not double it and give your Atari true stereo sound? Simple Stereo was a board designed by Chuck Steinman that adds a second POKEY chip with addresses 16 bytes higher in memory. (The trick to programming stereo POKEY is keeping in mind that the chip normally handles SIO as well as sound.) Today, you can buy a Simple Stereo board from Lotharek. Several games developed in the 21st century for the 8-bit support stereo sound; the best known of these is Yoomp!, as described earlier.

If you're a recording musician, you probably know about MIDI, a venerable protocol that lets synthesizers, digital pianos, and computers all talk to one another. The 16-bit Atari ST is known for its built-in MIDI ports. But the MIDI spec was ratified back in 1983, and several efforts were in play to bring MIDI capability to the 400/800, XL, and XE even then. Perhaps the best-known interface for the Atari 8-bit platform is Midi-Mate, which came with MidiTrack software and included MIDI and SYNC ports. There are also some schematics floating around for rolling your own MIDI interface. A quick Google search should bring up some posts archived from the beloved Cleveland Free-Net Atari SIG Historical Archive; start there if you're interested in putting an 8-bit Atari at the center of a retro-future recording studio.

Our next item of discussion isn't an Atari peripheral, but it's worth calling out for its ingenuity. An enterprising enthusiast by the name of Brian Peters made a dual POKEY chip synthesizer so you can compose electronic music on any system using the 8-bit Atari's distinctive square wave-like sound quality. It's a breadboard design for now, so don't expect a fully assembled product with a shiny case you can order from Guitar Center, but it looks like a must-have tool for making chip music. Skrasoft Systems also developed a packaged POKEY synth complete with knobs and modular ports; a limited run of 25 were sold back in 2010 through a site called analogbytes.com, which was still up at the time of this writing.

Figure 9.3: Skrasoft Systems' POKEY synth with knobs and modular ports.

Portronic's Stereo Phaser was a limited-production add-on board that connected via the monitor port and gave you a group of small paddle controls to generate various synthesizer sounds in a pseudo-stereo configuration, along with a pass-through (for the actual monitor). It's mentioned in the Atari 8-bit FAQ, but information on it is tough to come by. I counted exactly one AtariAge forum user (CharlieChaplin) who mentioned owning it.

Ben Heck's Atari Computers

Finally, let's discuss the person who is perhaps the most famous Atari 8-bit modder: Ben Heckendorn, also known as Ben Heck. He's created what are easily the best custom portable Atari 8-bits ever made. He's made three of them so far, and it's worth going through each of them here, because they're beautiful—and all three put the portable I helped build for *ExtremeTech* to shame, honestly. Ben's also done some beautiful work on versions of the VCS, the Commodore 64 (our arch rival), and some other systems. He even built a portable Xbox 360 with 1970s-Atari styling, complete with a woodgrain front panel like the original "heavy sixer" VCS.

Heck's first Atari 8-bit machine, the 800XE laptop, was based on an Atari XEGS game system. He tells the story in excellent detail at www.benheck.com/atari-800-xe-laptop/, but the gist is that he bought an OS chip from another modder called Mr. Atari. The chip contains a modified version of the OS that recognizes a hard drive, plus built-in BASIC. Heck used it, a Compact Flash–to–IDE adapter, a NiMH battery pack, and an 8-inch TFT display. He laser-engraved a keyboard, complete with raster-engraved lettering (instead of decals), and wired up the whole thing. Then he made a custom hinged enclosure with brushed aluminum panels and a burled woodgrain look. The laptop even contained two built-in "joypads" with fire buttons, a cursor disc, two speakers, and external joystick ports if you want to use the real thing.

The next time around, for what he called the Atari 800 Laptop 2, Ben used an XEGS again along with a MyIDE interface. He also claims he got a lot better at soldering, and instead of using the Compact Flash–to–IDE adapter, he just soldered in the Compact Flash slot directly. This time around, he made a keyboard that clicked, instead of a membrane-style version, and he dropped the woodgrain look in favor of a sleeker black design. He also used the same 8-inch TFT and battery pack as before, but was also able to add a headphone jack. The top panel features a raised brushed aluminum Atari logo, while the sides are done in silver chrome.

Heck's third Atari 8-bit computer build, the New Atari 800 Laptop, is more retro than the first two. This one was based on an XEGS motherboard as well, but with an XE 130 RAM expansion, a 2.5-inch IDE hard drive and custom OS ROM, a larger 15-inch glossy screen sourced from AEI Components, a new-old-stock Atari 800 keyboard, and a flush-mounted cartridge slot. Finally, the entire housing is done up the way you'd imagine Atari would have made an 800 laptop in 1981, complete with red backlit status lights (XE RAM, MyIDE hard drive access, and Power), four function keys in the original system's colors on the right, and a retro-style volume knob for the built-in speakers in the wrist rest. He even cut some grooves in the top panel like what you'd find on the top of an actual Atari 800.

Figure 9.4: The amazing Ben Heck's New Atari 800 Laptop, based on an XEGS and complete with a new-old-stock Atari 800 keyboard and retro-styled goodness. (Credit: Ben Heck)

As you have seen in this chapter, modding your Atari computer can be a fun project, and lets you do the kinds of things you could only dream of back in the 1980s. If you're handy with a soldering iron and a breadboard, the sky is the limit. If you're not, and you just want to buy a few prepackaged upgrades, it's worth it to head over to Lotharek's or Atarimax to see what's available. There are plenty of drop-in upgrades you can get that will maximize the potential of your machine. There's always eBay and the Atari forums as well.

It also depends on how hard-core you want to be about this. Many people using the Atari 8-bit today are doing it for nostalgic reasons. You may be happy with a simple SIO2SD interface or an Atarimax cartridge that lets you play your favorite childhood games. But maybe you want to be the only musician you know who wrote an entire album using an 800XL as a MIDI recorder, or you want to browse the Web with Lynx on an 80-column display upgrade for a 130XE. Whatever you may fancy, more power to you. Happy modding!

10 | Community

If you were an Atari fan in the 1980s, you may have been a kid like I was. Or maybe you were an adult, in which case you got to do things I didn't, such as go to local user group meetings about Atari computers. Maybe you were an early technology journalist, and were around to see the original announcement at the 1979 Winter CES. Either way, there was a large community of Atari computer users back then, consisting of programmers, publishers, fans, gamers, and more, thanks to local user groups, retail stores, BBSes, and trade shows.

For obvious reasons, the community today contains fewer people that use Atari computers on a regular basis. You'd have to be pretty dedicated to use an Atari machine as a daily driver—though from what I've seen in the forums, some do! Still, it's tough to get by without a proper graphical representation of the Web, as well as photos, gaming at 60 frames per second, streaming movies and music, and all of the other capabilities expected of today's computers. But the people involved today—like you, since you're reading this book—are the most dedicated and enthusiastic fans of them all.

Fortunately, there are places you can find all kinds of wonderful Atari 8-bit related content. In fact, many of these sites provided the resources necessary for me to write this book, and I'm continuing to read them over again for fun even as I put words to paper (well, screen). During this time, I've spent many evenings playing games on emulators and reading old issues of *Antic: The Atari Resource*. I gave away my own print copies of the magazines more than 15 years ago. I miss them dearly, and I'm glad I can read them online. Here are some of the best resources out there. Check 'em out, and tell 'em I sent you.

Websites and Forums

Atarimania.com is one of the best sites for Atari 8-bit ROMs, screenshots, manuals, brochures, ads, and other information. It has done a stellar job of gathering together materials for Atari computer hardware and software over the years. It covers each major Atari platform, including game consoles like the VCS, so you'll want to hit the 400/800/XL/XE section.

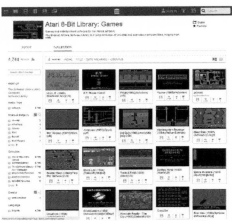

Figure 10.1: The Internet Archive's Atari 800 games page. There are a ton of 8-bit Atari resources here.

The Internet Archive (www.archive.org) is a long-standing repository of archived Web information, but in the last couple of years it has become a truly awesome resource for Atari 8-bit fans. It lets you play Atari 800 games right in your browser window at archive.org, and it contains hordes of old documents, videos, and other tidbits not always found in other places around the Web. Recent additions include two of Joe Decuir's engineering notebooks from 1977 and 1978, which include design concepts for the 400/800, several of the chips, competitive analysis with other machines, and even meeting notes from Atari headquarters.

Kevin Savetz has maintained a wonderful pair of sites, Atarimagazines.com and Atariarchives.org, for well over a decade. Atarimagazines.com contains the full text of the entire print run of magazines like *Antic* and *A.N.A.L.O.G.*, as well as selected issues from many other popular rags of the day. Atariarchives.org hosts the contents of dozens of popular 8-bit Atari books, including how to use them, how to program them, and how to otherwise get the most out of them.

Benj Edwards runs Vintagecomputing.com, a decade-old site dedicated to all kinds of wondrous early computers. He has plenty of Atari 8-bit coverage there, and also writes for PCMag.com, Fast Company, and other publications, usually with a tight focus on retro computing that often mentions the Atari 8-bit.

Atariage.com is of particular interest to computer users thanks to its lively forums, even if the site itself is more geared toward the video game consoles. The 8-bit forum in particular is active, with eight to 10 new messages per day. And the archive of postings is a veritable gold mine for anyone interested in buying, repairing, or modding an Atari computer or peripheral.

Speaking of forum archives, sometimes the original can be best: Usenet. The group comp.sys.atari.8bit was active for many years, well into the early 2000s before Usenet usage as a whole began to fall. All of those posts are still there, and you can find tons of info that hasn't made it over to more recent forums.

Atarimuseum.com hosts documents, catalogs, ad scans, and other memorabilia, for just about all popular Atari computer and video game system platforms throughout the years. Like Atarimania.com, it's a stellar resource if you want to browse PDFs of old magazines, brochures, and advertisements, as well as checking out the current top 50 lists to see which Atari 8-bit ROMs are the most popular at the moment.

AtariProtos.com is a fantastic resource for information on prototype Atari games (for all platforms, not just the 8-bit computers) that never saw a full retail release. As you may have seen earlier in this book, this was a common situation. The Great Video Game Crash of 1983, combined with the inner management turmoil at Atari and then the Tramiel takeover in 1984, all combined to create an environment where executives cut their "losses" on internal projects left and right. I shudder to think now at all the wasted work Atari employees put into these projects. Chances are, you played some "pirated" versions of games that were prototypes; many achieved significant notoriety at the time, because so many of them were practically finished and ready for release! At least we got to play them.

There are plenty of other Atari 8-bit sites I don't have room to mention here, but the above should serve as a solid start.

Podcasts

ANTIC: The Atari 8-Bit Podcast (ataripodcast.com) is the big one: It's an ongoing trove of information, much of it never heard before until now. Hosts Randy Kindig, Kevin Savetz, and Brad Arnold discuss all manner of Atari 8-bit computer lore. The hosts interview many of the key figures of the time, from early Atari engineers and software developers through those continuing to keep the community alive today (like themselves). I highly recommend checking out this podcast.

The famous Atari modder Ben Heck has had two podcasts, one of which is still going. As I discussed in the Mods chapter, Heck has made numerous custom versions of classic computers and game consoles.

Books

The following books perfectly capture the community feel of early 8-bit computers, even though none are dedicated entirely to the Atari. Each one is a ton of fun to read, and many of the authors are still active in the community now. I'm hoping to meet as many of them as possible as time goes on, just so I can thank them for their hard work and dedication to this hobby. Each book listed below either directly contains Atari 8-bit computer information worthy of reading, or is directly relevant to the rise and fall of the platform as a whole.

Atari, Inc. Business Is Fun (Curt Vendel and Marty Goldberg, Syzygy Press, 2012)

Perhaps *the* definitive book on early Atari corporate culture, historians Marty Goldberg and Curt Vendel lay bare the behind-the-scenes action that brought us these wonderful computers, at least through 1984, when most of the action had already happened except for the Tramiel take-over and the XE line. The book contains photographs of early notes from within the company and plenty of informative interviews. A newer companion volume, *Business Is War,* intends to tackle the Jack Tramiel era in more detail, although a release date wasn't available when this book went to press.

Chris Crawford on Game Design (Chris Crawford, New Riders, 2003)

Ever think about designing your own game? What goes into a stellar, tightly written, well-tested design anyway? Chris Crawford details some of his earliest projects—starting with Legionnaire and Eastern Front, and moving through Excalibur and Balance of Power, two cult-favorite 1980s titles. Crawford is also the founder of the Game Developers Conference (originally called the Computer Game Developers Conference).

Dungeons & Desktops: The History of Computer Role-Playing Games (Matt Barton, A K Peters/CRC Press, 2008)

This is perhaps the definitive work on the evolution of computer role-playing games. It includes plenty of historical detail and solid analysis of each RPG's significance, from the first mainframe and minicomputer programs through the early to mid 1980s megahits and lesser-known titles, before blossoming into the next golden age of games that came after the Atari 8-bit, like SSI's Pool of Radiance and BioWare's Baldur's Gate. It's also lots of fun to read, and contains notes on which games continue to have fans playing them today.

Hackers: Heroes of the Computer Revolution—25th Anniversary Edition (Steven Levy, O'Reilly, 2010)

This book, first written in 1983, gives the most vivid portrayal of the origins of the hacker culture. This would be the *real* kind of hacker, the one who wanted to figure things out and make the world a better and more interesting place. Even so, there's plenty of discussion of Space War—arguably the first real video game of any consequence—plus the origins of Sierra On-Line. I still have my early paperback copy, but the latest 25th-anniversary reissue is the one to get, with added subsequent visits to Richard Stallman, Bill Gates, and other luminaries.

Halcyon Days: Interviews with Classic Computer and Video Game Programmers (James Hague, Dadgum Games, 1997)

This was a digital book before anyone knew what ebooks were; it was published in 1997 and sold via floppy disk (!). Today it's available for free on the Web. It contains super-informative interviews with over a dozen programmers who worked on famous Atari games (among other platforms).

Home Computer Wars: An Insider's Account of Commodore and Jack Tramiel (Michael S. Tomczyk, Compute Books, 1984)

This out-of-print book, told from the perspective of Commodore, is key to understanding the home computer market of the 1980s. Michael Tomczyk joined Commodore in 1980 as a marketing strategist and assistant to the company's then-CEO Jack Tramiel, upon which he wrote up the design documents and guided the launch of the wildly popular VIC-20, a machine that led directly to the Commodore 64.

Racing the Beam: The Atari Video Computer System (Nick Montfort and Ian Bogost, The MIT Press, 2009)

Some folks sneered at the VCS even 30 years ago, back when the Intellivision and ColecoVision were clearly superior hardware. But the VCS started it all, and hung on for a long time. This book explains just how difficult it was to program games for it. Read this and you'll come away with a newfound appreciation for six of the most significant games ever to grace the platform, Combat, Adventure, Pac-Man, Yar's Revenge, Pitfall!, and Star Wars: The Empire Strikes Back—and a clearer understanding of TIA, the video chip in the VCS that directly lead to the Atari 8-bit line's ANTIC and CTIA chips.

Vintage Games: An Insider Look at the History of Grand Theft Auto, Super Mario, and the Most Influential Games of All Time
(Bill Loguidice and Matt Barton, Focal Press, 2009)

This is a good overview of some of the best and most significant titles to hit the scene. There is plenty of riveting detail, including notes on the development process and critical reception. There are tons of full-color screenshots and images of game boxes in the book, plus information on copycat games they spawned, not to mention their continued relevance today. Admittedly, the book focuses on games throughout the past several decades; the ones Atari 8-bit fans will want to read about are Pac-Man (1980), Castle Wolfenstein (1981), Flight Simulator (1980), Pole Position (1982), Space Invaders (1978), Ultima (1980), and Zork (1980); there are 18 other games covered as well.

The Ultimate History of Video Games: From Pong to Pokémon—The Story Behind the Craze That Touched Our Lives and Changed The World (Steven Kent, Three Rivers Press, 2001)

This book delves deep into the culture of early Atari, among other things. It's packed with insightful quotes from some of the most important figures to grace the video game and home computer revolution alike. It also spends a good amount of time on Atari's arcade and video game console business.

ZAP: The Rise and Fall of Atari (Scott Cohen, McGraw-Hill, 1984)

Atari fans will likely remember this book as the earliest one written, the first real history of Atari from an insider's perspective. Unfortunately, some of the info here has since been contradicted, as can be found around the Web and particularly in *Atari, Inc. Business Is Fun*. This book is still worth a look for some of its juicier details; just note that some of the facts are outright incorrect, and take it with a grain of salt.

11 | Atari Forever

Atari—the entity described in this book, both as Atari Inc. and as Atari Corporation—long ago ceased to exist. Thanks to a series of corporate mergers and buyouts, the Atari name lives on today, but with none of its original cachet. But Atari computers—notably the 8-bit line, though the ST does have its fans, and I imagine someone somewhere bought one of the PC-compatibles—will live forever in the eyes of enthusiasts, and have secured their proper place in the history of the tech industry. With an estimated two million lifetime sales, not everyone had one. But as we've seen in this book, there's a thriving and even growing community of lifelong enthusiasts to keep the flame alive.

The more time passes, the clearer the lens of history becomes. That's certainly true in the personal computer industry, which by most measures is still quite young at just over 40 years old. Even as it transforms in new and exciting ways—lots of people now think of the phone in their pocket as their main computer—for those who remember the beginning and how amazing it was at the time, that sense of wonder will never disappear. Instead, it crystalizes. So it is true with Atari, the beloved and confused company that brought us the first wave of popular arcade games and home consoles. While Atari didn't bring us the *first* personal computer, it brought us the first one you could use to play arcade-quality games, and that was so most fun to program.

I remember one long evening where Carlo and I played Crystal Castles for hours, never letting up except to eat whatever snacks my mother prepared for us. I'd have a day and evening like this, and it would become permanently imprinted in my memory as a "fantastic day." I lived and breathed these games, and if there was a day where I got solid hours of playtime in, and the game was fun to play, then chances are I still carry that memory right now.

Figure 11.1: An Atari 800, a pair of joysticks, and a boxed Space Invaders cartridge; I took this photo when I visited the Computer History Museum in Mountain View, California in 2008.

We'll never know what might have happened had Atari gotten its act together and continued to dominate the personal computer market in the 1980s, instead of so easily losing its footing and never quite regaining it. But the quality of the core hardware design speaks for itself, and to this day some of the games have yet to be equaled in quality, despite being far surpassed in graphics and sound. And thanks to this, we can all continue to enjoy talking about the hardware and playing games today. I always wondered what would happen as I got older and no longer used Atari computers. At the time, I couldn't have envisioned the emulator scene, eBay, and the stunning growth of the Internet, where all of us can gather and talk about our favorite 8-bit machines. It turns out that even after all this time, in many ways, I'm thrilled to know the sense of community is stronger now than it ever was before.

Now if you'll excuse me, I need to get back to Star Raiders. I've just completed hyperwarp, and I see a couple of Zylon ships on the radar display. Now I have a new sector to clear out—and a friendly starbase to defend for the Atarian Federation. See you on the other side of the galaxy.

Acknowledgements

Beginning with receiving my first Atari computer at age eight, over the next 35 years of my life many special people have created the conditions that led me to write this book. Dan Costa understood my enthusiasm from the get-go, green-lit the project, and provided the support framework necessary to get it done. Matthew Murray is a terrific editor who provided kind guidance and clear assistance throughout the process. Jason Ashlock delivered sound advice on navigating the byzantine publishing industry. Wendy Sheehan Donnell provided a steady voice and listened to me complain; I've learned so much from working with her over the years. Carol Mangis kindly assisted with the production, release, and promotion.

Going back earlier in time, Sascha Segan has been there with me since the beginning, for first calling my Atari 800 BBS on January 1, 1985, and then becoming a lifelong friend. David Friedlander called my BBS a few weeks earlier—I still remember it was December 1984, but I can't recall the exact date anymore—and also became a lifelong friend. Both were groomsmen at my wedding in 2013. Carlo Bonavita was my childhood and elementary school friend and the unspoken hero of this book, the one who played Atari 800 games with me the most often throughout. I played games in person and became online friends with many others thanks in large part to the Atari 8-bit, including Warren Wein, Peter Volpe, Michael Keylan, Chris Lue-Shing, Brian Natoli, Frank Ventura, Ben Ventura, David Passantino, and my elementary school friend Howard Gelling, who sadly perished in the World Trade Center attacks in 2001.

I would also like to thank my parents, without whom I would have never had the opportunity to immerse myself so fully in the world of Atari computers—or breathe air on this Earth, so there's that, too. Most important, my wife Allison has been wonderfully supportive throughout while I goofed off with old computer stuff strewn about the house, and served as an excellent (willing? maybe?) sounding board while I stomped about and spouted off about archaic computer trivia on a near-random basis.

Finally, I would also like to acknowledge some people I don't know personally, but who unknowingly have contributed to this work (and are footnoted accordingly throughout when applicable), and to my enthusiasm for what are now known as vintage computers. They include: Nolan Bushnell, Al Alcorn, Joe Decuir, Doug Neubauer, Matt Barton, Bill Loguidice, Kevin Savetz, Benj Edwards, Curt Vendel, Marty Goldberg, Jason Scott, Chris Crawford, Michael Current, Steve Fulton, James Hague, Evan Amos, Nick Montfort, and Ian Bogost. This is the "standing on the shoulders of giants" part, and I am forever grateful.

Index

A

N

O

P

Q

R

About the Author

Jamie Lendino is the Editor-in-Chief of ExtremeTech.com. Previously, he managed the consumer electronics and mobile teams at PCMag.com. He's written for the print, Web, and digital versions of *PC Magazine* for over 10 years, and has frequently covered the retro gaming community in both places. He has also written for *Popular Science, Electronic Musician, Consumer Reports, Sound and Vision,* and CNET. Jamie has appeared on NPR's *All Things Considered,* CNBC, Fox News, Reuters TV, and dozens of terrestrial radio stations across the country. He lives with his wife and daughter in Collingswood, New Jersey.

41448456R00175

Made in the USA
Middletown, DE
06 April 2019